the urBan treasure hunter

DATE DUE

A PRACTICAL HANDBOOK FOR BEGINNERS

michael chaplan

SQUAREONE
PUBLISHERS

The advice in this book is based on the personal experiences and research of the author. The author and publisher suggest that the reader check with local authorities before beginning a dig where there is any question regarding ownership of the site, ordinances or special restrictions regarding metal detecting or digging on public land, or removal or sale of archaeological finds.

This book is as timely and accurate as its publisher and author can make it; nevertheless, they disclaim all liability and cannot be held responsible for any problems that may arise from its use. Please do not use the book if you are unwilling to assume the risk as well as the adventure.

Cover Design by:
Phaedra Mastrocola and Jacqueline Michelus
In-House Editor: Elaine Will Sparber
Typesetter: Gary A. Rosenberg

Square One Publishers
115 Herricks Road
Garden City Park, NY 11040
516.535.2010 • 877-900-BOOK
www.squareonepublishers.com

Permission Credits

The photo on page 125 is reprinted courtesy of *Confederate Veteran's* magazine and the Sons of Confederate Veterans.

Tables 13.1, 13.2, and 13.3; Figures 8.1, 8.2, and 9.1; and the photos on pages 10, 12, 16, 60, 119 (Top), 123 (Bottom), 124, 150, 164, 163, and 167 are reprinted courtesy of People's Publishing Company.

Library of Congress Cataloging-in-Publication Data

Chaplan, Michael.
  The urban treasure hunter : a practical handbook for beginners /
Michael Chaplan.
    p. cm.
  Includes index.
    ISBN 0-7570-0090-8
1. Treasure-trove. 2. Metal detectors. 3. Cities and towns. I. Title.

G525.C338   2005
622'.19—dc22

2004016970

Contents

Appendices

To the memory of my father, Jack,
who instilled in me a sense of curiosity about the world—
and who showed me how to have life affirming adventures.

Acknowledgments

Input from the following sources is gratefully acknowledged for the successful production of this book:

- People's Publishing Company, for allowing me to use material that was previously published in *Western & Eastern Treasures* magazine.

- Digger Dave, for coin support.

- Rudy Shur and the staff of Square One Publishers, for their confidence in my project and their talented production of *The Urban Treasure Hunter*.

- Howie Schutcofsky, for the author photo on the back cover.

Preface

Who would believe it? *Treasure hunting* in New York City!

When I first became an urban treasure hunter in New York City in 1980, I realized almost immediately that this exciting activity was a perfect outlet for my natural curiosity and that it would supply me with plenty of adventures and interesting finds. I haven't been disappointed.

At that time, the prices of precious metals were going sky-high. Silver was up to $50 an ounce and gold had zoomed to the $800 level. That was just the motivation I needed to purchase a cost-effective metal detector and head for the nearest park. It took me a couple of visits to figure out what I was doing, but soon I was finding silver coins and gold jewelry, along with an interesting variety of collectible items. Remarkably, I was traveling only a few blocks from my home and I was finding *treasure*!

Since that first year, I've successfully branched out into other avenues of urban treasure hunting, pursuing the many possibilities that New York City has to offer a creative and adventurous person. My academic background and training in anthropology and archaeology have been valuable assets, allowing me to systematically research historical urban settlement patterns while applying field proven recovery techniques. I've been able to explore New York on all the levels of its existence, from a prehistoric Amerindian settlement right up to its present incarnation as one of the world's greatest cities.

Perhaps you're already familiar with my numerous how-to articles on the subject, which have been enthusiastically welcomed by treasure hunters looking for fast success in this satisfying and profitable outdoor sport. If not, glad to meet you!

If you're not already a treasure hunter, I would imagine that you probably became interested in this book because, like for so many people, that bewitching word "treasure" stirred the Indiana Jones in your soul. In days past, there were folks who dropped everything and headed for the hills to find riches even at just the *whisper* of the word.

Those old pioneers were a hardy lot. They may have been a bit superstitious, but when gold called, they ignored all obstacles. Many of us today have those same treasure hunting instincts, but need an accessible arena in which to apply them. Well, *The Urban Treasure Hunter* offers you the chance to begin taking your treasure dream seriously and to follow in the footsteps of those old-timers, but with new goals and new technologies to make new discoveries.

This book is additionally intended to offer a pleasantly rewarding way to use your recreational time while having some great fun. Too often, the uniformity of daily life can dull fulfillment of our human potential. Treasure hunting is just the type of activity to spark alertness and creativity by exploring the city where you live. It will also help you gain a new perspective on urban America.

During my career as an urban treasure hunter, I've seen the Big Apple like few people can imagine. Not only have I found myself in some pretty out-of-the-way spots, but I've also applied a treasure hunter's frame of reference to places that are commonly visited. It's been a very interesting pursuit that I look forward to keeping and that will continue to shape my daily outlook.

I consider this book to be a celebration of the experiences and successes that I've enjoyed, which I'm certainly very glad to share with you. I'm sure that *The Urban Treasure Hunter* will lead you to "the high road to adventure," which is a lot closer than you may think. So, get out there and give it your best shot! Who knows? Maybe one day, we'll bump into each other at some overgrown ruins surrounded by Super Civilization and compare notes!

Introduction

Something hidden. Go and find it.
Go and look behind the Ranges—
Something lost behind the Ranges.
Lost and waiting for you. Go!

—RUDYARD KIPLING, "THE EXPLORER" (1898)

Urban areas are the most diverse and rewarding treasure hunting frontier in America, and *The Urban Treasure Hunter* will show you how to harvest their treasures while also having some great adventures. There's no need to travel to steamy, faraway places to find treasure. It's right there in your own hometown.

Curiously, most people believe the fallacy that everything has already been found where they live, which is the precise mindset that has kept city-style treasure hunting the province of a canny new breed of urban adventurer. Believe me, treasure is found often enough by people who know how and where to look for it.

And that's what *The Urban Treasure Hunter* is all about. It offers a complete course of hands-on instruction for finding lost, hidden, and long-forgotten treasures where *you* live. The types of recoverable urban treasures that I'm talking about include rare old coins, lost jewelry, hidden money caches, valuable historical relics, criminal swag, antique bottles, and prehistoric Native American artifacts made of chipped stone. Delving into your city's past will provide plenty of challenging projects, and a metal detector will be your time machine.

The information presented in *The Urban Treasure Hunter* is based on my more than twenty years of adventure filled and profitable treasure hunting in New York City. This is where I came to the conclusion that all cities, big or small, must have certain "treasure zones" in common and that a how-to book about treasure hunting in the Big Apple would cover practically any urban treasure hunting situation. Since I first began writing about my treasure hunting experiences, I've been contacted by numerous readers from all over the country who have reported that my urban treasure hunting strategies have also worked well for them.

Actually, I consider this book a payback because many of the ideas and techniques it contains I picked up from fellow urban treasure hunters during chance field encounters when I was learning the ropes. Being a researcher and a communicative person, I took an interest in their adventures and fascinating finds, and asked them about any successful innovations they may have introduced into their search efforts. Because of what I learned from these treasure hunters, who included some very talented pros, I became a much better treasure hunter.

Finding treasure has always been a universal desire. When Mark Twain observed, in *The Adventures of Tom Sawyer*, that "there comes a time in every rightly constructed boy's life when he has a raging desire to go somewhere and dig for hidden treasure," he correctly identified a vibrant dream that most people have wanted to pursue.

Few people have been able to actualize this fantasy, however, due to the hectic world in which we live and the more immediate concerns that vie for our attention. Instead, we experience the thrill vicariously when we see a suntanned adventurer triumphantly recovering a long-lost treasure on television or in the movies. Well, that exhilarating success can also be yours!

Each chapter of *The Urban Treasure Hunter* is a map that will guide you in one of the many interesting and rewarding treasure hunting directions that await you in a city. For example, some of the topics that I will cover are the role of local history in your searches, cultivating a treasure awareness, dealing with the public, equipment and search strategies, research and project development, exploring city parks for treasure, caring for and marketing your finds, safety and "strange encounter" issues, and interpreting archaeological site reports. I also include a confidence building do-it-yourself project for constructing a very useful sifter.

You get the idea. It's really pretty easy to begin treasure hunting in areas that are surprisingly close to home and accessible to the general public. By the time you've finished reading this book, you should be ready to lead your own intrepid treasure hunting expeditions around town. Remember, cities are constantly changing and there's always something new to explore.

Undeniably, the urban environment is a very distinct arena for treasure hunting and one that has been relatively neglected in the popular literature. It just doesn't seem exotic next to such illustrious feats as Mel Fisher's discovery of the lost seventeenth-century Spanish treasure ship *La Señora de Atocha*, which had millions in gold and jewels on board, or the diehard search by legions of crusty old miners for the legendary Lost Dutchman Mine in the remote Superstition Mountains.

But the truth of the matter is that you can also do pretty well where you live and experience the same romantic thrill of discovery. Urban treasure hunting is a perfect example of looking in your own back yard when considering substantial treasure finds. There's plenty of treasure lying around in your city waiting to be found. And *you* can find it.

With the proper equipment, sensible expectations, and a guide that points you in the right direction, you may be the next person to hit it big. I am not promising any miracles, only a reward that matches your input, plus an interesting array of challenging adventures and feelings of personal accomplishment—which perhaps are the greatest treasures of all.

So, throw away those old ideas about not finding treasure in a city and join me in an exciting and profitable new challenge—as an urban treasure hunter.

Good hunting!

"Life which is lived without zest and adventure—is not life at all."

—F.A. Mitchell-Hedges, *British explorer of the 1920s*

🌿 1 🌿

An Urban Historical Perspective

Any person with a serious interest in urban treasure hunting should have a firm grasp of the dynamics that brought about the growth of cities in the United States. Many of the treasures you will be seeking will relate to past eras and to the gradual changeover from a rural society to an urban one. A historical perspective is necessary to clearly understand the social pressures and volatile periods through which your city went and the types of recoveries that are available from those times.

In this chapter, we will take a very broad look at why the United States became an urbanized nation. To learn the history of your specific area, visit your local library and museum.

THE FACTS

It should not surprise you to learn that the results of Census 2000 clearly showed that 79 percent, or more than three-quarters, of the United States's population lives in urban designated areas. The next census, in the year 2010, may show an even greater percentage. It's certainly obvious that the United States is an urbanized nation.

The United States Census Bureau defines as "urban" any territory that is designated as either an urbanized area or an urban cluster. Basically, an urbanized area has a population of at least 50,000 people, and an urban cluster has a population of at least 2,500 but not more than 50,000. As you can see, there are large and small urban settings. In all probability, you live in such a location or on the outskirts of one.

EARLY CENSUS DATA

The first national census in the United States, which was conducted in 1790, revealed a total population of just over 3.9 million people. There were only twenty-four towns in the country then with a population of greater than 2,500 people. Nearly all the nation's citizens lived along the Atlantic Coast, about equally divided between the North and the South.

At that time, the center of population growth was located 23 miles east of Baltimore, Maryland. New York was the leading city of the era, with just over 49,000 residents. The other most populous cities of the period were Baltimore; Charleston, South Carolina; and Philadelphia, Pennsylvania.

The concentration of the populace on the more secure East Coast served as a prelude to the rapid expansion by migrants into the wild and unsettled territory of the West in a search for land, financial gain, and new hope for the future.

THE 1890 CENSUS

One hundred years later, the 1890 Census of the United States disclosed that one-third of the growing nation's population of nearly 63 million people lived in an urban settlement pattern. The upsurge in urban living was caused by an increase in people moving to established cities and by the birth of new cities as intrepid settlers headed west.

Chicago, which had had a population of just 5,000 people in 1840, surpassed the 1-million mark only fifty years later. The new center of population growth was located 20 miles east of Columbus, Indiana.

IMMIGRATION AND INDUSTRIALIZATION

Historians consider the nineteenth century to be the most significant period of acquisition and settlement by the United States government. Immigrants, arriving in great numbers from countries where they had few economic and personal opportunities, took the challenge and streamed to the frontier and new destinies. Incentives provided by the great California Gold Rush and the Homestead Act spurred them on. It took only a hundred years for our country to acquire all the land that constitutes its current continental area.

The cities of the latter half of the nineteenth century posed increasing demands for manpower due to industrialization and the development of the transportation network. Factory owners built substantial housing for workers and their families. The factory town became a phenomenon that spread across the industrialized parts of the country.

A BETTER WAY OF LIFE

People flocked to the cities because living in an urban area gave them a stability they generally could not realize in an agricultural economy. Because of this advantage, the majority of immigrants to the United States in the nineteenth and twentieth centuries settled in cities, just as their predecessors had.

Many struggling ethnic groups started at the bottom of the social and economic ladder, but due to their idealism and hard work, they turned their cities into regional hubs of economic and social activities for the nation. In many instances, what began as a small fringe settlement has today become a sprawling metropolis, built by multiple waves of migrants. The entire sequence of evolution of a city can range from prehistoric Amerindian settlement through Colonial and Civil War city to today's Super Civilization.

The westward moving pioneers and adventurers acted out the same scenarios repeatedly as the towns and cities of the United States took form. The different regions around the country saw cycles of boom and bust, causing more people to move to the cities for economic opportunity and security. Cities represented hope, and it seemed to be the will of the people that an urban settlement pattern take preeminence in the United States.

The years following the Civil War ushered in the modern era of cities. City people evolved a pattern of life quite unlike those in the countryside and on the frontier. Rugged individualism was replaced with a concern for the general social welfare.

❧ 2 ❧

Treasure Hunting in a City

When people hear the term "treasure hunter," they picture either a diver exploring the blue depths for a sunken wreck or a batty old geezer baking his brain in a rattlesnake filled desert while seeking some legendary lost glory hole. Both of these images are correct in that they represent the type of treasure hunting pursuits that capture the headlines—and the romantic interest the subject inspires.

However, both these images also tend to put a lot of distance between today's average citizens and where they believe treasure can be found. This is because the average citizen lives in a city and not close to what is the popular image of a treasure hunting environment. Topping it off, most city dwellers also believe the myth that nothing is left to be found in twenty-first-century urban America.

In this chapter, we will explore why cities are lucrative places to go treasure hunting. We will also take a look at the type of people who become urban treasure hunters and how you can develop a "treasure awareness" to become an urban treasure hunter yourself.

It would be a real oddity for any urban area, no matter how small, not to have a cache or two waiting to be found.

WHY TREASURE HUNT IN A CITY?

Contrary to the popular myth, cities are excellent places to engage in treasure hunting, as they have so many spots to explore. There's probably even recoverable treasure in or near your own neighborhood in the form of hidden money caches, buried antique bottles, lost coins and jewelry, historical relics, and other valuables. Enterprising urban treasure hunters make these types of finds on a regular basis.

Finding silver coins makes any treasure hunting expedition a success.

William Calver and Reginald Bolton were the original urban treasure hunters in New York City, beginning in the 1880s and continuing into the 1900s. Their discoveries of prehistoric Amerindian, colonial, and Revolutionary War sites, along with numerous important relics, inspired public interest and many newspaper articles about "buried treasure." They were admiringly referred to as "The Explorers."

If you also include searching hidden nooks and crannies for prehistoric Native American artifacts, then you really have the opportunity to take your treasure dream seriously. And don't forget ghost towns, especially if you live out West (see page 11).

It's not hard at all to get started. The right equipment (see Chapter 6) and appropriate treasure identification references (see Appendices A and B) are readily available. Even a novice should have no trouble choosing an area of interest. With just a cost-effective metal detector and a natural sense of curiosity, as well as the knowledge of how to combine them, you will be ready to follow several different urban treasure hunting directions.

At the outset, you may concentrate your search efforts on just one type of treasure, but at some point, you will most likely run into something that will lead you to branch out into other areas. Sooner or later, you will also begin making important connections. The urban treasure hunting arena is quite substantial and interwoven, providing a perfect outlet for someone who is interested in history and also likes to explore.

A Ghost City

Out west, urban treasure hunting opportunities are not limited to the twenty-first century. Treasure hunters yearning for a taste of the Old West can search a famous "ghost city," such as Virginia City, Nevada, which exemplifies the boomtown cycle that I described in Chapter 1. During the mid-1870s, more than 20,000 silver-crazed people lived there, enjoying all the luxuries of a bustling, affluent American city of that era.

Virginia City first came to life when a giant lode of silver, called the Comstock Lode, was discovered in 1859. By 1865, the boom began to fade, but it was reawakened in 1870 by the cry of "Bonanza!" at the bottom of the Crown Point Mine. As a result, thousands of miners and speculators from all over the world began to arrive, causing the town to take on a very cosmopolitan appearance with fancy saloons, hotels, opera houses, gambling rooms, and elegant restaurants.

Everyone wanted a piece of the greatest silver strike in United States history. This included Mark Twain, who started his journalism career at the Virginia City *Territorial Enterprise*. But the 1880s saw the end of the silver boom, and the boomers moved on from what was once the premier mining city in America and known as the "Richest Place on Earth."

Now just a shadow of its former grand self, Virginia City has a current population of about 600 people. Many of the old buildings that are still standing are being utilized as museums. Fortunately, metal detecting is allowed in Virginia City, meaning this nineteenth-century ghost city continues to live for quixotic urban treasure hunters.

There's always a fresh angle to investigate in a city, since urban areas are constantly changing as the old is replaced by the new. If you're wondering what you can find in your city, aside from coins and jewelry, go to a museum that has exhibits on the history of your region. Many of the items on display were once in the ground. Through careful research, archaeological excavation, and accidental finds, they made their way to the public view.

You can apply similar research and recovery techniques, along with your own innovations, to create an impressive study collection. You can also sell what you find or donate artifacts to the local museum. It's your treasure!

I had the pleasant opportunity to take the third route once when I recovered an early broad-axe blade on the property next door to a historic Colonial-era house that was being used as a museum. Believe me, the museum curators were very glad to make that surprise acquisition and put the blade right into a display case.

Colonial-Era Areas

If you live in a state that has a Colonial history, your urban area was probably part of it. This time period is usually very well documented, so helpful background information will most likely be available. Since the early colonists were of European origin, their artifacts will be similar to the types of tools and implements we are used to seeing.

You will find easily recognizable items such as coins, bottles, buckles, silverware, buttons, chinaware, jewelry, and military items. Tokens and coins of this era are terrific finds, as was the brass New Yorke token of probable Dutch origin found by a treasure hunter using his metal detector in a pile of dirt at a lower-Manhattan construction site. This early token was probably minted between 1664 and the 1770s, when the spelling "New Yorke" was in vogue.

Or how about the Boston treasure hunter who came up with a silver 1652 Massachusetts Oak Tree shilling in a field behind an old school? He thought it was play money until his hunting partner rang the bell of reality and told him that he had a real keeper.

Amazingly, another New York urban treasure hunter found a small, bronze swivel cannon in a wooded area. He did the necessary research and legwork, and discovered that a Hessian regiment had been encamped there during the Revolutionary War.

I'm very proud of my two 8-pound solid-shot Revolutionary War–era cannonballs. I found one when I was following an old horse trail and decided to detect around a large boulder in the brush. There it was—about a foot down. According to my research, the 42nd Regiment of Royal Highlanders had seen action in the area. I found the other cannonball in a large pile of dirt that had been taken from a Wall Street construction site and dumped on the Brooklyn waterfront in Red Hook.

That Red Hook site was the scene of a mad rush because the word was out and urban treasure hunters were swarming in to get their share. Actually, quite a few cannonballs were recovered from that site, along with bar shots, a type of artillery projectile with either a half or a whole cannonball attached to each end of an iron bar. Bar shots were fired at a ship's rigging to take down the sails. The six bar shots found in Red Hook were the half-cannonball type and were sold to a collector for $400 each.

Every city in the United States has its own unique category of

This Colonial-era shoe buckle was a surprise find in an old stone wall in a woodsy section of the Bronx.

The men of the Royal Artillery were called "gunners." A well trained detachment of one officer and four enlisted men required about two minutes to sponge, load, and fire a heavy cannon. Light guns were expected to be fired at about two rounds of shot per minute in battle.

hunting areas for versatile urban treasure hunters. By the way, there are also urban treasure hunters in Europe. In London, a band of hardy souls called the "Mudlarks" hunt along the banks of the Thames River. This group's remarkable finds go back through the long history of England into Roman times. Now you're really talking time machine treasure hunting!

The Mudlarks are also responsible for some examples of medieval pewter toys recovered from the banks of the Thames and included in the British Museum traveling exhibition "Buried Treasure: Finding Our Past." This impressive showing, which can be viewed online at www.british-museum.ac.uk, is composed mostly of recoveries made by British detectorists who registered their treasure finds for possible government market-value acquisition, as mandated by British treasure law.

Although the medieval pewter toys recovered by the Mudlarks have little financial value, they are important as artifacts that illustrate everyday life in the Middle Ages. Among the other exhibition items are Iron Age gold jewelry, a Bronze Age gold cup, and the Snettisham Hoard.

Civil War Areas

If you live where the Civil War was a major historical occurrence, you should do very well. In fact, quite a few southern urban treasure hunters also dig for Civil War relics, which include rare types of buckles that have sold for thousands of dollars. Uniform buttons, bullets, and even artillery shells can also be part of a day's haul. Aside from the older parts of town, where anything can show up, land adjacent to the city that served as a battlefield or military camp is a ripe hunting ground—but not until you obtain permission from the property owners.

A good example of the type of recovery possible in these areas is the cache of Confederate artillery shells discovered in the Savannah River near Augusta, Georgia. This cache, which was probably hidden to prevent its capture by advancing Union troops, included dozens of Raines grenades. The Raines grenade was considered a rare military item until that recovery. Other significant Civil War munitions cache finds have been made around New Orleans and Richmond, Virginia.

However, searching for items such as shells and grenades can be

In England, among the most popular areas in which to metal detect for old coins and historical artifacts are farms. Some have been in cultivation for 2,000 years or even longer.

Treasure recovery from the Savannah River is challenging. The outgoing tide is strong, and ledges forming the channel wall contain deep undercuts waiting to trap divers.

risky because of the danger of accidental detonation. This has claimed the lives of several treasure hunters who were trying to disarm naval shells, which seem to maintain their stability longer than other types of Confederate artillery projectiles. You should proceed with extreme caution when encountering this type of artifact and report any such recoveries to the proper authorities.

WHY BECOME AN URBAN TREASURE HUNTER?

Why do people become urban treasure hunters? The answer to that question is very simple—for adventure and profit. Some people find that either the adventure or the profit that urban treasure hunting supplies is sufficient, but the majority of people who become involved in this rewarding quest enjoy equal amounts of both.

In today's world, where the uniformity of daily life grinds down creativity and self-esteem, being a treasure hunter is an inspiring alternative to doing "the same old thing" every day. After all, treasure hunters live for creative accomplishment by seeking out adventure, monetary reward, glory, and, in some instances, fame.

This exciting activity has what a mind needs to stay active and alert. What could be more fulfilling than working on a successful treasure recovery project that you design and carry through to completion by yourself or in association with a like-minded friend? However, most of the time, success depends solely on your input and nobody else's. The rewards, both psychic and monetary, are well earned because you had the idea, you did the research and the field-work, and you came home with the goods.

It's been said that the United States is a nation of spectators. However, even though the power of observation is crucial in treasure hunting, don't include urban treasure hunters in that group of spectators. By nature, treasure hunters are optimistic and inquisitive problem solvers who view life as exciting and challenging. Their minds are sharp and organized, allowing them to see things that most other people pass over. They are able to focus their attention and apply themselves to the job at hand with patience and perseverance. If they need a new skill, they learn it fast. Treasure hunters are doers who enjoy searching around because it can launch them into inspiring, off-the-beaten-path adventures where the triumphs can be quite astounding.

Such was the case for an enterprising urban treasure hunter who found $25,000 in $20 goldbacks from the 1920s. (Goldbacks were so called because when this currency was in circulation from 1863 to 1933, the United States Department of the Treasury backed it with gold.) He found this cache under a bathtub, stashed away in several old leather pouches, in an early-1900s Brooklyn house that was about to be torn down. He also recovered an antique European doll with human teeth that was eventually sold to a collector for $2,600. Not bad for an afternoon's work.

So, as you can see, treasure hunting in an urban setting is not a wild fantasy and can give a meaningful purpose to your spare time. It will also bring out the best in you. In addition, many of the treasure hunters I know appreciate the mental escape of the hunt, which clears their heads of daily stress. Urban treasure hunting can truly offer a multifaceted sense of fulfillment.

DEVELOPING A TREASURE AWARENESS

Now that you know the scope of city-style treasure hunting, you need to begin developing a "treasure awareness" to get things moving. In other words, you have to start thinking like a treasure hunter in order to achieve success. To help you in this process, I'd like to set the stage by passing along the most basic tenet of urban treasure hunting: "Anything can be anywhere." This also happens to be my personal treasure hunting motto.

I define "treasure awareness" as the mindset necessary to quickly recognize and assess the potential of making a good find. This entails interpreting features in the physical terrain, along with written and verbal clues about neighborhoods as they may relate to past eras and activities, and then coming to the logical conclusion that lost, hidden, or forgotten valuables can be recovered. This ability is self-perpetuating because many of your future successes will be based on your past accomplishments and what you learned from them.

I consider my treasure awareness something akin to an automatic pilot arising from my creative intuition, my field observations, articles and books I've read, and, of course, conversations with my fellow urban treasure hunters. All of this input has synthesized to make me very receptive to New York's constantly changing possibilities for finding treasure.

A General Benedict Arnold relic was found in Brooklyn at an old ruins and has been authenticated as a lead key tag attached to a seventeen-link brass chain. Inscribed on one side is "Arnold's Staff," while "Con. Army" is inscribed on the other. Also found were two dozen George II and George III copper coins. Anything can be anywhere!

To develop your treasure awareness, you will need to develop the following instincts and habits.

Seize the Moment

Urban areas are a hodgepodge of opening and closing doors for the treasure hunter. Many opportunities are transitory. Once you pass them by, you may never find them offered again, which makes vigilance an essential trait. My personal experiences continually validate this point.

For example, one day I was driving by a local reservoir that had dried up due to a severe drought in the region. When I saw all that long covered-up ground now exposed, my brain quickly started to receive treasure messages. The reservoir's age was a prime motivating factor, since it dated back to the 1880s. You don't have to be a

This reservoir, dried up due to a severe drought, offered plenty of treasure hunting adventure. The water control house in the background has a dedication date of 1889 inscribed on a center stone.

genius to recognize the treasure potential of this unusual situation. After all, people must have been throwing things in the reservoir for years, as well as losing coins and jewelry while swimming.

Subsequent library research, which I did within two days of seeing this terrific opening, provided me with enough background material on the reservoir and the surrounding park to support my original interpretation. Among the research material I found were photographs from the late nineteenth century showing lively picnic activity. This gave me the impetus to get some field exploration going soon, before the drought conditions changed.

After a week's time, a friend and I, armed with metal detectors, descended the slanted cobblestone walls of the dried-up reservoir to search through a century's accumulation of debris, which included many graceful bottles from the 1920s. The biggest surprise was finding nine rusted handguns, including a late-nineteenth-century Colt six-shooter. Our wonderment was short-lived, as we soon realized that a body of water in a city was a very safe place to get rid of incriminating evidence. We also found plenty of toy guns that had probably been brandished as "the real thing."

These guns were found in the reservoir using a metal detector. The one in the center is a late-nineteenth-century Colt revolver. The other two are modern Saturday night specials that were probably used for nefarious deeds and then discarded.

We searched that reservoir using a winding, "S"-type pattern to cover the 40 feet or so of debris that radiated from the shoreline. Many old marbles dotted the surface, and one deep signal from our metal detectors produced a Civil War military insignia. We didn't hit a silver or gold jackpot as we had expected, but the chance was certainly there. Exploring that reservoir was a first-rate adventure and reinforced another basic treasure hunting tenet: "What you find is not always what you're seeking."

I'm pretty sure that we were the first people ever to use metal detectors in that reservoir, and we may have been the last for a while. Within a month of our expedition, a large amount of rainfall restored the reservoir to its former condition—full. This is a very important lesson: When you see a treasure hunting opportunity, you need to get right on it, or else, in a short time, it might be gone.

Explore the Unusual

In another adventure, I encountered an old, rusty, strange looking pipe sticking out of a cracked concrete base in a remote wooded area. This struck me as odd because nothing else in the surrounding terrain matched. However, there had to be a reason people needed this pipe in such an out-of-the-way place.

Pursuing it further at the local library, I found documentation that the early German immigrant residents of the neighborhood had been very fond of their beer gardens, which strongly suggested that the mysterious pipe had once brought water to just such a late-nineteenth-century establishment called Schmidt's Woods. Over the years, because of neighborhood development and the construction of a major highway in 1934, all traces of the once-cherished beer gardens, except this pipe and its foundation, had disappeared.

After firing up my metal detector, I found some wonderful silver 1880s Barber coins and Indian Head cents, plus an exotic one-cent piece from British North Borneo dated 1882 that I like to think was lost by a merchant seaman. The Indian Heads were more numerous in one particular area, and my guess is that the patrons betted on their target practice skills. After all, Schmidt's Woods was located within a large park named Schutzen (German for "shooting") Park.

> The picnic groves and beer gardens of yesteryear gave hardworking bricklayers, butchers, and machinists a quiet green place where their children could romp, their wives could relax, and they could sit on a bench enjoying a cold beer with friends. A lost moment in time.

There were also three large apple trees in the surrounding dense vegetation. Apple trees often indicate an old picnic grove or farmstead. Even if they were just isolated trees, people are generally attracted to fruit trees and someone may have left something behind. Whatever the case, either the strange pipe or the apple trees should have been sufficient to start the treasure ball rolling. But what proved my vanished-beer-garden theory were the broken pieces of old beer mugs that came up as I dug for coins. Together, all of these clues made a case for further investigation and historical appreciation.

Exercise Your Creativity and Individuality

Your personal creativity and individuality will also help shape your treasure awareness. The ever-changing urban environment offers you a fine opportunity to try out a multitude of treasure hunting ideas. Combined with keeping an open mind and maintaining a broad perspective, your individuality of thought will take you to productive sites that other treasure hunters may never even consider.

That was my experience when I first started my treasure hunting career as a dedicated coin hunter. It seemed that practically every place I detected for old coins would pay off, making me wonder why more people were not using metal detectors. In actuality, there were plenty of detectorists (treasure hunters who use metal detectors) around at the time, but not where I was searching. My creativity is what brought me to untouched spots—and still does.

While refining your treasure awareness, you should always come back to a third basic urban treasure hunting tenet: "There is a positive correlation between finding treasure and searching in areas where there was people activity." For example, some human behaviors, such as recreational pursuits, are more conducive to the loss of valuables than others. Therefore, you should go to places where people participated in recreational activities and search around. The many vintage parks in New York City fit the bill perfectly and have yielded numerous old coins, lost jewelry items, and collectibles for diligent urban treasure hunters.

Denver, with its more than 200 parks, has a fine reputation regarding urban treasure finds. Among the parks in the Mile High City, fourteen date from before 1900, with the oldest going back to 1868. Over the years, Denver's large municipal park system has been described in treasure hunting magazines as offering "some of the best metal detecting to be found anywhere" and being "a paradise for coin hunters."

Backing up this statement, adept urban treasure hunters from Denver have reported finding a good amount of old silver Barber and Seated Liberty coins, along with an occasional gold coin, such as the $5 gold piece from 1903 found in City Park, which was built in 1881. No doubt, similar possibilities probably exist where you live. I like to follow Sherlock Holmes's rule, "The obvious is always overlooked," which is extremely helpful advice for all treasure hunting endeavors.

Re-create the Past

To be successful, you must hone the ability to recreate the past in your mind—and not be trapped in the present. It's up to you to be

Explore as many different treasure hunting directions as possible. After all, one thing leads to the next in ways you can't imagine.

"There is nothing more deceptive than an obvious fact."

—Sherlock Holmes, *"The Boscombe Valley Mystery"*

The old orphanage once had a baseball team, as well as both a boys' and a girls' band. All the children were taught to play an instrument, and every spring and summer brought festivals attended by children from other orphanages.

curious and to unravel the facts about your city's early years, such as the locations of old trolley and bus lines, trading posts, forts, picnic groves, battlegrounds, railroad depots, and steamboat landings. Of course, many of these have been built over, but you may be pleasantly surprised to find a bare patch of ground to reconnoiter.

My treasure awareness provided another productive adventure when I received permission from the administrator of an orphanage built in 1896 to search its huge, overgrown lawn with my metal detector. The old orphanage had been a serendipitous drive-by discovery that had really astounded me. Imagine accidentally coming across such a terrific hunting spot all tucked away in a quiet neighborhood in the outskirts of the city. My ongoing search of the grounds turned out to be a *Twilight Zone* experience due to the interesting artifacts I found, but even more so because of my associated research, which revealed the orphanage's purpose and history.

Historical orphanages have seen cities grow around them and can provide some great coin hunting on their extensive grounds. This "home" was built in the mid-1890s. Remember to ask permission!

Basically, according to a remarkable series of photo-filled newsletters printed in the 1920s, the orphanage was founded by caring Protestant immigrants from Germany for the children of their countrymen who had died while crossing the Atlantic. The children were part of the massive wave of European immigrants who passed through Ellis Island and into New York City's dynamic growing population in the late nineteenth and early twentieth centuries.

The home protected the children and provided them with a religious and moral upbringing. There were always about ninety children living there, and over the years, many coins, religious medals, and toy lead soldiers were lost in the great lawn. Today, the orphanage is used as a similar institution for neglected children of our present society.

Looking back, I'd have to say that this old orphanage ranks as one of my all-time-favorite hunting grounds. I feel very lucky to have found it. But as things go, the great lawn is now home to a hospital clinic and no longer presents the remarkable search opportunities that I experienced there.

Investigate Hearsay and Rumors

Sometimes your introduction to a potentially rich hunting spot will be through hearsay. Therefore, never discount any intriguing treasure lore about communities or "strange" individuals.

Even the most unlikely story may contain that spark that will ignite your imagination and lead to a wonderful discovery. Ask any urban treasure hunters who have been at it for a while, and they will probably agree and even tell you about a surprising clue and recovery connection they made.

For this reason, keep a record of your ideas. It's very easy to forget spontaneous thoughts and associated details. I guarantee that your growing treasure awareness to-do file will provide you with an ongoing list of projects—and the more projects you have active, the better your chances will be for success.

The orphanage's great lawn yielded many old coins, pieces of jewelry, and other personal items. Notice the double row of old maple trees lining the winding entranceway.

"When you have excluded the impossible, whatever remains, however improbable, must be the truth."

—Sherlock Holmes,
"The Adventure of the Beryl Coronet"

Study Your City's Criminal Record

Joe Bradish was a lesser known East Coast pirate who sailed his ship, *The Adventure*, around Long Island. Historical records state that he buried treasure caches at Montauk Point and on small offshore islands. Bradish was captured and hanged in 1700.

To develop your treasure awareness, you also need to learn about your city's criminal history. This could lead to finding long-forgotten caches of valuables. Urban areas located along coasts or river systems also have the potential for the recovery of hidden pirate loot.

Our country's history is overflowing with tales of thievery along its waterways. Many small offshore islands were often used to hide smuggled goods, stolen money, and other valuables. Stories abound about such infamous pirates as Blackbeard, Jean LaFitte, and Captain Kidd burying treasure along our shores.

If you live in a city that a famous (or maybe not-so-famous) pirate considered part of his territory, there's probably a good amount of established information on his lawless activities for you to sift through. Sometimes this research will point you toward specific places to dig and you may get lucky.

Even if your city is landlocked, it most likely had highwaymen doing on its roads and rails what their nautical counterparts did at sea. You've probably heard of missing payrolls from stagecoach and train robberies—Jesse James and all that. A reliable strategy to follow here is to imagine that you were living in the bandit's time and had something to hide. Where would you stash the goods?

This is exactly the strategy followed by two treasure hunters who recovered the loot from an old train robbery in New Mexico. They followed up on some clues in a treasure hunting magazine article about the missing loot—$40,000 in cash and an unknown amount of silver dollars—from a train robbery pulled off by the Bronco Kid and Kid Johnson. The two robbers had held up a Santa Fe–bound train south of Albuquerque in 1898.

Following the escape route of the desperadoes, the treasure hunters searched the most likely hiding places and, a hundred years after the robbery, found a portion of the stolen money. Grateful to the author of the magazine article, they rewarded him with a dozen silver dollars from the swag. Now, that's how it's done!

If you ever find yourself near the Catskill Mountains of New York, you can try to find some missing loot yourself. Dutch Shultz, the flamboyant and ruthless Prohibition-era gangster, is said to have buried approximately $7 million in diamonds, cash, gold pieces, and negotiable securities somewhere near Phoenicia, New York. This particular treasure quest has kept some hard-nosed treasure hounds busy for years and is exactly the type of treasure lead from a city's criminal past that you should try to ferret out.

Expand Your Search Horizons

When researching treasure hunting opportunities, don't restrict yourself area-wise. Some of your treasure hunting projects may take you right to your city's limits or even beyond. This is very typical because urban treasure hunting will be your entry to all types of treasure hunting, and will also provide you with the skills and confidence to hunt in practically any environment. It's really up to you to decide what you're looking for and to then plan your expeditions accordingly.

Speaking of city limits, they seem to be stretching further out as today's urban areas continue to grow and rural property is developed into suburban housing tracts and shopping malls. This situation presents some good get-there-while-you-can opportunities to conduct exploratory expeditions into newly developing areas. What could be better than a first shot at some new turf?

A few smart urban treasure hunters from Memphis, Tennessee, made this sensible connection and now regularly hunt the suburbs by following the bulldozers and earthmovers—with good results. Among their recoveries have been coins and artifacts from both the pre– and post–Civil War eras. Currently, their key finds are old Spanish reals, silver coins from the late 1700s and early 1800s. Coins from Spain were once legal tender in America, even after the first mint was established in the United States in 1792.

No one is sure why these classic silver coins are turning up on the outskirts of a rapidly expanding Memphis, but treasure hunters speculate that they were left by early settlers and Native Americans using the Cherokee and Pontotoc trails, which run through the area. This is a plausible explanation based on a good sense of local history. In addition to the Spanish silver, some United States gold coins have also surfaced. Another good reason to come back and search some more! I would say that there's an interesting piece of Americana being revealed in Memphis.

Keep Up With Current Events

Your treasure awareness should also include keeping up with any unexpected treasure finds reported in the media to have been made by people not even looking for treasure. That's how it is—sometimes things just turn up. There's always something to learn from these surprising events, with the possibility of follow-up opportunities to capitalize on. You never know what riches might have been missed.

When an occasional accidental cache discovery makes the headlines, it always creates some "treasure hunting fever."

For example, not too long ago, the newspapers reported the story of a woman in Santa Rosa, California, who found thirty gold coins while digging in her backyard. The oldest coin was dated 1884 and the most recent 1910, indicating that her neighborhood would certainly be a good area to investigate. I'm sure there's probably an interesting story behind this recovery. And there may be more caches just like it waiting to be found.

Actually, I find these out-of-nowhere types of recoveries to be inspiring, since they demonstrate that every time you're out hunting, you have the chance to find something unexpectedly valuable and interesting.

The Santa Rosa find also debunks the popular treasure hunting misconception that only making "big strikes," not finding a number of small caches hidden by people of more modest means, is typical of success. On the contrary, persistent treasure hunters make the latter type of find more often than you might imagine because a lot of treasure is hidden in urban America.

Another way of keeping up with treasure hunting opportunities is to keep track of park renovations. In New York City, the various contracts awarded for park renovations are listed in "The City Record," which is available in a paper version and online. Every so often, visit the parks slated for renovation to see what's going on because sooner or later, the earthmovers will show up and get down to business. Be ready!

To really enhance your treasure awareness, I strongly recommend that you subscribe to any of the treasure hunting magazines listed in Appendix C. These publications offer interesting and instructive articles written by other urban treasure hunters who are glad to share information about their finds, their search techniques, and the equipment they use. The value of having a constant flow of field-proven and inspiring how-to information on which to base your projects can't be overstated.

Interpret Natural Features

An integral part of developing your treasure awareness is learning to understand your city's natural features. In many instances, the topography has been so altered that being able to reconstruct the terrain using your knowledge and imagination is necessary in order to tap into whatever treasure you're seeking. The ability to read the particular elements of the landscape and to evaluate when and how they were disturbed is an important skill to master.

A good illustration of this might involve the type and placement of trees where you're searching. This could be along an old boulevard, in someone's backyard, or in a wooded section. Remember, many trees grow only in specific parts of the country, and the trees growing in your search area that are not native to the area were probably brought there for a reason, usually for landscaping, shade, or fruit bearing purposes.

Scattered piles of rubble are all that remain of a once-magnificent early-nineteenth-century mansion that now lies in ruins deep in an urban woodland. Imagine the potential here!

Encountering a straight row of the same species of tree in an uninhabited or out-of-the-way place should make you pause and consider how often anything in nature is that linear. Most likely, this was the location of some outdoor recreation area or structure such as an old picnic grove, dance hall, roadhouse, or even overgrown entrance road to a ruined mansion.

Don't be put off if the trees are not extremely tall. The height of a tree does not always indicate its age. Some tree varieties grow very slowly, so a tree doesn't need to be tall to be old. Further research using a tree identification guide, old maps, and field exploration is definitely in order.

What if an area has very sparse vegetation or is completely barren—what could that mean? My immediate reaction would be to wonder *why* it's that way. In all probability, the spot was the focus

This vacant lot in an old neighborhood may have been used in the past for traveling carnivals, fairs, and patriotic celebrations. A coin bonanza is not unlikely here, nor is locating an old privy or making bottle finds. Look for pieces of antique glass and crockery as clues.

of some human activity that denuded it. Perhaps it once served as a baseball sandlot or fairground. Both of these possibilities should send you running for your metal detector because of the potential for super finds in old silver coins.

I've encountered inconspicuous locations like the above in remote sections of the city. Finding them was like hitting three of a kind on a slot machine. In one small, dusty lot that measured approximately 150 feet by 100 feet, I found more than 2,500 coins, many of them silver. Research supported my treasure awareness here by revealing the lot's use as a fairground beginning in the 1920s and as a site for War Bond rallies during World War II.

To learn about the natural features (such as the terrain, trees, plants, animals, or insects) of your city, I recommend the Peterson series of guidebooks. The Peterson books are very detailed, easy to use, and enjoyable, and will definitely enhance your treasure awareness. Any urban treasure hunter would clearly benefit from adding a naturalist's skills to his or her repertoire for deciphering the environment.

Searching near a nineteenth-century mansion's desolate ruins revealed a buried empty pot at a depth of 1 foot. That's about as close as you can get—and a real heart stopper!

Become a Photographer

Another useful strategy for sharpening your treasure awareness is to take photographs. Having study photos of a proposed site will enable you to plan an expedition while not actually being at the site. In addition, keeping a photographic record of the ground you cover during an expedition will allow you to avoid duplicating work the next time you're able to return to the site.

You should also make it a practice to take photos of large parks during the different seasons so that you can study how the use patterns change. Certain topographical features may be more prominent or heavily used in different seasons. For example, I know of at least two instances where the rolling hills of a public golf course become a winter wonderland for skiers and sledders. After the snow melts, a simple eyeballing walk can produce some good jewelry and coin finds on the larger hills, where the more spectacular wipeouts occur.

Searching a likely
sleigh riding hill from
bygone days with a
metal detector produced
this 1889 silver dollar.

On one such walk, my treasure awareness kicked in and I was rewarded with an 1889 silver dollar after surmising that a small, out-of-the-way hill had also been used for sledding in bygone times. It just had that look! I started detecting at the bottom of the hill and almost immediately got a loud signal in my headphones. After digging down about 4 inches, I scooped out a handful of dirt that included a large silver disk that turned out to be a silver dollar. Even though I had expected to find something, this magnificent coin was a big surprise.

Being an urban treasure hunter will allow you to see your city the way few other people do. Your day-to-day perspective will grow to include all its nooks and crannies, and you will find yourself searching under bridges, wandering through marshes, exploring huge parks, and going deep into construction sites. You'll follow trails far into the woods, stroll along the waterfront, and match your step with those of the tourists filling the downtown streets. You'll circle lakes, ramble in fields, and chug along old railroad tracks. You will see it all, and along the way you'll meet some very interesting people.

❧ 3 ❧

Public Relations

The same as with many other endeavors in today's world, urban treasure hunting often places you in contact with the public. Whether you're negotiating with a client over your services, interviewing the longtime resident of an area for research purposes, or dealing with an ethnic group that regards a public park as a piece of its homeland, using good human relations skills and behavior will ultimately increase your success and enjoyment.

In an urban environment, where people have learned to be suspicious of strangers and their motives, your ability to clearly explain your purpose and methods will be a strong asset in gaining access to important information and searchable property. In this chapter, we will discuss how to define yourself, how to explain what you're doing, and how to interact with the public and property owners.

DEFINE WHO YOU ARE

One of the first things you should do before hitting the streets with your metal detector is work on your self-definition. I choose to think of myself as a law-abiding adventurer who searches for long-lost or hidden valuables, who is careful to respect the rights of others, and who in no way would be considered a pirate. Pirates are a variety of treasure hunter who don't care if they trespass on or destroy the property of others to gain a profit. This small segment of the treasure hunting population makes things difficult for the vast majority of treasure hunters because of their foul methods and reputation.

MEET THE CAST OF CHARACTERS

Using a metal detector in a city is like waving a people magnet. In many instances, curious people will come over to see what's going on. Some of them will be genuinely interested in what you're doing and have intelligent questions or even substantive leads to offer. Others will be "clowns" with dumb remarks who want to borrow your machine to supposedly look for something they lost.

You may also find yourself crowded by annoying kids who bombard you with inane conversation. Then they may want to keep what you find.

The way I handle the public depends on how I'm approached. People who treat me with respect get the same back. I'm certainly not opposed to having a short, friendly, informative conversation with a polite person.

The rude types usually don't get much of a response from me, or I tell them, "I can't talk and detect at the same time. Please stay out of my way." Then I just ignore them. They soon get the message and leave.

AVOID SHOW-AND-TELL

A good-hearted treasure hunting companion of mine once found a really fine gold ring in Brooklyn's old and distinguished Prospect Park. Soon after, a ten-year-old boy came over and asked, "Hey, mister, what did you find?" My friend was so thrilled with his discovery, he took out the ring for show-and-tell, and the little dear immediately grabbed it and ran away.

There is an important message in this story: *Never* show people anything valuable that you find. It opens you up to being hassled by people claiming to have just lost the item—even though it is more than 100 years old and was buried 6 inches down. Use common sense. You're better off letting the public-at-large believe you are a harmless eccentric looking for pennies.

One way to avoid people problems is to put off going to heavily used parks until the weather is poor. This piece of advice definitely applies to tough parts of town. Drizzle and cold weather will keep the majority of people away from outdoor recreation, allowing you to hunt undisturbed.

TRY TO BLEND IN

Your urban treasure hunting adventures can take you into many diverse neighborhoods, and looking nondescript is a worthwhile goal wherever you go. Some local inhabitants are sensitive to outsiders in their neighborhood. After all, your most noticeable attribute, even before you start detecting, is your physical appearance.

Successful urban treasure hunters are very aware of the concept of "fit"—that is, whether you look like you belong in the neighborhood. My experience has been that fit is very important in the better sections of town, where people tend to be very touchy about outsiders and who is sharing their recreation space.

Strategically, I try to dress like the average neighborhood person who is out for a day in the park. In more upscale areas, that means looking like a typical jogger or some other type of middle-class sport enthusiast.

Eliminate all the rough edges from your presentation. For example, never use a hunting knife for digging in such neighborhoods. It will cause people to feel uneasy about your presence, especially if there are young children around. You will lose your social invisibility, and you might even be asked to leave by patrolling private security guards. I learned this by experience.

In tough areas, I affect a harder, more streetwise look by wearing an article or two of camouflage clothing and worn jeans. I also use my K-Bar combat knife for digging to discourage certain members of the local population from becoming too interested.

It's really best to let the public at large think you are just a harmless eccentric looking for pennies and old tokens.

REQUEST PERMISSION TO HUNT ON PRIVATE PROPERTY

On certain occasions, you will find it beneficial to hunt on private property. Asking permission to do this is like anything else in life. The worst that can happen is that you will be turned down, which does occur. Your chance of getting the go-ahead, however, is improved by a neat and nonthreatening appearance, as well as by a coherent verbal presentation.

When approaching a property owner, it's very important that you be able to clearly explain what you expect to accomplish. In addition, show the property owner some similar items you found elsewhere to prove that you are legitimate. Be specific. Most property owners will be suspicious of what appears to them to be a "fishing expedition" with no clear goal or time frame.

One approach you can use is to explain that you are an amateur historian interested in the city's past and that you believe the land being discussed, due to its history, is a prime site for the recovery of some telling relics and coins. You could then offer to show the property owner how your metal detector works, emphasizing that you will not harm the land in any way.

Even though a hunting knife may be your favorite digging tool, today is not the day to have one hanging from your belt. Leave the knife at home and bring a trowel or gardening tool instead. Don't look like Rambo when asking permission.

If your target is old bottles, assure the property owner that you will not turn the property into "crater city." Make it clear that you take great pride in the neatness of your recovery techniques.

Don't Be Greedy

When seeking permission to hunt on private property, be flexible. If the property owner offers you access on terms and conditions that are not exactly what you want, accept them anyway and be thankful that you got in. Don't be greedy and argue for a better deal. This will alienate the property owner and might cause a change of mind. Also, ask the property owner if there is something that the family may have lost over the years. If you find it, you can return it.

Sometimes, the only way you can get onto private property is to offer a split of what you find. Half of something is better than all of nothing. Hold off on making this offer, however, until you've exhausted all the other positive points of your presentation.

Occasionally, property owners give an unqualified go-ahead at the outset, but then "request" a payment of some sort afterwards. Be prepared for this with a reasonable offer. You may want to return, so establishing good will is important. For casual, spur-of-the-moment searches, don't complicate things by asking for a written agreement. A quick verbal understanding is better. Just go for it.

In general, it's not a bad idea to give the property owner an old coin or bottle that you recovered there as a token of your appreciation. People tend to be very curious about what can be found on their land. Once a rapport has developed, they may even tell you some important facts, filling in research gaps or offering new leads. They might even open up doors to hunting adjoining property.

Work to Build Trust

I got into hunting on private property quite by accident. One day, I was coin hunting in an old park near where I live and a guy came over to ask me about my metal detector and its capabilities. It seemed that in the course of demolishing an antiquated carriage house, he had broken open a child's penny cache concealed in the wall and was now curious about what else might be there.

After talking for a while, the man invited me to the carriage house site to investigate further, which I did. All I found were some more Indian Heads in the rubble. None of them were particularly valuable, but it still was an eye-opening experience.

As it developed, however, this gentleman introduced me to his father, who became a valuable resource to me concerning the neighborhood's history over the last sixty years. His father also arranged for me to search bordering property by speaking to his neighbors.

This incident demonstrates an important aspect of searching private property—the building of trust. There should be nothing about your manner that would discourage trust. After you receive permission to search someone's property, you should announce yourself when you arrive and when you leave. Talk about your activities in a way that promotes good will and that leads to sustaining the property owner's interest in your project.

Accept Rejection Gracefully

If your request to search someone's property is rejected, accept the decision gracefully and without any negative feelings. After all, it's a property owner's right to say no—and that should be the end of it. When turned down, move on to another project. There are plenty of others out there. Who knows? Maybe one day the land will be sold and the new owner will be more amenable to your request. Until then, know that you tried your best.

I strongly advise against any clandestine activity to search property whose access you've been denied because you can be arrested and may have to spend time in jail while waiting to be bailed out. You might also have to worry about a civil suit for property damages.

ADVERTISE YOUR SERVICES

Some urban treasure hunters, including myself, actively advertise our treasure hunting services to help people find lost or hidden valuables. A helpful aid in this endeavor is a business card clearly stating who you are, your telephone number, and the services that you can provide.

Distribute the card to homeowners and construction site bosses, and post it on neighborhood bulletin boards. In addition to getting your message across, this will help give your treasure hunting enterprise an air of social responsibility. You can also earn dividends by way of fees for your work, but I'll cover that in more detail in Chapter 13.

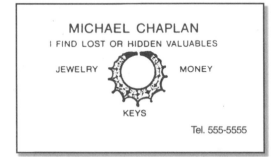

MICHAEL CHAPLAN
I FIND LOST OR HIDDEN VALUABLES

JEWELRY   MONEY

KEYS

Tel. 555-5555

An attractive business card with your telephone number will boost your respectability when approaching people for information and advertising your treasure hunting skills on neighborhood bulletin boards.

PLAY BY THE RULES

Be very careful to know and respect your local ordinances regarding digging in public parks. Don't expect the parks department to feel kindly towards you after some idiot made a prize lawn look like gophers invaded. Always fill in your holes. Beyond that, use common sense regarding when and where you dig. If you have to apply for a yearly permit, do so. Remember, you will be paving the way for the urban treasure hunters who follow and how they will be received.

OFFER COMMUNITY SERVICE

There are many socially beneficial ways of pursuing treasure hunting in a city. For instance, you should consider helping historical societies recover artifacts from the land to which they have access. In one instance, I was asked to locate a time capsule that was believed to have been buried somewhere around the foundation of a historical society headquarters, which was an old public school built in 1869.

After about two hours of probing and detecting, I came up with the very bare remains of a small metal box. Time and the elements had destroyed the container and any message from the people responsible for the original construction project. The recovery project was tremendous fun anyway, and I was glad to have volunteered my services.

Some treasure hunting clubs form search-and-recovery teams that work with law enforcement and other agencies needing metal detecting expertise. These clubs have been helpful in finding lost and stolen property and have been instrumental in uncovering important trial evidence. Some clubs have assisted the National Transportation Safety Board in aircraft accident investigations, and others have been of great help in locating valuables for homeowners following devastating earthquakes and fires in California. There are a lot of socially constructive things that urban treasure hunters can do.

The main point to remember when dealing with the urban public is to be civilized and alert. With this in mind, you should not have any problems in 95 percent of encounters. Even further, you might find yourself the happy recipient of a productive idea offered by someone intimately acquainted with the neighborhood.

Your actions and recovery methods will affect how the local citizenry and city officials view your activities. If you want to continue digging in peace and prosperity, never violate the rights of others. Anything detrimental you do will negatively influence how all local treasure hunters are perceived. So, make it easy for everybody and act responsibly.

Sharing your expertise through community service activities will bring additional interesting projects your way and help you earn the recognition you deserve as a valuable resource to the community.

Joining a club helps to promote treasure hunting as an organized outdoor sport. The oft-repeated headline, "Local Metal Detecting Club Helps Police Locate Crime Evidence," has created a lot of good will.

❧ 4 ❧

Hazards

Treasure hunting in an urban environment has its risks as well as its rewards. These risks increase or decrease depending on where you do your searching. A characteristic of urban areas is that they are composed of neighborhoods, some of which are good, but others of which are problematical. This is the main key to level of risk.

Most cities have a good selection of potential hunting sites, and you can find yourself in the best or worst parts of town, with many sections somewhere in between. Your paramount consideration should always be your personal safety. Sure, it's nice to find a lot of "goodies," but not at the cost of being attacked and robbed. Nothing you could ever find is worth losing your life.

In this chapter, we will discuss the varied risks of urban treasure hunting and what you can do to minimize them.

ACROSS THE TRACKS

My experience in high-crime areas has been that there are certain categories of people who are more inclined to come over and ask what you are doing in what may seem an aggressive manner. Most of the time, you are approached by either the local wise guy or adolescents who see you and your metal detector as a diversion from just hanging out.

When this type of person comes over, I generally respond by saying as little as possible about my potential finds or the ones I've already made. Sometimes, if pressed, I will briefly mention that I'm doing an article on the history of the neighborhood and am hoping to find some old subway tokens for an accompanying photo. No metal detector demonstrations here.

In addition, I never make a recovery while I'm being watched by any "characters." If I did, one of the consequences might be having a few extra people shadowing my every move for the next several hours. Believe me, it happens.

The usual progression of events is that the "crew" generally loses interest after a few minutes and departs. I reinforce their decision to leave by telling them that what I'm doing is similar to fishing. I say that I have my good days and my bad days, and today looks like a loser.

However, the allure of these tough areas is that hardly anyone attempts to do any treasure hunting there, while the potential for good finds is excellent. Some old parks in rough areas served as the center of local social activity during earlier and better times, and are loaded with old silver coins and gold jewelry. On the downside is the possibility that you might get mugged.

My advice is that if you're not up to the verbal jousting and encounters with desperadoes associated with tough areas, *don't go.* You have to decide for yourself whether a particular project is worth it. Just remember how appealing a target you make, lost in concentration with your shiny and expensive looking metal detector.

If you decide the project is worth it, take a few precautions. Get there early. This is a proven method for avoiding trouble. If you arrive at 6:00 in the morning and stay until 10:00, chances are you will miss the criminal rush hour.

Don't wear any gold jewelry, and immediately put away all the valuables you find. You can look at them later. Winos, junkies, and assorted other criminal types might get the idea you're a walking moneybag if you become careless in that respect.

To illustrate my last point, one treasure hunter I know was detecting in Crotona Park, a dangerous but productive area in the Bronx, when he unearthed an 1882 silver dollar that was about 4 inches down in the dirt. Standing there admiring it, he attracted some toughs who claimed that one of them had lost the coin the day before. My buddy tried to explain that the coin had been buried deep in the ground and could not have been the "lost" coin, but as he spoke, he sized up the situation as rapidly going downhill and surrendered the silver dollar. It was a wise move.

"At least once in every man's life, death looks him straight in the eye and passes on."

—Colonel Percy Fawcett, *British explorer of the 1920s*

Luckily, my friend had his car parked nearby and escaped unharmed. Lesson learned—I hope. This brings up another couple of precautions you should take: It's not a bad idea to leave your wallet in your car, plus to keep a spare car key hidden under the chassis in case you do get robbed.

One intrepid treasure hunter I know who specializes in tough areas has an inventive way of dealing with bothersome people. He always carries some old, rusted nuts and bolts with him. These junk items provide him with an "out" when he is questioned about his finds. He just reaches into his pocket, takes out the junk, and says, in an annoyed and frustrated manner: "Nuts and bolts. Nuts and bolts. That's all I ever find!" At this point, the interrogators usually laugh at this "eccentric"—who actually does remarkably well. Most times, his response is enough to discourage any further attention.

HUMAN FLOTSAM AND JETSAM

Homeless people, squatters, and derelicts will generally leave you alone. However, under certain circumstances, you can find yourself in real hot water. My closest call came in Thompkins Square Park on the lower east side of Manhattan. I was there with a hunting buddy because the park has a record for producing some terrific coin recoveries dating back to the 1830s.

The park's history is quite remarkable, since it was used for many years during the early nineteenth century as a campground for new arrivals in New York City. It was also the site of a major riot in the 1860s.

We were there on a beautiful summer day when my partner came too close to an area being used as a squatter's camp. It was sort of a "hobo jungle," with cots, discarded furniture, dilapidated beach chairs, and a campfire going. The reaction of the inhabitants was unpredictable and fast when a crazy bag lady started screaming: "Thief! Thief!"

My buddy was surrounded by the squatters and accused of being a marauder out to steal from them. I ran over to help, and luckily we were able to talk our way out of the predicament while hastily retreating. It really was a very close call and a frightful experience. It also strongly influenced my planning of future expeditions to that park: I have not gone back since!

"Adventures are a sign of incompetence."

—Vilhjalmur Steffannson, *Norwegian arctic explorer of the early twentieth century*

Remember, urban street people have their own set of rules and values. They are more inclined to hit and stab first, and then ask questions. Somehow, my buddy and I violated their turf and etiquette—or at least, the bag lady thought so—and we almost paid a severe penalty. We did the right thing by leaving immediately.

NEVER WORK ALONE

That last incident demonstrates the importance of another precaution to take when going into tough neighborhoods: Don't go alone. It's always a good idea to have someone around to watch your back. Always travel with one or more companions when hunting on the wrong side of the tracks.

In these risky parts of the city, it's not a bad idea to be able to signal your partner in case a problem occurs. I like to carry a pheasant call for this purpose. A pheasant call is a hunter's call that produces the raucous cackle of the cock pheasant. This is quite an unusual noise that can be heard for some distance. Some urban treasure hunters carry a canister of Mace with them. Check your local laws, and learn how to use Mace if you choose it as your fail-safe. Don't make things easy for the crooks by gassing yourself.

ALWAYS STAY ALERT

Sometimes, what seems like a good-natured crowd may form to watch you detect. However, you will still need to be alert because someone could use the opportunity to size you up as a victim. In these situations, once again, it's best to move on.

For obvious reasons, *never* go into areas where street gangs are known to operate. This will almost always prove to be a no-win situation, with your most minor loss being your detector. Also, be very careful around bushes. You can be pulled in and vanish very easily.

Another simple precaution to take is not to leave any equipment unattended on the ground. If you're the type of person who carries everything along, get a fanny pack for storage. That way, nothing will be missing at the end of the day.

Also, you might want to dull your expensive looking detector's appearance by covering its shiny logos with gray duct tape. You really don't want to provide any extra visual stimulation that will attract malevolent characters.

WILD AMERICA

An additional hazard of urban living is wildlife. I've hunted in over-grown areas where the size and number of rats running around amazed me. They've never been aggressive toward me because I don't put my hands into ground or tree holes, where they live. If I get a positive signal from a hole, I probe the opening with a digging tool. The "rat rule" goes like this: "If you see one, there are at least twenty others that you can't see." Be forewarned!

Stray dogs can also be a problem. Sometimes, particularly in large parks, they form packs and can appear quite menacing. If you see a pack coming your way, leave the area and get to a spot where you have some protection. One treasure hunting friend was cornered by dogs in upper Manhattan's Inwood Park while searching rock grottos for Native American artifacts. Luckily, he had his metal detector with him and turned up the volume to create a barrage of loud noises that scared them away. That was quick thinking on his part and a useful tip to pass along.

New York City doesn't have any wild poisonous snakes that I know of, just the occasional escaped pet poisonous snake. All the snakes I've encountered have been harmless. But your part of the country might have some dangerous snakes. Take the necessary precaution to learn snake identification, then keep your eyes open.

Insect pests are a problem that everyone shares. The biggest annoyance I've encountered is the common mosquito, particularly after several days of rain. Large numbers of their eggs hatch from pools of standing water. Most of the time, their irritating bite is the only problem. But you should be aware that some species carry disease, such as the various types of encephalitis, including West Nile virus, which you don't have to be in the tropics to contract.

Luckily, an effective safeguard is readily available. There are quite a few different kinds of bug sprays available with varying degrees of protection. The most effective ones have relatively high concentrations of the ingredient N,N-diethyl-meta-toluamide, commonly known as DEET. A spray formula that is 20-percent DEET will provide adequate protection and enable you to work in areas from which other folks run.

Bug spray also discourages ticks from finding a home and a meal on your body. These little monsters—which are not insects, but rather

Venomous snakes bite about 8,000 people annually in the U.S. However, only 12 percent to 15 percent of these bites are fatal. There are four varieties of venomous snakes to watch out for: rattlesnakes, water moccasins, copperheads, and coral snakes.

Surveillance data from the Centers For Disease Control and Prevention report human West Nile virus infections occurring in thirty-seven states. Most infections take place in August and September.

arachnids, like spiders—are responsible for the spread of Lyme disease, Rocky Mountain spotted fever, and other serious diseases. Despite their names, these diseases can be contracted in all regions of the country, including urban areas. When disengaging a tick, be sure to remove all the mouth parts from your skin or you may end up with an infection. Sounds great, right? If you frequently search in areas that are bushy or full of scrub vegetation, like I do, don't underestimate the value of a good insect repellent.

Regarding ticks, I also recommend that once you get home, you put all your clothes in the freezer for fifteen minutes. This will kill any ticks that may just be walking around your clothes at the moment, but may attach later on. Don't forget to run your clothes through the washer and to clean up the freezer!

Bees, wasps, and hornets are minor problems if you aren't allergic to their venom. Then the only problems with them are their painful stings. In general, though, play it safe and give them plenty of room when you move through flowery or wooded areas or when you work in abandoned buildings or old ruins, where you may brush up against a nest. If you get stung under these latter circumstances, you may become further injured by tripping over rubble and debris while trying to escape.

You should also be careful around spiders. All spiders are poisonous, but there are two types living in urban areas that can cause you a great deal of grief. These are the black widow and the brown recluse spiders. Both are easily recognizable by their distinct abdominal markings of an hourglass and a violin, respectively, but I don't recommend getting close enough to positively identify them. These species tend to make their homes in habitats that people created by dumping refuse. They may also be encountered in abandoned buildings, woodpiles, cans, mattresses, and outhouses; under porches; and in a variety of other spots where treasure hunters often investigate. If you do get bitten by one of these spiders, head for an emergency room fast because you will need medical intervention as soon as possible.

Of course, the word "wild," when used to describe America, can have another meaning, too—"weird" or "strange." To learn about the "wild America" I stumbled upon in a trek through one of New York City's woodsy parks not too long ago, see "Strange Encounters" on page 43.

Searching old, abandoned miner shacks out west places you at risk for contracting Colorado Tick Fever. Symptoms include fever, headaches, and muscle aches that usually last for about a week.

Strange Encounters

An *Indiana Jones* component of being an urban treasure hunter in New York City is encountering voodoo ritual artifacts while searching around in the large, woodsy parks. This seems to be something that most treasure hunters experience, and we enjoy comparing notes on these "strange encounters." Here's how one such unexpected episode led me on a mysterious journey into the supernatural.

Picture this scenario: I was out detecting along a woodsy network of old horse trails when I came to the junction of four paths. Nothing too unusual about that—so far. But as I walked through, out of the corner of my eye I noticed a bright orange colored object under an oak tree about 7 feet into the brush.

Moving closer for a better view, I recognized the object as an upside-down clay flowerpot being used as some sort of alter. And on top of it, staring back at me with shiny white cowry shell eyes, was a weird looking stone head. As an experienced woods hunter, I was pretty accustomed to coming across things that people stashed in the bushes. However, this was a whole new experience and I felt like Robinson Crusoe when he first saw Friday's footprint. I was not alone, but who—or *what*—was with me?

I walked over and was just about to pick up the

Finding this mysterious stone fetish led the author into the strange world of urban voodoo. Note the 2-inch blade protruding from the top of Legba's head. Who has the antidote?

stone head when I noticed a sharp, 2-inch metal blade protruding from the top, partly concealed by a crown of grassy herbs. This made me pause and reflect on the potential downside of what I was getting into—such as being poisoned and then learning that the only known antidote was in Peru. By adding the right background music, this could have been a great intro for a movie called *The Detector of Doom*.

Now, I'm not one to haphazardly put my life in danger, but I do have a strong sense of curiosity that has led me to some memorable adventures. So, I carefully placed my prize in a plastic bag that I had with me. Also on the altar was a smooth, fist-sized rock, a shiny new penny, and more herbs, covered by a sticky, sweet smelling goo that was probably honey. After a final hesitation, I pocketed the coin and went on my way.

Later, at home, I started to research the mysterious stone head by looking through tribal artifact books, hoping to find a match or something solid to pursue. My interest in this area is extensive and I've attended quite a few auctions and exhibits where primitive curiosities were on display, but none included anything like this fetish.

The next surprise came a week later, when I revisited the site and saw that the smooth stone

This wooden voodoo doll was found standing amid the roots of a large oak tree. Sometimes it is intended for an outsider to take these ceremonial objects in order to finalize the magic.

had been used to smash the pot. They had come back! It was a baffling situation because so far, my research had dead-ended. The closest I had come to finding a match was a photo of a nineteenth-century Congo nkisi nail figure. A strange curio, to be sure, but it was a whole-bodied wooden figure studded with both blades and nails.

After three months, I was finally put on track by a radio talk show guest who suggested that I contact a particular *bruja* (sorceress) at an up-town *botanica* (occult goods store) in Washington Heights. At last! Here was someone who would be able to explain my puzzling find and the equally mystifying significance of the pot smashing.

The small shop was on a quiet street off busy Broadway. When I entered, chimes hanging on the door melodically signaled my arrival as a musky incense wafted up to greet me. I stood there for a moment, slowly exploring this realm of the super-natural with my eyes. One wall had high shelves packed with glass jars holding assorted roots, seeds, and bark. To the left, a large table was crowded with colorful statues of saints, while the cabinet next to it held a group of carved African figures. The rear counter was an eye-catching sight with a line of burning red and white candles. Some had $20 bills under them. I could tell this place was the real thing.

The striped blue curtain behind the counter parted and a stocky, gray haired woman appeared. Walking toward me, she asked, "How can I help you, my friend?"

"I'm looking for Graciella," I replied, somehow knowing that I was already speaking to her.

An open-palmed gesture with both hands was her response, and I began to tell her why I had come to see her. She patiently listened to my story and seemed deep in thought as I unwrapped my find and put it on the counter. Graciella then nod-ded her head toward the burning candles and said in a hushed voice, "You have been chosen."

"How's that again?" I asked, trying to make sure that I had heard her correctly.

She repeated her ominous statement and went on to tell me that this particular idol repre-sented Legba, "one of the seven *orishas* [African powers]" and the most feared deity in the cult of Santeria. Just as I had thought: I was dealing with some type of voodoo!

Graciella carefully explained how I had be-come a participant in a sacred Santeria ritual, and that it had been intended that I take Legba in order to make the spell work. When the *Santero* (Santeria practitioner) had returned and saw that

Legba was gone, he had immediately smashed his flowerpot altar to finalize the magic. Everything had gone as planned, and his petition to Legba—whatever it may have been—would be granted.

Great! But back to this "being chosen" business. "What else does that mean?" I asked with mounting interest.

Graciella's froglike face broke into a partial smile and she said: "That is not very clear because you are an *aleyo* [nonbeliever]. Most likely, you have done a lucky thing. Treat Legba well and he will protect your home from evil. Keep him behind your front door and give him sweets and cigars." That was just the type of reassurance I needed to hear. It sounded like I had a good shot at becoming King of the Zombies!

The door chimes signaled that new visitors were arriving and that it was probably time for me to leave, so I packed Legba up and thanked Graciella for her time. She looked me straight in the eyes and said, "Good Luck!" in a surprisingly loud voice. I departed feeling as though I had just become a candidate for "Ripley's Believe It or Not."

Now that I was on track, I continued digging up Santeria's long roots, which are buried deep in West Africa and the mystical Chango cult. Chango's large pantheon of gods is widely worshipped in the region, with its central focus among the Yoruba tribe in Nigeria. According to Yoruba beliefs, Legba is a mischievous trickster who delights in sending foes in unknown and bumpy directions. He also opens and closes all doors to opportunity and guards "the crossroads of life," which is probably the reason I found him at the junction of four paths. Basically, Legba covers a lot of important ground and you don't want to get him angry.

These primal beliefs are centuries old and were initially brought to the New World via the slave trade. These beliefs first surfaced in the Caribbean in Cuba, where people still whisper about the power of *Lecumi*, as they call it there, and then spread throughout South America, particularly into Brazil, where they are referred to as *Macumba*. And now, what was formerly thought of as exotic mumbo jumbo from the Caribbean has finally filtered into Hometown USA.

My experience with Legba turned out to be just the tip of the iceberg. From that point on, my encounters with voodoo and other occult ritual artifacts have seemed to become almost routine in my explorations around town. As a reality check, other urban treasure hunters with whom I discuss

The author with typical urban voodoo ritual objects found in New York City. The bell is for calling the spirits and the wax female figure represents a victim. Have a nice day!

this strange new phenomenon report similar experiences. Many of us are digging up "spells" buried in small jars under the roots of large trees. These jars contain coins, kola nuts, and notes rendered unreadable from being soaked in perfumed oils. Apparently, the New York City park system has become a haven for voodoo worshippers.

I consider these strange encounters to be first-rate urban anthropology fieldwork and I look forward to any new and interesting experiences that treasure hunting may bring me. My goal is not only to find things, but also to be part of action learning experiences. I haven't been disappointed.

So, as you can see, it's really not necessary to be on some steamy tropical island where King Kong might live or in the jungles of Africa or South America to have any chance of meeting up with voodoo. I would think that any urban area, no matter what its size, has hidden nooks and crannies where these strange rites are carried out. And I'm also sure that some of you reading this have your own hair-raising stories to tell.

Yes, I know it's all part of being an urban treasure hunter, but sometimes I do ask myself, "What next?"

Urban treasure hunters have to deal with some strange situations. What would you do here?

PROBLEM PLANTS

Some people think that because of all the concrete and tall buildings in their city, they won't encounter any toxic plants such as poison ivy, sumac, or oak. How wrong they are. These noxious shrubs love the city, or so it seems from the large amounts of poison ivy that I've seen growing in New York City's parks and other undeveloped areas. It's a particularly good idea to become familiar with how they look rather than how they feel.

I know one treasure hunter who philosophically accepts a yearly case of poison ivy on his hands as an unavoidable consequence of his undertakings. The poison ivy usually spreads, probably because his immune system has been sensitized. Of course, he could avoid this problem simply by learning how to recognize poison ivy and, if necessary, by using a rake to clear an area before getting down to business.

Wearing gloves also helps prevent coming into contact with poison ivy. However, if the gloves become contaminated, they will need to be isolated and washed, or even discarded, because urushiol, the inflammatory plant oil in poison ivy, adheres to fabric for up to five years and may cause a problem at an unsuspected moment. This once happened to me in the middle of the winter, during a January thaw, when I used some contaminated gloves from my car trunk and came down with a severe case of poison ivy. Another lesson I learned the hard way!

Identifying poison ivy (*Rhus radicans*) can be perplexing, as it can take the form of a low creeper, a long vine with a 20-inch circumference, a shrub, or a small tree. Even the leaves vary.

GLASS AND RUSTY METAL

While on the subject of gloves, I would have to say that one dangerous practice I've been surprised to see so many urban treasure hunters engage in is barehanded digging in the ground. This is a very risky thing to do.

If the top of the ground is littered with sharp pieces of glass and rusty metal, chances are that's what is also underneath. You take a considerable chance of getting seriously cut by not wearing some type of lightweight work gloves. Pain, infection, and severed nerves can be the consequences of ignoring this advice.

PLUMBER'S ITCH

Here is a health hazard for you folks who live in the Gulf or South Atlantic states, particularly for people who often dig under old porches and in other dank areas. Plumber's itch is a parasitic condition whose medical name is "cutaneous larval migrans," or "creeping eruption." The common name evolved because plumbers are the usual victims.

Plumber's itch is caused by coming into contact with soil that has been contaminated with dog feces containing dog hookworm eggs. When these eggs hatch, they develop into larvae, which bore into the skin on your hands or elsewhere. Since you're not a dog, the con-

Most cases of Plumber's Itch resolve without long-term adverse reactions. Mortality from this odious infection has not been reported.

fused larvae start to wander around in curving paths under your skin, which most people find annoying.

Again, wearing gloves can help avoid the problem, as can taking care where you sit. Light infections can be cured by freezing the infected area and then extracting the larvae. Heavy infections require treatment with pharmaceuticals and monitoring.

DANGEROUS MICROBES

Soil can also contain dangerous microbes, such as the *tetanus bacillus*, which can cause a deadly medical condition to develop quickly if you become infected through a cut. I once read about a bottle digger who died from tetanus. This was sorry news to hear because the condition can easily be prevented with a simple vaccination that provides protection for ten years.

Microbes that you will have no protection against are the viruses that cause acquired immune deficiency syndrome (AIDS) and hepatitis C. I bring this up because I've seen plenty of syringes lying around on the ground in city parks, and the injection drug user population has a very high rate of infection with these serious blood-borne diseases. So, if you see a syringe, just leave it alone.

AN UNSETTLING MOMENT

"There is but one step from the grotesque to the horrible."

—Sherlock Holmes, "The Adventure of Wisteria Lodge"

Some situations are not hazardous, but rather fall into the category of being unsettling. One such scenario occurred as I was zigzagging my way through a wall of 9-foot-tall phragmites weeds surrounding Jamaica Bay. I saw something that sent a chill up my spine. It was something that I had always dreaded encountering while exploring New York's many nooks and crannies. There it was—two pink feet protruding from the ground cover. A body!

"This is not my day!" I muttered, as I braced myself before going over and taking a closer look prior to notifying the police. I had to know what I was dealing with, so I picked up a stick and poked one of the feet. No movement. However, on closer inspection, there was something about the feet that didn't look quite right. They appeared to be made of a synthetic, rubbery plastic. There were also the garishly painted red toenails. I started to become suspicious.

After moving some debris, it became clear that I had actually found a smiling, life-size, inflatable fantasy doll that some kook had dragged into the weeds for a good time and then tried to conceal. What a relief! I had to laugh out loud—for the joy of not having a gruesome tale to tell, even though it first appeared that I had stumbled on some really grisly business. I bid the doll adieu and continued on my way, taking great delight in watching a northern harrier hawk swoop low over the marsh. The trials of an urban treasure hunter!

Urban areas can present a variety of hazardous scenarios for the unsuspecting treasure hunter, but once informed and properly equipped, you're ahead of the game. Try to use common sense when dealing with these problems. They are all surmountable or avoidable, and not anything that should cause you to give up the quest. Basically, do your treasure hunting where and how you feel the safest, wear gloves, and watch out for nature. The following table can provide you with a quick reference to the various hazards you may encounter.

TABLE 4.1   COMMON HAZARDS AT-A-GLANCE

Being an urban treasure hunter can be exciting and fun, however it does come with its share of risks. While some risks are minor, some may be a bit more hazardous. The following chart lists some of the most common hazards an intrepid urban treasure hunter is likely to run into on any given expedition. I recomend that you review this chart carefully. By asking questions, being observant, learning to listen, and always being prepared for the unexpected, you can and will minimize these dangers. Should you feel uncomfortable in the environment you are working in, do not hesitate to leave. Also, remember to always carry a small first aid kit with you.

Hazard	Signs	Solutions/Options
Dog(s) Attacks	Growling, bared fangs, roving dog packs.	Carry a high frequency whistle to disorient dogs. Leave the area immediately, but don't run.
Electrical/Power Lines	Posted signs indicating the presence of electrical wires. Wires or cables running out of the ground or hanging down from a pole or tree. Sparks.	Never dig near exposed or loose wires or cables. Leave the area immediately if water is present. Report downed wires to your local utility company.
Falling Objects	Dead trees, construction sites, abandoned buildings, and crumbling tall structures.	Wear a hard hat. Avoid such environments.
Gas Pipes	Smell of gas. Gas is usually carried through narrow black pipes.	Do not bang or hit pipes. Do not try to dislodge any connected pipes.
Holes	Construction sites, abandoned buildings, vacant lots, forested areas, overgrown fields.	Be mindful where you walk. If you are uncertain, probe the ground in front of you first or walk around it. When investigating holes, use probes first and wear gloves.

Hazard	Signs	Solutions/Options
Insects, Biting/Stinging	Swamps, woodsy areas, fields, brush, and bodies of water. Warm weather. Discarded garbage. Bee hives and/or wasp nests.	Use insect repellent containing at least 20% DEET. Do not wear brightly colored clothing or scented lotions. Keep your distance.
Mosquitoes (West Nile Virus)	Any place that contains stagnant water such as abandoned tires, pools of water beneath air conditioners, tarps, and ponds. Swamps, woodsy areas, fields, and brush.	Use insect repellent containing at least 20% DEET. Avoid being in the field at peak mosquito-biting periods (at dawn, dusk, and early evening). Check with your local health department.
Plants, Poisonous (Ivy, Oak, Sumac)	Swamps, woodsy areas, fields, weedy lots, and brush.	Learn to identify and stay clear of local toxic plants. Wear gloves. Carefully dispose of any contaminated gloves.
Plumber's Itch (Skin infection caused by parasites)	Found in moist, warm soil or sand where there are deposits of cat and dog excrement. On beaches and under porches in warm weather areas.	Avoid skin contact with infected ground. Wear latex gloves. Avoid such areas.
Rats	Found throughout urban areas, especially areas containing discarded rubbish. Look for rat burrows in the ground or actual rat sitings.	Wear gloves. Probe holes with a trowel.
Sharp Ground Objects	Can be found throughout various settings.	Wear thick-soled shoes or boots. Wear gloves.
Snakes, Poisonous	Different species live in various parts of the country. Location of area determines these snakes' habitats.	Learn which areas may be inhabited by snakes. Wear gloves. Seek immediate medical attention.
Spiders, Poisonous/Scorpions	Different species live in various parts of the country. Found in old structures and piles of rubbish.	Learn which areas may be inhabited by such spiders and scorpions. Wear gloves.
Street People	Locations considered crime areas, drug- or gang-related hangouts. Individuals that may look or behave oddly.	Learn in which areas they are and avoid them. Cross a street to avoid confrontations. Avoid eye contact. Hunt with a partner.
Syringes (Viral Diseases)	Areas used as drug hangouts such as city parks. Areas with discarded rubbish.	Wear gloves. Avoid handling any syringes.
Tetanus	Rusty nails or sharp objects in the ground.	Tetanus vaccination provides 10 year protection. Wear thick-soled shoes or boots. Wear gloves.
Ticks (Lyme Disease)	Swamps, woodsy areas, fields, tall grass, sand, and brush.	Use insect repellent containing at least 20% DEET. Cover exposed skin. Check yourself often. Freeze your clothing for 15 minutes when you get home. Check with your local health department.
Tough Neighborhoods	Locations considered high crime areas, drug- or gang-related hangouts.	Learn which areas they are and avoid them. Hunt with a partner.
Voodoo Rituals	Ritual artifacts such as makeshift altars, candles, high concentration of animal remains.	Leave the area.

❀ 5 ❀

Legal
Considerations

As is true for everything else you do in life, it's your responsibility to conduct your treasure hunting activities in a lawful manner. Therefore, for your own protection, and to stay out of trouble, you should become familiar with all the relevant laws of your city and your state, along with those federal acts that may impact where you may pursue treasure hunting. Otherwise, you could be in for some deep trouble. This chapter presents a general overview of the types of laws in force at the local and state levels that affect urban treasure hunting. It also discusses the federal laws with which you should become familiar, including the primary federal law, the Archaeological Resources Protection Act of 1979.

Take the time to learn all the fine points of the laws governing your activities; don't wait until you need to know them in a crisis. There's no excuse for not knowing or not obeying the law.

LOCAL LAWS

Let's begin with local law. I would recommend first checking with your city hall or parks department to find out if there are any ordinances or special restrictions regarding metal detecting or digging in your city's parks. If digging is allowed only seasonally or in restricted areas, comply with the regulations. For example, in New York City you need to register for a yearly permit, which states the terms and conditions for using a metal detector in the city's parks.

Another good source of information concerning your local laws affecting treasure hunting is your local metal detector dealer. Your dealer should know the whole story—the good, the bad, and the ugly—and probably can even provide regrettable examples of what happens to people who choose to ignore the law. In recent years, it seems that a significant number of urban parks have been closed off to metal detecting because a number of selfish people have violated the letter and spirit of the law by illegal and careless digging. However, access to these parks is slowly being won back through the hard work of member clubs of the Federation of Metal Detector and Archaeological Clubs. (To learn about this organization, see below.)

Then there's the matter of common trespass laws to consider. Trespass is defined as the intrusion onto property or premises owned by another person without the permission of that owner. These premises can be land, a structure, or both. Trespass can be on the surface, above the surface, or below it. Furthermore, you can be arrested for trespass even if there are no signs posted.

The laws concerning trespass differ among jurisdictions, so the law abiding urban treasure hunter should never enter private property without permission. Doing so can get you arrested, plus can incur whatever other penalties the law prescribes. It's a road you don't want to travel.

Federation of Metal Detector and Archaeological Clubs

The Federation of Metal Detector and Archaeological Clubs (FMDAC) is a nonprofit, noncommercial, nonpartisan organization that is dedicated to preserving the sport of metal detecting. Founded in 1984, the FMDAC currently consists of 135 clubs in forty-two states.

FMDAC members support a code of ethics that promotes responsible metal detecting practices, along with respect for property and the providing of community service. A quarterly publication, *Quest*, is distributed to members and is also available on the organization's website at www.fmdac.com.

People new to urban treasure hunting, as well as those who have been enjoying it for a while, might want to seek out their local chapter for some camaraderie and a clear perspective on potential treasure hunting activities in their local area.

For further information about the FMDAC and its affiliates, write to Frank Colletti, National Secretary, at 1439 Stephen Marc Lane, East Meadow, New York 11554. The telephone number is 516-481-9244.

STATE LAWS

Most states have enacted laws designed to regulate excavation activities on public lands for what are considered "archaeological resources." These laws vary from state to state and are continually being amended. Your state archaeologist is the best source for the most up-to-date information on your state's historical preservation laws.

The states vary, however, in their interpretation of antiquity when describing restrictions on recovering historical relics. In Illinois, for example, archaeological resources are any items remaining of past human life or activities that are of archaeological interest and at least 40 years of age. In Kentucky, the items must be more than 100 years old.

Regarding state parks, be aware that metal detecting restrictions may vary from park to park in the same state, with some parks being fully open to metal detecting while others are totally or partially off limits. You should never presume that the same rules apply to all the state parks in one state. It's always best to inquire first because you may have to register for a metal detecting permit. In addition, also note that federal land is sometimes mistakenly believed by the public to be state land.

Despite severe penalties and people being apprehended, site looting still persists. For example, Caddo burial sites in East Texas continue to be the target of looters because Caddo pottery and pipes are highly desired market items. The Texas Historical Commission is energetically trying to educate people about the damage being done to the archaeological record of Texas.

FEDERAL LAWS

Don't get too carried away by your success in your neighborhood or local state park and try to pursue treasure hunting on nearby federal land. A federal law called the Archaeological Resources Protection Act (ARPA) of 1979 (Public Law 96-95) states, in Section 6(a): "No person may excavate, remove, damage, or otherwise alter or deface any archaeological resource located on public lands or Indian lands unless such activity is pursuant to a permit issued under Section 4 [of the act]."

An archaeological resource is defined in Section 3(1) of the act as "any material remains of past human life or activities which are of archeological interest." According to Section 3(1), this includes "pottery, basketry, bottles, weapons, weapon projectiles, tools, structures or portions of structures, pit houses, rock paintings, rock carvings, intaglios, graves, [and] human skeletal remains." To be protected, the item must be more than 100 years old. However, according to Section 7(a)(3), the surface collecting of arrowheads is allowed, but you sure better know the difference between an arrowhead and a spear point—and hope that the ranger agrees.

Three men were caught metal detecting in Blakely State Park in Alabama with old rusty nails, part of a cannonball, and a toy gun from the 1800s in their possession. They were charged with criminal trespassing, excavating antiquities, and violating park regulations. They did some jail time, paid $2,000 in fines, and were put on two years probation.

Rangers apprehended a man digging in the woods of Ocmulgee Indian Mounds, near Macon, Georgia, assuming that he was illegally searching for artifacts. However, the man was actually burying $1.6 million and said that he didn't trust banks. He was still arrested for an ARPA violation and the money was seized. Authorities are investigating where the loot came from.

ARPA, according to Section 12(c), applies to "public land [and] Indian land," but not to private land. Public land includes the National Park System, National Wildlife Refuge System, National Forest System, Bureau of Land Management lands, military bases, and any other tracts held by the United States government. Public land and Native American land may seem like good places to find arrowheads, but I wouldn't advise searching on them. Stick with the casinos for trying to make a score on Native American land.

ARPA is not concerned just with on-site violations. In Section 6(b), it also prohibits the selling, purchase, or exchange of archaeological resources removed from public or Native American lands in violation of the act or of any other federal law, rule, regulation, or ordinance. This means that even if you only purchase archaeological artifacts, you should first ascertain their source. There have been felony prosecutions for violation of this subsection, too.

The penalties for violation of ARPA are stern. For first-time offenders, according to Section 6(d) as modified by Public Law 100-588, enacted November 3, 1988, if the damage, which includes the cost of restoration, is less than $500, the offender may be fined up to $10,000 and/or sentenced to up to one year in jail. If the damage is more than $5,000, the penalty can go to $20,000 in fines and/or two years in jail. For a second violation, the penalty can reach $100,000 along with five years in jail.

A further penalty for violating ARPA, according to Section 8(b), is forfeiture of all vehicles and equipment used to perpetrate the violation. Most states, particularly those in the Southwest, where site looting is rampant, have parallel statutes protecting state lands. The feds take ARPA very seriously, and you will be in for a lot of grief if you don't.

ARPA also provides a reward, in Section 8(a), for information leading to the arrest and conviction of persons violating the act. This reward amounts to half of the fines paid, though it cannot exceed $500. That's right—you can be turned in by a bounty hunter!

Another ARPA subsection, Section 6(c), is also of particular interest to treasure hunters, since it mandates: "No person may sell, purchase, exchange, transport, receive, or offer to sell, purchase, or exchange, in interstate or foreign commerce, any archaeological resources excavated, removed, sold, purchased, exchanged, transported, or received in violation of any provision, rule, regulation, ordinance, or permit in effect under State or local law." The weighty upshot here is that you can even be prosecuted by ARPA for breaking a local law.

As an example of how ARPA is enforced, three men were arrested in Richmond National Battlefield Park in Virginia in the act of digging Civil War relics at 1:30 A.M. They were convicted of violating ARPA and received stiff penalties, including forfeiture of their vehicles and equipment. All three had to do time, as well as pay heavy fines and, no doubt, large legal fees. In addition, they were saddled with two years of supervised probation, during which they were prohibited from entering any federal, state, or local parks.

The United States magistrate who presided over the case said: "This is not a simple case of trespassing and petty larceny. This is a major crime, a breach of hallowed ground! The violators have stolen a bit of the legacy of every man, woman, and child in this country." That's what you're up against. Case closed.

OTHER FEDERAL ACTS

There are other federal acts designed to preserve prehistoric and historical sites of which you should be aware. Like ARPA, these acts need to be observed to the letter of the law.

The American Antiquities Act of 1906

The American Antiquities Act of 1906 was enacted to preserve the sites and artifacts that were rapidly being destroyed in the western United States at the time. It created eighty-two monuments of prehistoric and historical significance, and set penalties of fines and imprisonment for violations pertaining to the unlawful excavation and collecting of "antiquities" on these sites.

The Historic Sites Act of 1935

The Historic Sites Act of 1935 established a national policy for preservation. It created the National Historic Landmarks Program, the Historic American Buildings Survey, and the Historic American Engineering Record under the auspices of the National Park Service for the purpose of determining and preserving historical and prehistoric sites. Never intrude on posted historical landmark sites. We should all be very glad that our historical heritage is being preserved in this responsible manner.

The National Historic Preservation Act of 1966

The National Historic Preservation Act (NHPA) of 1966 was passed by Congress to maintain a list of buildings, sites, districts, structures, and objects of local, state, or national significance in American history. This list is called the National Register of Historic Places, and the properties it includes are protected from treasure hunting.

KEEPING WHAT YOU FIND

As a person who recovers lost and hidden valuables, mostly of unknown origin, you also need to know the laws pertaining to keeping what you legally recover. Ignorance is not bliss.

Suppose one day you come up with a significant cache. What do you do—or not do? My first advice is to make the recovery in an inconspicuous manner. Don't become front-page news.

If you do become noticed, as sure as a fish can swim, someone—or even a whole group of people—will come forward to say that what you found belongs to him or her. Before you know it, this person or group will hire a sharp, percentage-seeking lawyer, and the courts will tie up the treasure until a "proper" disposition can be decided upon—however long that may take.

Meanwhile, you will have to hire your own clever attorney to protect your rights. If you found the goods on public land, the local bureaucrats will also want a piece of the pie. Most likely, the state will get involved, and ultimately, the only ones to benefit from the find will be the lawyers—and possibly your heirs.

Taking all that potential turmoil—plus the thousand urgent marriage proposals—into consideration, your best bet is to be discreet. I can't stress that enough. It will prevent legal headaches and harassment from the vultures who will undoubtedly file nuisance suits against you, hoping to make an out-of-court settlement on *your* find. If you examine past dispositions of found treasures that have become public knowledge, you'll understand why anonymity is the best policy to follow.

TREASURE TROVE LAW AND THE COURTS

"Treasure trove" is the legal term for currency, coins, precious bullion, gold, and silver found hidden in the ground and for which no owner can be determined. Basically, the Doctrine of Treasure Trove states that if any such item is found on private or public property, it can be declared treasure trove if it was hidden long enough ago so that the original owner is unknown and presumed deceased.

While some states recognize treasure trove law, all do not. Some of the states that don't instead declare that all found property must be treated as lost, misplaced, or abandoned. Other states insist that each case be treated individually, with a final decision made by a judge.

When a find is declared a treasure trove by a court of law, it belongs to the person who discovered it, with no strings attached. An exception is made if the finder was trespassing or in violation of some other federal, state, or local statute. In such a case, the goods may be awarded to the landowner or seized by the government.

However, if someone comes forward claiming to have hidden the valuables and can prove it, the courts may declare the find "concealed property" that the original owner had intended to reclaim. In that case, the loot is returned to the owner. The court also tends to award found treasure to original owners who can prove it was lost or misplaced. Other treasure trove categories include abandoned property and property embedded in the soil, such as antique bottles and artifacts with historical value. These are usually viewed as the property of the finder—as long as no laws were broken to recover them.

Experienced treasure hunters know that court decisions are unpredictable. They are influenced not only by the Scales of Justice, but also by politics as well as other factors, some seemingly obscure. Your best course of action is to avoid a court decision at all costs. Therefore, once again, don't become front-page news.

Finding treasure can be tricky business, and holding onto it can be even trickier. An important point to take away from this chapter is that how you conduct yourself can lead you either into time consuming and expensive litigation or to the peace of mind that sudden riches can provide. It's your choice. But the better choice is to go out there with an optimistic, law abiding attitude. You protect your rights by respecting everyone else's.

Two British metal detectorists found the largest hoard of Roman coins ever discovered. The 9,212 coins date from 31 B.C.—A.D. 325 and were found in a farmer's field near Glastonbury. Under British treasure law, the hoard has been declared treasure trove and the detectorists are eligible for compensation, which can amount to several hundred thousand pounds.

6

Tools of
the Trade

The type and quality of tools you choose for your treasure hunting will significantly affect your success. On the other hand, just possessing the right equipment is no guarantee of finding riches. You need to understand the purpose of your tools and become proficient in their correct use. You also have to keep them in good working order. Tools that are supposed to cut must be kept sharp and ready for action. Batteries should be checked on a regular basis and be backed up with spares.

Don't be the person who has everything, but nothing works. That's too frustrating and could cause you to lose interest. Anything in life upon which you depend has to be properly maintained or else the show will never get on the road. Treasure hunting is a prime example.

I believe in being prepared for any type of situation, while at the same time staying as unencumbered as possible. You certainly will never need to carry all your equipment with you, but you should definitely have those tools that relate to the project at hand. In this chapter, we will cover what equipment you will need and how to best apply it. You will even find instructions for building your own sifter.

In addition to equipment, we will discuss some other treasure hunting essentials. These include proper attitude and reasonable expectations. We will also examine the importance of applying yourself to learning the basics of treasure hunting and how your treasure hunting outlook will eventually blossom into a personal style. Finally, we will review how to explore the various treasure hunting niches available in your city.

Learning the fundamentals of treasure hunting is an eye-opening process that every urban treasure hunter has to go through and that should prove to be adventurous and rewarding. As one old, grizzled beach hunter told me when I first hit the Coney Island sand, "Look, pal, just do what you see everyone else doing." Good advice for the novice!

TOOLS FOR URBAN TREASURE HUNTING

The tools required for urban treasure hunting are readily available, are not hard to use, and fit easily within most recreational budgets. In this section, we will discuss the metal detector and its components (searchcoil, batteries, headphones, and carrying case); digging, cutting, raking, and probing tools; sifters; and magnets.

We will also take a look at how a camera can be useful for a variety of treasure hunting–related projects. Basically, these are all the tools upon which I rely for my treasure hunting jaunts around New York City. For a quick, at-a-glance chart of these tools, see Table 6.1.

Metal Detector

The author treasure hunting with his metal detector at Bowling Green Park, the oldest park (1733) in New York City and located in the middle of the Wall Street Stock Exchange.

Probably the most versatile tool for treasure hunting (aside from your brain) is the metal detector. With this electronic marvel, you will be able to find old coins, lost jewelry, nineteenth-century dumpsites, hidden caches, fascinating historical relics, and a large assortment of objects considered collectibles. Using a metal detector has a special way of blending the past and the present.

Your best source of information on metal detectors is your local metal detector dealer. To find one, check the yellow pages under "Metal Detecting Equipment." These dealers generally carry several different brands and models. They will also know about the ground

TABLE 6.1 AT-A-GLANCE TREASURE HUNTING TOOL CHART				
Tool	**What It Is**	**Models**	**Prices**	**Comments**
Metal detector	A portable electronic device for finding metal objects (such as old coins, historical relics), good hunting areas (such as 19th-century dumpsites), and metal containers holding hidden caches of valuables.	Turn-on-and-go (for beginners) Middle-range Top-of-the-line, ultra-high-tech (for serious treasure hunters) Specialty (for purposes such as detecting on beaches, gold prospecting, relic hunting)	$200 $300–$600 $1,000 and up $600–$1,000	Beginners should choose a turn-on-and-go detector. Stick with the major manufacturers. Look for a volume control and a built-in speaker. 4 pounds or less is best for fatigue-free, all-day hunting.
Searchcoil	The circular, signal emitting, target sensing head of a metal detector.	Standard, 8- to 10-inch (for general detecting) Large, 11-inch and up (for sizable items) Small, 4- to 6-inch (for better signal separation)	$100–$150 $100–$150 $70–$100	A standard-size searchcoil comes with all detectors. Learn to use your detector with its factory supplied searchcoil. Metal detector searchcoils are interchangeable only within each brand.
Searchcoil scuff cover	A durable, lightweight plastic cover for the searchcoil.	Variety of shapes and sizes to fit the different searchcoils	$5–$10	Necessary for protecting the searchcoil against abrasive ground hazard damage.
Batteries	The power source for the metal detector.	Alkaline AA Nickel-cadmium (nicad) rechargeable AA 9-volt batteries	4-pack, $3 4-pack, $10 2-pack, $5 Alkaline	Nicad battery packs come standard with some detector models. Alkaline batteries last longer and won't suddenly lose power. If you use nicads, keep track of their hours of use and monitor their strength with a battery tester. Always keep alkalines ready as backups. Dispose of all batteries properly.
Headphones	A headset for blocking out external noise and hearing deep, faint signals you might otherwise miss.	Standard-size with large ear cups Lightweight Walkman-type with small, foam ear pads	$20–$100 $5–$40	Experiment and use what works best for you.

Tool	What It Is	Models	Prices	Comments
Carrying case	A protective case for storing and transporting your metal detector and its accessories.	Soft-padded vinyl Hard suitcase	$40–$70 $100–$150	Also good for keeping an expedition organized.
Hand trowel	A 1-foot-long, pointed digging tool for recovering coins and other buried items.	Standard Long-handled	$8–$20 $8–$20	Own a spare or two in case of loss or breakage.
Hunting knife	A sturdy knife with a single-edge blade, sharp tip, and hand guard for digging up coins and other small buried items.	6-inch blade	$20–$50	A sharp hunting knife always comes in handy for the urban treasure hunter.
Shovel	A common digging tool for moving large amounts of earth when searching for old bottles or buried caches.	Army surplus folding Full-size, long-handled	$8–$15 $15–$40	It's convenient to always have a shovel in your car trunk.
Pitchfork	A very effective, long-handled, forklike tool for quickly turning the ground for broken-glass evidence when bottle digging in an old dump.	Standard 4-tine spading	$15–$25	This tool is often overlooked by the novice urban treasure hunter.

Tool	What It Is	Models	Prices	Comments
Hand rake	A small tool with metal teeth for quickly and gently scraping away layers of earth when excavating in an old privy.	Standard	$8–$12	Use it with a gentle touch.
Breaker bar or crowbar	A sturdy metal bar for breaking through subterranean walls when excavating in an old privy.	Standard	$15	Remember to wear protective work gloves when using this tool.
Walk board	A wood board for walking over a privy excavation hole, or as a sturdy platform for hauling out buckets of dirt or bottles.	$1\frac{1}{2}$- x 6-foot	$5	Inspect your walk board regularly for cracks.
Bucket	A plastic or metal pail for hauling dirt or bottles out of an excavation site.	Standard	$4–$10	Make sure your hauling rope is tied tightly and inspect it regularly for fraying.
Rake	A long-handled gardening tool with metal or wood teeth for quickly clearing away leaves and other ground debris.	Standard	$10–$20	Folding models are also available.

Tool	What It Is	Models	Prices	Comments
Hook	A wire clothes hanger with a small hook bent into one end for probing holes in trees and stone walls, and poking around old ruins.	Homemade	Negligible	Easy to make. One day you will need one, so be ready.
Machete	A large bush knife for clearing overgrown vegetation and cutting through extensive root systems.	18-inch blade	$20	The U.S. Army Regulation GI MIL-SPEC machete should handle all projects quite well. Don't alarm the public by carrying your machete around unsheathed.
Sifter	A metal-screen sieve for separating out small treasure objects from excavated soil.	24- x18-inch	$15–$20	See page 75 for instructions to build your own sifter.
Long probe	A thin, "T"-shaped, stainless steel rod with a bullet-shaped head that is inserted into the ground to determine underground conditions when bottle digging or looking for buried caches.	5- to 6-foot	$20–$25	A very useful tool that will help avoid unnecessary digging.
Magnet	A small (1- x 4-inch), heavy-pull-capacity magnet for retrieving iron objects from hard-to-reach places (such as old wells, frozen lakes).	50-pound lifting capacity	$20	Going fishing with a magnet in urban bodies of water can be quite an adventure.
Camera	A small, good-quality picture taking device for keeping a photographic record of recoveries and researching prospective hunting sites.	Point-and-shoot Single lens reflex	$80–$150 $175 and up	A knowledge of photography is a great asset to the urban treasure hunter. Treasure hunting magazines prefer articles with photos.

conditions around town and can help you select an appropriate machine.

It's certainly in your best interest to choose a model made by a major manufacturer that has been providing the treasure hunting community with quality products for a number of years. The chances are that such a manufacturer will be around to service your needs in the future. (For advice on getting your metal detector repaired, see below.) Among the major manufacturers are Bounty Hunter, Fisher, Garrett, Minelab, Tesoro, Troy, and White's. All of these manufacturers' latest models, along with consumer product reviews, can be found in *Western & Eastern Treasures* and *Lost Treasures* magazines.

These magazines are a wealth of information regarding the various detectors available and what they can do. For subscription information for these magazines, see Appendix C. In addition, I recommend that you take a look at the interesting assortment of treasure hunting websites on the World Wide Web, including *TreasureNet*, a highly informative website at www.treasurenet.com that has links to various manufacturers' sites.

Dr. Gerhard Fisher patented the metal detector in 1937 as the "Metallascope." He is considered the "father of the metal detector" and was the first to undertake large-scale production of the machine.

PURCHASE CONSIDERATIONS

If you can count three hobbies for which you've purchased expensive equipment but that you no longer pursue, use some caution when selecting a metal detector. The prices for detectors that actual-

Where to Get Your Metal Detector Repaired

If your metal detector develops a mechanical problem, you are always better off sending it to the manufacturer or to a factory authorized service shop. These places will have all the proper diagnostic tools and the expertise to correct the problem without needless delay. The only exception might be if the battery clips come off. Then, either you or a local television repair shop can do a simple solder job to get you back in business.

Remember, any time a detector seems to malfunction, check the batteries and their connections before sending the unit off. Also, be aware that the urban environment has many underground power lines that can make your detector appear to malfunction or act erratically. For example, if all of a sudden your machine starts to behave strangely or give off false signals, try changing your location. That may be all that's needed.

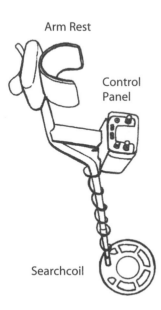

Arm Rest

Control
Panel

Searchcoil

Metal Detector

A metal detector will
be your time machine for
expeditions into your
city's historical past to
recover the valuables
and relics of yesteryear.

ly produce start at about $200. These low-end, turn-on-and-go
machines are good for learning and developing a hunting style.
They are very easy to use and will definitely find treasure, if you are
persistent. I started out in 1980 with a basic, low-cost machine that
did a great job, to the amazement of my fellow detectorists who
were using the "big guns."

On the other hand, if treasure hunting has really gotten into your
blood and you plan on devoting serious time to it, choose a more
advanced model. Middle-range units sell from $300 to $600. Top-of-
the-line, ultra-high-tech models begin at about $1,000. The better
machines are now microprocessor controlled and have more high-
tech features, such as:

- *Multiple frequencies.* A technology that uses a range of high and
  low detecting frequencies, rather than just one frequency, to allow
  enhanced target sensitivity, discrimination, and detection depth.

- *Target identification.* A meter that indicates the probable identity of
  the detected object (for example, ring, coin, pull tab, piece of foil,
  bottle cap).

- *Coin tone.* The production of a distinct audio tone to signal the
  detection of a coin.

- *Target depth.* A meter that indicates the depth from which the signal is originating.

- *Notch discrimination.* The ability to set the machine to precisely
  include or exclude certain metallic objects (for example, gold rings).

In addition, the better models detect considerably deeper in
highly mineralized ground, which has a substantial iron content that
may interfere with a machine's signal sending and receiving circuit-
ry, causing a reduction in detecting depth.

A top-of-the-line detector might not be the best for you if you're
just starting out, however. There are too many bells and whistles that
will reduce your learning curve. These machines are really more suited to experienced operators. I recommend that if you're a newcomer,
you start with a turn-on-and-go machine to build your confidence
and enjoy some quick successes in the field.

Some urban treasure hunters pursue a few different hunting

directions, including some for which they utilize specialty detectors. Specialty models offer features and performance levels designed for a specialized type of searching, such as beach hunting, gold prospecting, or relic hunting. The majority of urban treasure hunters I know, however, stick with a more versatile, all-purpose detector that can shift gears as the need arises. That's my type of machine because a day of city-style treasure hunting can take you into a few different search environments.

There are two features that you should consider when choosing a metal detector—a volume control and a built-in speaker. Why? Suppose your headphones fail. You would be stuck without any way of hearing your detector's signals and would have to call it a day. I've seen it happen. In addition, be wary of the weight of the machine. Any detector that weighs more than 4 pounds will start to drag you down after a few hours. Try to keep your detector light.

The winter holidays and spring are the prime times to buy a detector, since the manufacturers tend to offer cost-effective package deals. These packages often include an extra searchcoil, a carrying case, digging tools, and even a how-to book on the subject.

FUNCTIONALITY

My idea of a functional metal detector is one that can penetrate the ground where *you* live to detect a quarter-size object at 5 inches. Most old coins are found no deeper than that, unless there has been an excessive buildup of surface material, such as in a deep-woods area. Interestingly, the roots in grassy areas tend to trap coins and you might be surprised to come up with one that is a couple of hundred years old but only 2 to 3 inches down. I was once amazed to recover a 1720s Woods Hiburnia halfpenny at 2 inches down. You never know.

Detecting those older and deeper coins is a real skill to be mastered, even with the latest high-tech equipment.

Searchcoil

The searchcoil, or loop, is the circular signal emitting and target sensing head of the metal detector that is swept close to the ground. This highly sensitive component acts similar to a radar antenna, sending out and receiving electronic waves that bounce off metal objects. These waves are what cause the positive signal in your headphones.

Searchcoils and their protective caps are available in a variety of sizes for different treasure hunting projects.

Searchcoil

Protective Cap

The basic factory supplied searchcoil is generally between 8 inches and 10 inches in size. Searchcoils of this size are the best for all-around detecting and are well suited for coin-size objects. Of course, you can change the size coil you use on your machine to enhance the detection of specific targets or to reduce junk overload in trashy areas. Junk overload occurs when a large concentration of metal trash is scattered either above or below the ground, causing the metal detector to chatter continuously. It can also be caused by a buried car battery or a rusty iron grill.

Large coils (11 inches and up) are best for sizable metal targets such as cannonballs, strongbox caches, old tools, and guns, since they can penetrate much deeper to detect these objects. The downside is that large coils are heavier and also tend to be less sensitive to coin-size targets. In addition, when numerous targets are close together, large coils tend to pick up multiple signals, making it more difficult to pinpoint the target. Large coils are generally the choice of relic hunters who search for any metal object and detectorists who have the luxury of searching for coins in clean ground.

Small coils (4 to 6 inches), on the other hand, may be more productive in areas with many small metal objects, such as a trashy park. They allow a better separation of close-together targets so that each sweep of the coil will not pick up multiple signals. Small coils are also lighter, easier to maneuver, and better at pinpointing targets in trashy areas. However, the trade-offs are that it takes longer to cover an area with a smaller-size loop and it won't give you as much depth. The bottom line, though, is that it's better to find part of something than nothing at all.

There are also after-market coils in various sizes and shapes. These coils are claimed to add extra inches of ground penetration. However, they can be expensive. It's probably best to use the factory supplied coil, which was designed to be the most responsive for everyday coin hunting, until you become familiar with your detector and determine your detecting niche.

I recommend getting a searchcoil scuff cover to protect your coil from damage caused by sharp rocks and other abrasive objects. This durable, lightweight plastic cover is certainly much less expensive to replace than the coil. On occasion, you should remove the cover and clean out any accumulated sand or soil that may be affecting signal reception.

Batteries

I prefer using alkaline batteries in my metal detector because they have the longest life. Some people use nickel-cadmium (nicad) rechargeable batteries for economic reasons and also because they are supplied with certain units as standard equipment. The only drawbacks of nicads are that they hold a charge for only about half as long as alkalines and they go dead all of a sudden rather than gradually. You should always keep track of hours of use when you have nicads in your machine.

By carefully following the charging directions and by routinely monitoring their strength using the battery test indicator in your machine, you should get cost-effective service over a long period of time from nicads. Still, to avoid having to quit detecting early when out in the field with nicads, bring along some alkaline batteries just in case. Also, you might want to purchase a stand-alone battery tester, one that precisely measures the remaining battery strength under medium and heavy loads. Consider your metal detector a heavy drain of power for this test.

Batteries

Remove the batteries from your metal detector when it is not going to be used for a while, to prevent any possible damage from leaking.

Headphones

Headphones are a necessity in the majority of hunting circumstances for making the most finds with your metal detector. They block out external city noise and enable you to hear faint signals that you might otherwise miss by relying solely on your detector's small speaker. They will also offer you some privacy because everyone in the vicinity will not hear your machine beeping, which sometimes causes onlookers to gather.

Most urban detectorists use standard-size stereo headphones with large ear cups that have separate volume controls. There are many models from which to choose. Some offer built-in deep-target signal enhancers, but these are pricey. A word of warning here: Be very careful not to adjust the volume too high or you could seriously damage your hearing.

For average detecting excursions, I prefer the more-lightweight Walkman-type of headphones. With these, I'm not sealed off and I'm able to hear what's going on around me—a particular need when detecting in overgrown areas or tough neighborhoods. What's more,

Headphones

Headphones are a necessity to hear the faint whisper of those deep old coin signals.

lightweights are more user-friendly during periods of extended detecting and hot weather.

If your detector doesn't have a volume control, position your lightweights on your head about an inch or so forward of your ears to compensate. This system is quite effective and comfortable. Good-quality lightweights are pretty comparable to standard headphones when it comes to performance. However, if you hit a hot spot, switch back to your full-size headphones for the best deep-search recovery results. As for anything else, it pays to experiment and find out what works for you.

Carrying Case

Carrying Case

A carrying case for your metal detector will protect it from damage and help keep your other expedition equipment organized.

A very useful accessory for your metal detector is a carrying case. You need to protect your investment from damage while transporting it and when the machine is not in use. I prefer the soft-padded vinyl type of carrying case rather than the hard-suitcase variety. If you travel by public transportation, the case will also hold all of your tools and will prevent unneeded attention from being drawn to your activities.

Tools for Digging

Hand Trowel

The standard one foot long hand trowel is quite adequate for coin recovery in a city park. Always fill in your holes!

In addition to a metal detector and its accessories, you will also need tools for retrieving coins and other similar-size items. A small, sharp hand trowel commonly found at metal detector dealers and gardening stores will adequately do the job. A hunting knife with a 6-inch blade is also very effective.

Some coin hunters use a screwdriver, but I prefer a tool with a cutting edge because of the occasional need to slice through roots and other obstacles in the ground. Field experience will show you what works best for you.

For bottle digging, a shovel is a necessity because of the amount of earth that you may need to move. Depending on your mode of transportation and the size of your project, this can be either a small Army surplus folding shovel or a full-size, long-handled model. In addition, I've found that a pitchfork is very practical for a quick, exploratory turning of ground to find broken glass and crockery, which may indicate an old bottle dump.

Tools for Excavating

When excavating deep in an old privy, or outhouse, a small hand rake used for gardening is excellent for quickly and gently scraping away layers of earth to be hauled out. To augment this gentle approach, have a sturdy breaker bar or large crowbar handy to get through subterranean walls, which sometimes can be problematical. And don't forget a walk board, a plank for safely walking over a hole and to use as a platform for hauling out buckets of dirt and bottles.

Hand Rake

A hand rake should be used with a gentle touch when excavating for old bottles.

Tools for the Woods

For metal detecting in old picnic groves or wooded areas in general, other important tools for the prepared urban treasure hunter to own are a rake that folds up, a wire clothes hanger that has been straightened out and has a small hook bent into one end, and a machete. Each has a special function. The rake facilitates a quick clearing of leaves and other ground debris. The long wire with a hook is for safely probing holes in trees and stone walls, and for poking around the occasional old ruins that you will come across. The machete is very helpful for removing overgrown vegetation and tangled root systems. These three tools are very convenient to carry in your car trunk. Just in case!

Sifter

Another integral part of your treasure hunting gear is a sifter. Using this effective device is much better than simply eyeballing an excavated area. Small artifacts, which can easily be overlooked, become trapped in a sifter. Professional archaeologists always use sifters and have made some very valuable and important finds while routinely sifting excavated soil.

Pieces of ceramic from the nineteenth century or earlier may show up in your sifter. An attractive reward!

With the high prices being asked for some Revolutionary War and Civil War buttons, plus the collector interest in old coins, antique poison bottles, and Bisque dolls, which frequently come out of old urban dumps, sifting can give you a feeling of confidence that you are getting *everything*. Also, some projects, such as recovering Colonial-era or prehistoric shell trade beads (wampum), are only possible with a fine sifter.

One of the best things about sifters is that you can build one yourself. For a materials list and directions, see following page. After constructing your own sifter, you'll have feelings of confidence and self-sufficiency that will be reinforced every time you use your sifter and make an interesting recovery. I guarantee it!

Long Probe

The long probe is a very important tool in treasure hunting. It is used mostly for projects involving deeply buried items. A thin, "T"-shaped, strainless steel rod with a ground-penetrating bullet-shaped head, the long probe is available in different lengths. A 5- or 6-foot probe is about right for most projects and quite useful for deciphering underground conditions when looking for antique bottles or buried caches. Probing also eliminates unnecessary digging.

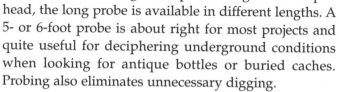

With practice, you will learn how to use your probe to differentiate among the various soil types and ground components (sand, loam, clay, ashes), and the assorted types of objects found in them. You can also read the contents of what you hit by looking at the tip of your probe for samples. My advice is to get out in the field and practice, to learn the way rocks, iron, wood, and glass feel at the end of your probe. Probing should be pursued with an organized plan and with a pressure light enough to stop a downward thrust when making contact with something.

Probes are also useful for finding the locations of old building foundations and for exploring deep, rocky crevices into which you really don't want to put your hands, but where something valuable may be stashed.

Probing is recommended before starting any major excavation.

Magnet

A heavy-capacity magnet is a useful tool, though one you won't use every day. I'm talking about a magnet that can hold at least 50 pounds. Surprisingly, such a magnet is quite small—only about 1 inch wide by 4 inches long—and can be easily lowered with a strong nylon rope

Building a Sifter

Building an easily transportable and low-cost sifter is a relatively simple project. It requires just basic carpentry skills (measuring, sawing, nailing, drilling) and materials that are easy to obtain.

Basically, all you need to do to construct a sifter is to buy and cut wood for the frame and join it together. Attach end brackets at the corners and staple the screen to the bottom. Add handles and leg supports, and presto! You have a sifter.

First, though, you have to decide how big a sifter you need. The size depends on variables such as your strength, your average project size, and whether or not you work alone. If you generally go solo, I recommend a very functional size of 24 inches by 18 inches. This is my own personal preference. When totally assembled, such a sifter weighs about 6 pounds. It should cost between $15 and $20 to construct, and will take about two hours of your time. Remember that if you build a sifter too large to handle by yourself, you may end up never using it. Sifting is hard work, so make things easy by not overestimating your work capacity. If your needs change, you can always build a larger one.

When buying the wood for the project, you can buy long pieces and cut them to size yourself or you can have the lumberyard cut the pieces to size for a small extra charge. When joining the

A sifter's frame should be strong, yet lightweight enough for one person to use without struggling.

pieces for the frame, there are many types of wood joints that you can use. The most basic and easiest is the simple butt joint, in which two pieces of wood are nailed together to form an "L" joint (see Figure 6.1). Assembling a butt joint involves more than just banging in some nails, however. To increase the frame's holding power at the joints, drive the nails in on a slight angle rather than straight and parallel to the grain. Then add metal end brackets for extra support. This will ensure that the sifter is long-lasting.

When you buy the screening material, you should definitely have it cut to size at the hardware store. Ask for "hardware cloth." They'll know what you want and will show you the different-size hole diameters. I prefer $\frac{1}{2}$-inch-size holes for most city-style projects. This diameter is perfect for sifting a lot of ground with great efficiency because the holes won't get clogged up. For projects in which you're searching for very small or thin objects, such as gold chains, $\frac{1}{4}$-inch-size or smaller holes are better.

Hardware cloth is very strong, and if handled carelessly, it can cause a bad gash from the jagged and sharp edges. Therefore, after you have attached it to the frame with wire staples, I recommend sealing in the outer fringes by nailing narrow wooden reinforcements over them directly to the frame's borders. This protects you from accidents, prevents the screen from developing weak points, and gives the sifter a small platform to hold it off the ground for light work.

While you're at the hardware store, I suggest you also buy two metal carrying handles to attach to the short sides of the sifter frame. These handles will make the sifter easy to carry and will supply anchor points in case you want to suspend the device by a rope from a tree or a tripod.

Once your sifter is ready for action, secure the legs on the ground at an appropriate angle (see Figure 6.2). Load the frame about half full with soil,

then lift up the sifter by the handles and shake the fill. Use gloves to protect your hands when removing any large rocks and smoothing out the fill. When everything that can go through the screen has done so, carefully pick through the remaining debris and remove any treasure articles.

Building a sifter is not a difficult or expensive project, and you should be able to turn out a piece of equipment that's functional and will help you make many good recoveries. It's easy to use. It's light enough to be carried and worked continuously without causing fatigue. It takes down easily for storage. But most importantly, it brings home the bacon!

MATERIALS

Frame

WOOD

2 pieces 24-x-3$\frac{1}{2}$-x-$\frac{3}{4}$-inch wood for long sides

2 pieces 18-x-3$\frac{1}{2}$-x-$\frac{3}{4}$-inch wood for short sides

2 pieces 24-x-$\frac{3}{4}$-x-$\frac{3}{4}$-inch wood for screen reinforcement on long sides

2 pieces 18-x-$\frac{3}{4}$-x-$\frac{3}{4}$-inch wood for screen reinforcement on short sides

HARDWARE

24-x-18-inch piece of hardware screen with $\frac{1}{2}$-inch-diameter holes

2 brass carrying handles with screws

4 (1$\frac{1}{2}$-inch) end brackets with screws

Package of #5 wire cloth staples

Package of 1$\frac{1}{2}$-inch ringed nails

Support Legs and Handle Grips

WOOD

2 pieces 24$\frac{1}{2}$-x-2$\frac{1}{2}$-x-$\frac{3}{4}$-inch wood for legs

1 piece 20$\frac{1}{2}$-x-2$\frac{1}{2}$-x-$\frac{3}{4}$-inch wood for horizontal leg stabilizer

2 pieces 14$\frac{1}{2}$-x-2$\frac{3}{4}$-inch wood for handle grips

HARDWARE

6 (2-inch) machine bolts

6 wing nuts

12 washers

Nails

INSTRUCTIONS

1. Purchase the wood and hardware.
2. Cut the wood to size.

Frame

3. Assemble the frame by nailing the long sides to the short sides with ringed nails. Use butt joints (see Figure 6.1).
4. Attach the screen to the bottom of the frame with wire cloth staples.
5. Trim any protruding wires or bend them inward.
6. Nail the screen reinforcements to the bottom of the frame over the screen edges.
7. Center an end bracket on the outside of each of the four corners and attach with the included screws.
8. Center a brass carrying handle on each of the short ends of the frame and attach with the included screws.

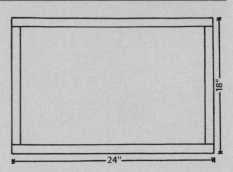

Figure 6.1 A sifter frame constructed using four butt joints.

Figure 6.2 A completed sifter.

Support Legs

9. Drill a bolthole, centered, in each leg $1\frac{1}{2}$ inches from one end.
10. Drill a bolthole, centered, in each long frame side $2\frac{1}{2}$ inches from one end.
11. Assemble the leg unit by nailing the horizontal leg stabilizer to the $\frac{3}{4}$-inch surface of both legs 6 inches from the end that does not have the bolthole.
12. Attach the leg unit to the frame with the machine bolts and wing nuts, placing one washer by the bolt head and one by the wing nut.

Handle Grips

13. Drill two boltholes, centered, in each handle grip 2 inches and 4 inches from one end.
14. Use the holes drilled in the handle grips as guides for drilling corresponding holes in each long frame side on the end away from the leg unit. Position the handle grips so that $8\frac{1}{2}$ inches extend beyond the short frame side.
15. Attach the handle grips to the frame with machine bolts, wing nuts, and washers. File and/or sandpaper the handle-grip edges until they're smooth enough to be comfortably used.

into spaces where you think it may pay off, such as into an old well or off a pier into a long-used harbor.

Since a magnet doesn't attract precious metals, it's mostly a tool for the relic hunter and the cache hunter looking for metal containers. In cities, many a small hoard was hidden by the early immigrants in an iron box stashed behind a wall. One day, you may encounter this type of scenario, and it's good to be prepared.

Magnets cost less than $20 and are the type of tool with which you can really be creative. For example, try going fishing with a magnet in an urban lake or pond. Guns and other weapons are typical finds.

If you happen to live in an area where lakes freeze over in the winter, you can use your magnet to recover the augers and other gear that fishermen lose through the ice. Advertise your services, and you may corner the market.

Magnet

Camera

A small, good-quality point-and-shoot camera that can also take close-up shots of finds is a very useful tool for the urban treasure hunter. A single lens reflex camera fitted with a close-up lens will also do an excellent job. There are many books available on close-up photography techniques, sometimes called "macro photography." Check your local library or bookstore. You might also want to take an adult education course in photography to learn some fine points. Just tell the teacher what your particular interest is and ask to be lead in that direction. That's what I did with some pretty good results.

Cameras are also useful for doing research, such as scouting out a prospective hunting site. You can study the photos you take to determine any potential hot spots. In addition, if you decide to write an article about your adventures for a treasure hunting magazine, you will be able to supply unique photos, which editors like to include.

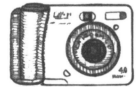

Camera

PREPARING FOR URBAN TREASURE HUNTING

Once you have your metal detector and other tools, you'll have to figure out where and how to use them to achieve the most success—and to have the most fun. This includes paying attention to the basics. Nobody starts out as an expert. No doubt you'll soon develop your own techniques and insights. If you consider the following suggestions, I'm sure you'll make the most of your metal detecting adventures.

Practice the Basics

The metal detectors available today are quite sophisticated and should pay for themselves, depending on how often they are used and how skillful and lucky their operators are. Your attitude will also play a significant role and can really affect the degree of success you attain. So, to maximize your detecting adventures, you need to spend sufficient time practicing in the field to learn how to use your machine correctly and how to interpret what it indicates. In treasure hunting, there is no substitute for personal observation and participation.

A coin signal that fades or disappears while digging is due to the coin being moved from its original horizontal position to a vertical on edge position along the sides of the hole. This will create a smaller target for your detector.

I've encountered some unnecessarily disgruntled rookie detector users in the field who felt frustrated and complained that their machines were not producing. At first, I found this strange because they were using some very expensive computerized deep-seeking models. Observing them, I soon confirmed that they were not operating their detectors properly or had the controls set incorrectly—with the most in the first category.

When I inquired if they had read their instruction booklets or learned some basic search techniques, the typical reply was, "I've read the booklet once" or "Why? Everything is supposed to be automatic." This attitude and the resultant lack of knowledge will get you nowhere, and I'm sure your misunderstood detector will soon wind up in a closet with your old high school baseball uniform.

The smart treasure hunter makes sure to read the instruction manual a few times—and thoroughly. This is a necessary step to get the most out of the machine. Reading the instruction manual one time is really not enough to understand the fine points of changing the control settings or developing the correct coil sweep. Yes, it's true that many of the newer models can work on autopilot, but you still have to learn the fundamental hunting skills. Generally, it takes about twenty-five hours of fieldwork with a new detector to understand its nuances.

Practicing the basics, such as pinpointing and learning the difference between a shallow and a deep signal, will refine your skills and definitely pave the way for you to make deeper and better finds.

This, in turn, will build your confidence. If you go treasure hunting and leave your confidence at home, you might as well stay home also. You need to believe in yourself—and in your equipment. Successful detecting is really in great part a result of having a proper understanding of how to operate your machine.

You may be as fortunate as I was when I started out by locating some bountiful hot spots that nobody has ever worked before. With my next-to-the-bottom-of-the-line detector, I found more than 5,500 coins during my first year, including a nice array of old silver coins. I should point out here that I was not working beaches, where lots of modern change can be found, but rather dry land, because I was looking for the good, old stuff.

That first year gave me plenty of inspiring practice, and I soon learned how to use my machine to its utmost potential. Those early adventures also taught me exactly what I wanted in a more advanced machine, one that was suitable to my developing needs in New York City's multifaceted urban treasure hunting environment.

Field-Test the Discrimination Control

The discrimination control setting on a metal detector allows the detector to selectively reject undesirable metal objects while still responding to valuables. It is a necessary feature in urban environments due to the large amounts of metallic trash such as foil, pull tabs, nails, and bottle caps in the ground. Still, you definitely don't want to use more discrimination than is absolutely necessary, which is an error of inexperience, since this may cause you to pass over gold items.

High discriminators generally don't find much gold because the first metals to be eliminated when increasing the discrimination setting are the least conductive electrically. After iron, this category includes nickel and gold, which have about the same conductivity. Therefore, you should do some field-testing to find the highest discrimination level on your detector that does not reject these two metals. If your detector misses nickels, it will also miss gold rings. Another factor to consider is that some machines tend to lose depth at the higher discrimination levels.

If you begin to find some good coins mixed in with the junk, a proven tactic is to pick up the trash as you dig, allowing you to reduce your discrimination. After a while, you will find proportionately more keepers because you will have fewer junk items masking the coins and jewelry.

Don't Expect Miracles

There were times, and still are, when Lady Luck wasn't cooperative for me. Everyone has off days, when the finds are mundane and far between. During these periods, my advice is to try to maintain a reasonable level of concentration and not become careless.

A lack of finds can be seen in a positive light because of the importance of eliminating dead ends from your search perspective. You learn from these experiences. Think of your unproductive efforts as successful field research that will add to your understanding of your city's treasure hunting potential. Tomorrow is another day, so don't give up.

YOUR DETECTING NICHE

Most detectorists specialize in a particular hunting environment. This generally is due to the availability of nearby hunting areas and their levels of productivity. Sometimes it's just a reflection of where the detectorist likes to pass the day.

Some folks like the security of athletic fields and parks, where coin and jewelry recoveries are frequent and replenished by a lot of new recreational activity. Other detectorists concentrate on the shoreline, as they have put in the required work learning how to read the tides, weather, and sand patterns to get consistently good results.

I happen to believe in versatility and becoming familiar with an assortment of detecting environments. My favorite hunting arenas, however, are the old bridle paths and trails in the wooded sections of the city.

I also like to travel around New York City exploring what each neighborhood has to offer, which can lead to some memorable adventures and interesting recoveries. It's also common knowledge that infrequently visited parks in tough parts of town can pay off well. I've met a few courageous detectorists who specialize in these parks.

One very accessible and profitable detecting location that is often overlooked is the strip of grass between the sidewalk and the street. Older neighborhoods are definitely the better choice for this type of

After finding a medal or any other item with a hole drilled in it, try to find the broken chain that once held it.

hunting. Try detecting around old bus stops for some fast action—if nobody's beaten you to it.

Over the years, these inconspicuous but beckoning strips have accumulated a surprising assortment of metal valuables. Whether it's because people drop things as they reach into their pockets for their car keys or because kids play in the grass, the result can be serendipitous urban detecting at its best.

The prime indicators of age for this particular treasurescape are old sidewalks made of flagstone or sidewalks cracked and buckled due to the unmanaged growth of tree roots. These are serious clues that mean the neighborhood is sufficiently old to make some good recoveries. My finds here have included numerous old coins, assort-

Sidewalks broken or buckled due to the roots of large trees usually mean that old coins and tokens should be found along the curbside. Further research on the neighborhood's history would be in order here.

ed advertising and transportation tokens, rings, antique skate keys, and even an artillery button from the War of 1812. I made this last amazing find while I was waiting for the traffic light to change.

Of course, I'm not alone in this curb hunting pursuit. A group of detectorists in Kansas City, Missouri, has taken this same approach. Treasure awareness led them to try their luck downtown along the "parkways" that line the boulevards fronting some early-twentieth-century apartment houses. Their finds were fast and plentiful, which was to be expected, since they had chosen an area that few other treasure hunters visit due to safety concerns. One day's hunt produced 310 coins, including Barber silver and Indian Head cents. To top it all off, these detectorists still have a few miles of solid, enjoyable coin hunting left along these wide, grassy inner city islands.

Historical buttons help tell a city's story. The War of 1812 artillery button (center) was detected along a curb in New York City. Anything can be anywhere!

YOUR PERSONAL STYLE

Through trial and error, most detectorists seem to develop an individual hunting style. For example, some like to "butterfly" around a target area. Others prefer to choose one particular spot and work it intensely. In actuality, the best method is a combination of the two, the first for locating a hot spot and the second for conducting a more thorough search. Many successful detectorists use that sequence with great efficiency.

Once you've located a hot spot, you need to make the most of it. As an example, here's what I do when I locate a concentration of coins in a park. First, I detect in increasingly larger circles around them, like the spirals on a seashell. This tactic serves the dual purpose of centralizing the coin zone while sharply focusing my attention. While gradually widening the search area, I am able to see how far and in which direction the coin zone extends.

Next, I form a grid pattern in the target area using some kind of marker (see Figure 6.3). This entails dividing up the target area into small square sections of arbitrary but uniform size for a thorough and overlapping search configuration. I use golf tees as markers and make my squares about 3 feet by 3 feet in size. As I work my way

When working a grid, proceed slowly with a close-to-the-ground overlapping sweep of your coil.

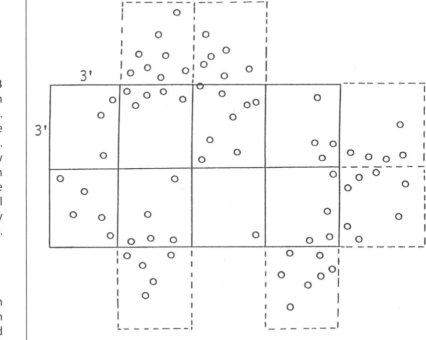

Figure 6.3
A sample grid pattern used in an old picnic grove. The solid lines indicate the initial exploratory pattern. The dotted lines show the sections added on to follow the flow of the coins (the circles). All the squares are roughly 3 feet by 3 feet in size.

News of the Lindbergh baby kidnapping on March 1, 1932, shocked the world. The convicted kidnapper, Bruno Richard Hauptman, lived in the Bronx and was known to frequent a particular picnic grove.

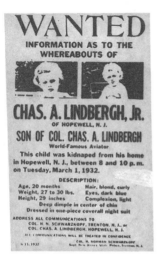

through the squares, I move the tees to form new squares. If you don't have tees, you can use stones or twigs.

Laying out a grid pattern is a classic method for getting the most out of a hunting site and has practical application for all of your treasure hunting endeavors. Hunting in an organized manner is definitely more effective than wandering around aimlessly, which can cost you old coins and other valuables that you should find but may miss, even in a productive area.

I conducted my most memorable grid search in a long-forgotten picnic grove. A good tip and then some research brought me to a woodsy section of the Bronx. I was there to search for the still-missing $31,000 in ransom money from the infamous Crime of the Century—the Lindbergh baby kidnapping of the early 1930s. Luckily, I met an old-timer on one of the trails who knew the whole story very well and showed me where the kidnapper, Bruno Richard Hauptman, and other German immigrants used to go every weekend to eat wiener schnitzel and be serenaded by um-pa-pa music. My

guide was quite up there in years, approaching ninety, but still had strong feelings about the case. As he
pointed around, he said, "That rotten bum Hauptman
deserved the chair!"

The first coin I found was a 1910 Barber half near
a vine-covered picnic bench. "This could be good," I
thought to myself, and it wasn't long before I had my
grid set up and was pulling old coins out of the
ground. I also found a cache of Depression-era dishes
buried in a metal container between two trees. Actually, I was ready for big bucks when I first saw the metal
lid about a foot down. No doubt the picnickers had
used these decorative dishes every week, but then, for
whatever reason, forgot about them. An intriguing find.

Since working a grid takes time, I recommend
holding off until the hunting site has demonstrated
that it will produce. It's best to find a high-yield or
high-potential spot before working over the ground so thoroughly. In
addition, don't develop a mindset where you demand that the piece
of land pay off. You have to learn the point of diminishing returns for
the work involved.

A cache of 1920s floral-
design dishes was found
in the old picnic grove
frequented by Hauptman
during a search for the still-
missing $31,000 in ransom
money from the infamous
Lindbergh baby kidnapping.
A fascinating project!

YOUR FELLOW URBAN TREASURE HUNTERS

Part of the metal detecting experience in a city is the other treasure
hunters you will meet out in the field. Some of them will be very
interesting people and talented detector operators. I never pass up a
chance to go over and say hello, see their equipment, and perhaps
learn what they are finding and where.

I also inquire about other parts of the city that I'm researching in
a casual information exchange. Most of the time, it's an enjoyable
and constructive conversation, although some people are wary about
discussing their digs. Such is life. On occasion, however, I've received
some exceptional leads, including one on a five-month-long irrigation construction project in a large historic park in Brooklyn.

The bulldozers had stripped the surface layer down to the clay
on 40 acres of land that had always been considered prime hunting
turf anyway. The word was out, and treasure hunters from all over
the city were picking the site clean of easily detectable coins and

A total of $14,600 of the
Lindbergh kidnapping ransom
money was found buried in
Bruno Richard Hauptman's
garage. Still protesting his
innocence, Hauptman was
executed for the crime on
April 3, 1936. Regarding the
missing $31,000 ransom money,
The New York Times headline
the next day summed up
this final frustration with,
"Hauptman Silent to the End."

relics dating back to Colonial times. After hearing about this spectacular Coin Rush, I joined to get my share. A first view of the site revealed large mounds of dirt scattered over the landscape. The only downside was the opportunistic, crack-smoking security guard who demanded that everyone rent hunting time or buy a "season ticket," both at a considerable price. It became a rather testy situation, but everyone was able to find some bargaining power, and there were always a few people detecting the site. By some estimates, there were more than 100 detectorists who kept coming back.

Some treasure hunters at this site were glad to talk about their finds, while others were very cautious because the scheming security guard was also trying to get a piece of everyone's action. The guard kept asking me about an 1868 Napoleonic silver piece that he saw me pick up. Another digger had a problem with the guard over a set of gold teeth he found in a pile of dirt. The run-ins with this leech were constant. Then one day, the shouting lunatic shot himself across the chest with a flare gun that he had been waving around and had to be taken away in an ambulance half unconscious and moaning. We all had a good laugh about that. It was an incredible saga that had New York City written all over it.

This last episode is a good example of how amicable communication can lead to some interesting and rewarding experiences for the inquisitive urban treasure hunter. The next time you see another member of our electronic fraternity, I suggest you go over and ask, "What's going on?" It might well result in some wonderful hunting opportunities.

Everything considered, your metal detecting expeditions should prove to be quite enjoyable. Make sure to respect the rights and property of others. Learn good recovery techniques, and leave the ground as you found it. Nothing will wear out your welcome faster than leaving unsightly and dangerous holes.

Be civilized and civic minded. If you find something of historic value, share the knowledge and show it to the experts at your local museum or university. I'm sure they will be very glad to see it. As your search skills and finds increase, you'll have the satisfaction of pursuing a fascinating, as well as rewarding, pastime.

"The ridiculous and the tragic often go hand in hand."

—F. A. Mitchell-Hedges,
British explorer of the 1920s

7

Picking Up
the Trail

Research will be the backbone of your treasure hunting success. All urban areas have undergone gradual and persistent change while developing from a small settlement into their present state of civilization. If you are going to be a successful urban treasure hunter, you must learn and use creative research skills to trace the goings-on of yesteryear. In this chapter, we will discuss the research resources available in most urban areas, the information they will provide, and the skills and tools you will need to make the most of them.

GETTING STARTED

Fortunately, most urban areas have a good supply of research resources. These include the public library, historical societies, universities, museums, and such very important primary sources as senior residents and back issues of local newspapers. The basic techniques you will need to use to reap the most benefits from these resources are observation, reading, note taking, interviewing, and creating a working file of relevant material. Your file doesn't have to be elaborate. It can consist of just a large envelope or file folder for filing articles and a notebook for recording field notes, ideas, data for prospective investigations, and the results of your searches while following particular leads. This will provide a necessary degree of organization to your research efforts.

I can't overstate the importance of being organized. As for most pursuits in life, being methodical in your treasure hunting will pay

You have to look at your hometown with a creative new perspective.

off. In addition, vigilant urban treasure hunters are always alert to new developments relating to the history of their city. These include such occurrences as accidental treasure finds that make the head-lines, now or in the past, and the dredging up of old shipwrecks, which may affect shoreline and land hunting as the story develops.

How can an accidental treasure find reported in a back issue of a local newspaper be important? Here's an example. An article published in *The Huntington Bulletin* titled "Golden Treasures of Long Island" recounts an 1842 incident in which a Revolutionary War hoard of Spanish doubloons and English guineas was found by a pig on a farm in the Dutch Kills section of Long Island City. It seems that while the pig was rooting around for food, it turned up an earthen crock filled with gold coins. The report goes on to say that the total monetary value of the find at the time was $40,000. An astute urban treasure hunter would definitely see this information as worth some follow-up. There may be another crock to be revealed by modern-day construction.

To illustrate how an old shipwreck may be important, take the case of a salvager who claimed he found the remains of the British payroll ship *H.M.S. Hussar* in the waters of the East River off the South Bronx. This frigate sank in 1780 on its last voyage from Beekman's Wharf in lower Manhattan to Newport, Rhode Island, after it was wrecked in the treacherous waters of Hell Gate. Confirmed shipping records indicate that approximately $500 million in coins and precious metal bullion went down with the *Hussar*. Over the years, riptides may have carried the treasure to the shore, where waiting detectorists can now make some exciting finds.

RESEARCH RESOURCES

When starting out as an urban treasure hunter, don't attempt to cover every bit of information on your area of interest at once. This will only bog you down because of the large volume of research material most likely available. Let things evolve gradually—unless you have a definite project in mind.

The best way to begin is by reading a general social history of your city to gain a good historical perspective. This background knowledge should provide you with some preliminary ideas and leads for possible expeditions. It will also give you a sense of

A good research strategy is to study the older history books and maps of your city for promising leads. Just one small fact could be the clue that brings success.

how things developed from what they were in the past to what they are today.

If anything promising jumps out at you right away, choose that specific area for a project. If not, I suggest starting with your own neighborhood, since you probably know something about it already. Believe me, you have just as good a chance of making a hit across the street as across town. Good resources to check for information on your neighborhood or your city include the historical society, the library, the history room, the Internet, maps, and knowledgeable old-timers.

Don't be hesitant about following your intuition.

The Historical Society

When a neighborhood is particularly old or interesting, it may have a historical society that meets regularly to discuss the membership's research projects and to show slides of "how it used to be." Observation has shown me that members of local historical societies are longtime city residents who share your interest in the past, and who are quite willing to reminisce about "the good old days"—to your benefit.

Some of the members most likely are also very intense collectors of historical memorabilia and may be able to supply you with interesting facts and personal material you cannot get elsewhere, such as old photos or train routes. The historical society will probably also have a good reference file or even a library with books to borrow or photocopy.

My experience with this type of research resource has been good. However, I would advise you to be low-key in your approach. It's not necessary to say you're looking for some long-forgotten recluse's gold. Coming on too strong could close an important door.

Reading monographs and back issues of newspapers, and looking at old photos and postcards will help a lot of hazy areas to become filled in. Most importantly, these activities will provide you with the informational background to ask intelligent questions—without which you won't be able to proceed much further.

Some historical societies offer occasional tours of their neighborhoods. Make sure you're on the next one. These are invaluable because amateur experts will point out details such as local architectural styles and recreational patterns that you may never learn about otherwise.

Old-timers are informational gold mines. You will hear facts and stories that can't be found in any history book, such as the locations of long-forgotten swimming holes, carnival sites, and picnic groves—maybe even a good cache hunting lead about a local packrat who was observed digging holes before he died.

On one neighborhood tour that I took, part of the program was meeting some of the older residents. During the visit, two senior citizens rapturously told me about some swimming holes and picnic groves in the nearby woods that they had enjoyed as children more than seventy years earlier. This information has been quite helpful and has provided me with prime target areas to hunt for old coins that are only ten minutes from where I live.

The Library

One of the best assets an urban treasure hunter has is the public library. To avoid spending your valuable time in the wrong place, you should always first investigate any available written material and photographs concerning a potential hunting site.

Most branch libraries keep a small file on their particular neighborhood's history. These files usually contain a variety of helpful material, including short historical articles and a log of newspaper clippings describing significant local events. Within this last group may also be reports of unsolved robberies and other instances of money disappearing, the location of traveling carnivals, photos of long-gone manmade or natural structures such as outdoor dance halls and caves, and early maps showing former street names and boundaries of parks.

These neighborhood files often also contain old letters. I once found a letter written in 1923 by a schoolteacher, Rachel Martin, who mentioned a spot called Sunset Hill located by a stand of beech trees in the nearby woods. Rachel and her friends used to go there on picnics and watch the beautiful sunsets. I knew the location, but nobody in the area today refers to it as Sunset Hill. It's just an overgrown place in the woods that people ride by on horseback. That letter set the stage. I figured that the name "Sunset Hill" probably had its origins in the nineteenth century, so I optimistically went over there one afternoon with my detector and found an 1855 Seated Liberty quarter—and enjoyed a beautiful sunset. Another piece of research that paid off!

One interesting fact here: You would be surprised to learn how many libraries were built on the sites of old parks, making the surrounding grounds excellent prospects for coin hunting with a metal detector. However, remember to ask permission first.

Of course, in addition to neighborhood files, the library may also have books, even major works, about your urban area. So much the better.

The History Room

If you can't find sufficient books or files about your local area at the local branch of your library, go to the main branch. Many main branches even have a special room devoted to the history of their city, county, or borough called the "history room." I use history rooms regularly.

Suppose I'm thinking about coin hunting in a park that has been around for a long time and want to get an idea of what my possible finds might be and where in the park would be the best places to search. I would go to the history room and ask for a folder on that particular park. In New York City, I have never been told that such a folder does not exist. In fact, I'm usually presented with a splendid array of information, including a very complete local history and physical layout that may date back seventy-five years. This is generally quite sufficient for forming a logical plan of action.

Occasionally, these park folders also contain an archaeological site report describing a prehistoric Native American camp once located on the land. More recent information might be where a lake was located before it was filled in due to repeated drownings; the location of the original concession stand near where patriotic celebrations were held; if the land was ever used for troop encampment or battles during the Revolutionary or Civil wars; and whether the park was landscaped using soil from another part of town with its own significant history. All of these bits of information will have positive implications for your success.

Never underestimate what the library has to offer. In many instances, the history room librarian is a buff on the area at large and will be glad to supply you with important facts and information resources. It pays to be congenial and to sound interested in your project. Remember that other people may pick up on your enthusiasm and offer you helpful ideas.

On one occasion, I thought it quite strange to be detecting Civil War–era military relics along the old bridle paths in my local park. Upon conducting some research, however, I learned that there had

New York City's Jackson Pond is a good example of a filled-in urban pond. Dating back to the mid-1800s, this "swimmin' hole" was drained in 1932 after witnessing some tragic drownings. Search the surrounding bushes with a metal detector to find old coins lost by swimmers changing for their dip.

been a Union Army training camp, Camp Banks, established nearby in the 1860s. It was very interesting to learn that so many men from the area had joined up.

This information about Camp Banks was given to me by a friendly and interested librarian in the form of a book that was a chronicle of local events since the early 1850s. This book also contains a list of the oldest homes in the neighborhood and mentions the location of a long-gone Civil War–era racetrack near Camp Banks, which is now a big schoolyard. A construction project here would have soaring potential!

Actually, military relics can show up anywhere around the country, and you don't even have to be on a battlefield to find them. Consider the treasure hunter who found a New York Militia belt plate (circa 1840 to 1850) on the east side of Chicago. We can only guess at how it ended up in Chicago, and looking for the answer would make an interesting research project—one that might lead to more finds.

The Internet

The Internet has become a great resource for the urban treasure hunter. You can find information there on practically any topic relating to your city. You may also find maps. Other websites offer equipment reviews and chat rooms for discussing projects with other urban treasure hunters from around the country. Appendix D provides a list of useful websites that you can try for starters. Many of the sites have links to other websites. If you don't have Internet access, go to the library for half-hour shifts at the computers there.

Maps

Another key to locating potential hunting sites is a good map. Therefore, knowing how to read a map is an indispensable skill. I'm not necessarily talking about an authentic and detailed "deathbed" treasure map, but a common street map of your municipality. However, if anyone offers you the former, don't turn it down!

A good street map will show all the undeveloped land in your city, and it will do so quite explicitly, in green color. This will include big and small parks, marshes, the land surrounding highways, empty lots, and a multitude of other locations.

It's not a bad idea to have two street maps published by different sources, such as the Chamber of Commerce and the local auto club. Undeveloped land missed on one may be indicated on the other. Some of my best treasure hunting adventures have resulted from using maps in this way.

In my opinion, the best urban street map series is published by Hagstrom. "Comprehensive" is the only way to describe these maps. The New York City map includes many sites left out of the common tourist maps, and I've located some incredibly secluded undeveloped spots that were just the smallest green dots. If you buy only one map, this is the one.

In addition to street maps, other types of maps that may prove useful are old maps, topographical maps, and plat maps.

Old Maps

Another type of map you will need is one old enough to show the original street names for the area you're researching. Sometimes neighborhood newspapers print these in special Fourth of July anniversary issues. These maps will definitely come in handy when you receive a lead from a source that gives only the old street name for the location. In such cases, these vintage maps will clear up the impasse quickly. They're also very useful for pinpointing "dead" railroad lines and stations.

You should expect to spend hours studying old maps.

When I'm in need of an old map, I go to the history room at the local library and ask for it. Most frequently, I'm shown a copy of *Beer's Atlas*, a series of street maps printed for nineteenth-century urban areas starting in about 1870. There's probably one for your city as well.

These atlases are very detailed and will give you an excellent idea of how your city looked over 100 years ago. After making a photocopy of the map, I'm in business to pursue the information any way I need. It's really very interesting to see how things have changed over the years, especially from a treasure hunter's point of view.

Topographical Maps

Topographical (topo) maps are extremely useful to treasure hunters because they clearly depict a city's geological features. Natural structures of relief such as mountains, valleys, and hills show up as brown lines. Water courses are indicated by the color blue. Manmade transportation networks such as roads and train lines appear in black. Older topo maps are also useful for researching former roadway and building locations.

Current topo maps are relatively easy to obtain. They are available in map and outdoor stores, and can be downloaded from the United States Geological Survey's website (http://mapping.usgs.gov/topo). For older topo maps, my source is the geology department of one of the universities in town. This department has copies of all the geological maps ever made for the region and is usually very willing to provide access to them to the public. I always call ahead to make an appointment so the material is ready and waiting.

Plat Maps

Essential maps for privy digging for old bottles are the nineteenth-century fire insurance maps that were issued by the Sanborn Map Company of Pelham, New York, starting in the late 1860s. (For a complete discussion of privy digging for old bottles, see page 152.) Called "plat maps," they covered all parts of town, both commercial and residential, for thousands of towns and cities across the United States. An important record of urban growth, these maps were originally used by fire insurance companies to establish premiums. As a result, they provide everything an urban treasure hunter needs to know about a city lot, including all the structures on the property, such as privies, cisterns, and wells. Treasure hunters often use a Sanborn map with another old map, such as a *Beer's Atlas*. The key is to locate the property line so you can start probing in a grid pattern.

You can track plat maps down at the main branch of the library or the appropriate government agency in your city, or get a copy directly from the Sanborn Map Company (800-352-0050). Another way is to put "Sanborn Fire Insurance Maps" into a computer search engine for a listing of other information resources where they can be obtained, such as university collections.

Personal Interviews

Another important tool for obtaining useful information is the personal interview. An interview may have to be arranged in advance or it can be conducted on the spur of the moment, out in the field, when the opportunity presents itself. The latter situation is probably more common among experienced urban treasure hunters.

What usually happens is that somebody sees you poking around with your metal detector and comes over to tell you about a good place to search for things or about finds already known to have been made in the area. Sometimes, this is an older person who has quite a bit of knowledge and spirit, and can talk about yesteryear's events like they happened two days ago.

You should consider this a gift from above because here is a person who lived through the time period whose valuables you are seeking and who is willing to share his or her knowledge. It may not be hard to prime the pump here, but you do want to direct the flow of facts.

Be ready for this type of miracle by having appropriate questions at the tip of your tongue. For example, find out how long the person has lived in the neighborhood and for what he or she remembers the land being used. Did the person or an acquaintance ever find anything interesting? Who? What? Where? When?

Ask if there were any people who were known locally to be miserly, reclusive, or otherwise eccentric. Are there any interesting legends or lore concerning the community or the nearby woods? Always be calm, polite, and patient. Some old-timers tend to ramble a bit.

These impromptu interviews can also be initiated by you when someone who seems appropriate just shows up—for example, taking a walk where you're hunting. Using this last technique once resulted in my being led to an old, dried-up spring in the Bronx's huge Van Cortland Park, where neighborhood residents took morning baths during the 1920s, when the spring was flowing. My informant was a pleasant elderly lady who was a child back then and went there with her parents. She thought it would be interesting for me to know this fact. She was so right.

TAKE NOTES

Taking notes is a good idea at prearranged interviews, so come prepared with writing materials. However, sometimes it's difficult to write, talk, and think of follow-up questions all at the same time. It may also be distracting to the person being interviewed. You can easily solve this problem by using a tape recorder. I use a miniature one that is inexpensive and fits easily in my pocket when I'm on the move. At other times, it serves the important function of quick note taker and is a very valuable part of my research efforts. After I've entered a sufficient quantity of notes, I transcribe them to their proper places in my files. Just remember to always check your batteries before an interview.

BE COURTEOUS

When you interview someone, whether on the spur of the moment or in a prearranged chat, your manner should always be gracious.

Help the interviewed person feel at ease so he or she can readily waft down Memory Lane. An associated skill to interviewing is listening, so make sure you pay attention to what the person is saying. Don't let your thoughts race ahead to other topics. Slow and easy does it.

You want the interview to flow without stress, so give the person an opportunity to finish his or her thoughts. Plan enough time for the interview, and always arrive at the appointed hour. Showing up an hour early can be as annoying as arriving an hour late. Also, dress neatly so you don't alienate the interviewee.

Of course, at the conclusion of the interview, thank the person for his or her time. Also, suggest that a follow-up session might be in order at a later date. If you acted civilized, there probably won't be any problem with that.

RECORD KEEPING

Not all the answers to your questions will come from outside sources. By keeping detailed records of your finds and observations, you will build a body of knowledge that you can use to make predictions of future success and to evaluate past performance.

For example, I know how many wheat cents (pennies minted between 1909 and 1958) I've ever detected, and I also know, through my field experience, that wherever "wheaties" are found, there should also be silver coins. By dividing my total wheat cents ever found by my total silver coins ever found, I can calculate a ratio for the number of silver coins found per number of wheat cents found. In my case, the ratio is approximately 1 to 6. This means that if the area in which I'm coin hunting produces pre-1959 pennies, then statistically for every 6 wheat cents I find, I should find 1 silver coin.

Another way to predict your progress is to divide the total coins you have ever found by the total silver coins you have ever found. This ratio is your unadjusted chance of finding a silver coin per any number of other coins you find. For example, if you have recovered 6,500 coins of which 325 were silver, your silver finding ratio is 1 to 20. This means that for every 20 coins you find, 1 will be silver. Now you can predict you success in finding silver coins.

You can make ring-to-coins-found ratios or whatever else you feel is important to know. My personal ring-per-coins ratio is 1 to 190

(1 ring found per 190 coins found), which is not bad for a land hunter. Information, like these facts gained from your own hunting statistics, will make you more aware and self-confident regarding how you're doing.

Develop a System

A good idea is to count up and tabulate your coin finds on a quarterly basis. When I first started out as an urban treasure hunter, I did a tabulation after each coin hunting expedition. Gradually, however, I learned that this type of precision is not really called for unless you're tracking a specific hot spot.

Maintaining a yearly tally of your coin finds will provide you with an accurate record of accomplishments along with some predictable trends.

A three-month time period is sufficient to show any developing trend, which you can then evaluate. Over the years, and after recovering thousands of coins, my percentages have been relatively stable. Table 7.1 is a career summary of my urban coin finding percentages (UCFP).

From my conversations with other urban treasure hunters who keep similar records, I've established that these percentages are pretty universal and what you might expect to experience over a year's time of city-style coin hunting. Of course, there will be times and finds that will skew your data one way or another, but your totals should range near the percentages given.

TABLE 7.1 AVERAGE YEARLY PERCENTAGES OF COINS FOUND BY TYPE	
Coins	Percentage of Total Coins Found
Pennies	74.0%
Nickels	4.7%
Dimes	13.9%
Quarters	7.3%
Half dollars	Less than 1.0%
Wheat cents	26.5%
Silver coins	4.5%

Keeping an accurate record of noncoin treasure discoveries is also important. You should keep track of when and where you find them, the materials from which they are made, and whether the find is associated with any other category of treasure or a specific feature of the landscape. Such facts are always helpful in planning future expeditions.

Learn From Your Hunting Partners' Finds

If you team up with like-minded friends for treasure hunting adventures, make sure to pool your information. Knowing what other people are finding can only benefit your own hunt strategizing and eventual finds.

Some urban treasure hunters join metal detecting and bottle digging clubs. This is a very good idea if you want to learn from the successes of experienced members. Don't necessarily expect them to show you their private digs, but do expect an enthusiastic welcome from a group of people who enjoy treasure hunting within a club format and are willing to teach you some fundamentals out in the field. Your local metal detector dealer will be able to tell you how to get connected. Or, contact the Federation of Metal Detecting and Archaeological Clubs (see page 52).

Evaluate Your Finds Yearly

Aside from the benefits of being organized, evaluating your success on an annual basis offers the satisfaction that comes from actually knowing the cumulative amount and variety of your recoveries. Treasure hunting is one endeavor in life where your success often depends solely on you. If you do well, having the numbers in black and white will enhance your feeling of accomplishment.

Some folks pursue treasure hunting only for the thrill of the search and recovery. I think this shortchanges your success because it's a bit one-dimensional. Evaluation is necessary to give yourself the psychic rewards that will spur you on to greater achievements.

At the end of my hunting year, I always prepare an annual report. This consists of my UCFP, plus a number of other indicator categories including:

• Number, denomination, and dollar value of coins found.

- Number, denomination, and dollar value of silver coins found.

- Number of rings found.

- Number of gold and silver jewelry pieces found.

- Number and origin of foreign coins found.

- Number of Seated Liberty, Barber, and Indian Head coins found.

- Number of tokens found.

- Oldest coin found.

- Number and type of prehistoric Native American artifacts found.

- Number and type of antique bottles found.

- Interesting historical relics found.

- Oddities found.

- Other items of note found.

- Memorable events experienced.

You can add any other category that you feel is meaningful to your annual report. An annual summary takes very little time to prepare and provides a good review of your year's accomplishments. The next step is to make it cumulative for every year you have spent treasure hunting. The results will provide you with an excellent and useful record of your total progress, which you can use to plan future expeditions and research. When you have finished your accounting, use some of the money you found during the year and take your family out for an awards dinner to celebrate. You deserve it!

8

Learning From an Archaeological Site Report

Urban treasure hunters should learn and employ some of the methods used by archaeologists. It's certainly a good skill to be able to read and understand a professional site report, as this is frequently encountered while doing research. Such a report can give you insights into how a project was inspired, surveyed, mapped, and excavated. In a museum, you see the end product without a description of the techniques used to make the recovery. In this chapter, we will review the different sections of an archaeological site report and discuss the type of information that they offer.

THE INTRODUCTION

A typical archaeological site report starts with an introductory section that provides justification for the choice of the site based on archaeological principles, topographical interpretation, and physical evidence located through test pitting or other means. It names the archaeologists who introduced the site at a meeting of their state's governing archaeological society and mentions the approval of the membership for pursuing excavation.

The "Introduction" also includes the time frame for the "dig." In addition, if the site is located on public property, it mentions that a parks department permit had to be obtained for work to proceed. If the site is located on private property, it usually thanks the landowners for their cooperation and good will.

Any proposed hypothesis as to what excavation of the particular

City workers in Toronto were doing some grading on soccer fields in Moatfield Farm Park and found archaeological evidence that led to an excavation, which revealed a vanished thirteenth century Iroquois village. Archaeologists believe that this was a large village inhabited by 300 to 500 people.

site was meant to achieve is clearly stated in the "Introduction." Using an actual New York City coastal parkland site report as an example, we would learn that the site had been known to amateur archaeologists for many years and yielded a considerable amount of stone tools and midden (refuse heap) debris from the early part of the Late Woodland Period, which extended from A.D. 1000 to 1200. (For a complete discussion of the Woodland Period, see page 143.)

Reviewing the data in this coastal parkland site report and comparing it to what was already known about previously excavated coastal sites and Woodland Period lifestyles led to the logical assumption that the proposed site at one time had been a seasonal Native American camp during warm weather, when shellfish was plentiful and easily gathered. Therefore, ample reason existed to proceed with excavation.

THE SITE

The next section of an archaeological site report is usually titled "The Site" and is composed of subsections relating to the site's physical description, history, excavation, stratigraphy (underground vertical soil profile), features, recovered artifacts, houses, and food remains. It also supplies the site's exact location in latitude and longitude, and positions the site relative to a permanent boundary or physical feature, which is important information for any interested member of the public who would like to visit the site.

Physical Description

The physical description of a site covers all the pertinent topographical features including access roads, ravines, marshes, springs, bodies of water, elevated areas, forest cover, and grasses. It also notes any modern-day construction-related activities that may have affected the land, such as a bulldozer skimming the surface.

After reading the "Physical Description" subsection, you should have a very good idea about what was found at the site in terms of landscape. The New York City coastal parkland site report includes an interesting discussion on how a study of Woodland Period geological features revealed direct water routes from Long Island Sound, providing access to the site's central fresh water supply. This was, and still is, a small lake where canoes can be beached. Unfortunately, these entry points have been obliterated by highway and community development projects over the past fifty years.

The site report also points out that the camp was located in a ravine that may have provided protection from the strong northerly winds coming off the Sound during the winter, making year-round habitation possible. Proof of this could be supplied only by finding the remains of seasonally available foods and indications of winter-type shelters.

History

The "History" subsection of a site report describes known historical facts about the site. It discusses the land use patterns, such as farming or early Colonial settlement, that may affect the archaeological interpretation of any of the artifacts or manmade features observed.

The sequence of land ownership is also important and provides the necessary framework for a complete study of the site. It frequently also sheds light on historical events and cultural evolution. Out of all this information, a name for the site usually arises. Many times, when a site is located on private property, it takes on the name of the owner, such as the "Jones Site." If the site is near a prominent topographical feature, such as a lake, it may become known as, say, the "Maple Lake Site."

My name for the New York City coastal parkland site is the "Shared Site," which I feel is appropriate due to the harmonious settlement pattern of two contemporary early Late Woodland tribes (circa A.D. 1200), one indigenous to New York and the other from Delaware, who shared a small lake and marsh every year during the spring and summer.

Over time, the two tribal groups seemed to have developed a cooperative relationship and even prospered by uniting seasonally for communal shellfish collecting. The adjacent waters of Long Island Sound afforded them abundant catches of scallops, clams, and oysters. They also hunted the surrounding forest for deer, bear, turkey, and other game.

Interestingly, during the Archaic Period (8000 to 2000 B.C.), some 3,000 years before the Woodland Period settlement, people also used the lake. In archaeological parlance, the site is said to be an "open

An historic period occupation of a prehistoric site can cause some problems in how the site data is interpreted, since its original appearance and structure have been disturbed.

site" because of its long continuity of use by different groups. A "closed site" is a site that was occupied by only one group for a relatively short time span.

Excavation

Excavation of an archaeological site near Milwaukee has revealed evidence of prehistoric occupation dating back to 250 B.C. Aside from artifacts and other cultural material, a mass grave containing twenty-nine individuals was found. An intriguing circumstance.

The "Excavation" subsection of a site report describes the method of excavation used. The method must be adaptive to the site's individual characteristics and is usually selected according to the data gathered in a preliminary survey. At the Shared Site, test pitting showed the soil to be uniformly stratified, so the level stripping method was employed. This method separates features and artifacts through the use of arbitrary levels of excavation—for example, by following a particular soil layer or archaeological time horizon, or by simply digging to a convenient depth, such as 6 or 12 inches. The Shared Site was broken into a grid pattern, the natural subsurface contours of the land were followed, and each layer was thoroughly examined by sifting during removal.

Due to the site's clearly demarcated stratigraphy with a relative lack of subzones to aid in sequential dating, an archaeological technique called "time succession interpretation" was utilized. This technique involves analyzing the trait variations of the cultural materials, hearth construction, and any other visible features encountered from the top to the bottom of each zone.

The "Excavation" subsection also reviews the order of the excavation work, starting with the preparatory removal of the surface trash and proceeding to the outlining of the site's baseline dimensions, the setting up of a grid system, and finally the filling-in of trenches after all the artifacts have been collected and the subsurface features noted. At the Shared Site, sixty 5-by-5-feet squares were excavated for a total surface area of 1,500 square feet.

During excavation at the Shared Site, written and photographic records were carefully kept of all the artifacts found and of any changes in the major soil zones that might aid in assessing the cultural remains sequence. Also, a diligent watch had to be maintained for architectural remains such as fireplaces, storage pits, and house postmolds (dark stains left in the ground by decaying wooden house posts).

Lastly, the "Excavation" subsection notes any components that were revealed by the excavation, such as sharply defined midden areas and house structure outline patterns. These components are also noted on the map of excavation (see Figure 8.1). The "Excavation" subsection also mentions when the dig was terminated.

When an excavation is correctly done and the site report properly prepared, you should be able to reconstruct the site, with each artifact and feature in its proper place. This will provide a meaningful interpretation of the cultural activity at the site.

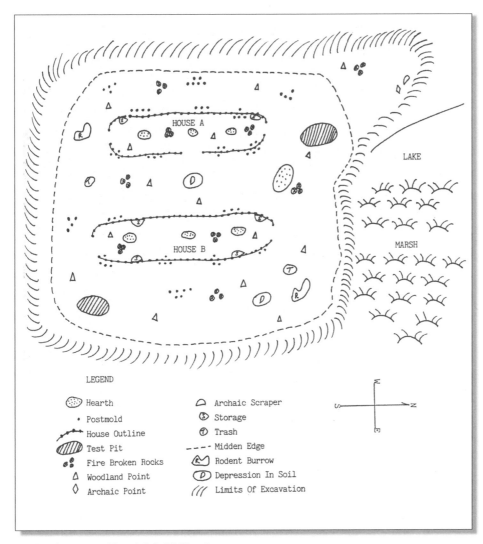

Figure 8.1

The map of excavation for the Shared Site.

Reprinted courtesy of People's Publishing Company.

Stratigraphy

The "Stratigraphy" subsection of a site report profiles the soil of a site and its contents in terms of vertical zones and their horizontal dimensions. Each zone is given a letter label, with the labels following the normal alphabetical sequence. The zones differ from each other primarily in texture and color, size of soil grains, and presence or absence of manmade artifacts and other camp remains.

The soil profile map for the Shared Site (Figure 8.2) is a perfect example of how a mosaic of soil compositions is archaeologically described and interpreted. As you can see, the Shared Site is composed of four different zones, all of which contain cultural material and food refuse, establishing them as zones of habitation to a greater or lesser degree. A typical site report might describe these zones as follows:

• *Zone A.* Street level and covered by a leafy mulch with small islands of grass and weeds. Dark brown soil due to an accumulation of organic matter. The surface was lightly scattered with glass, metal, and paper refuse. The remains of a late model car were removed by a city towing vehicle.

Measured from the surface, Zone A continued to a depth of 5 inches and contained fragment remains of clam, scallop, and oyster shells; refuse bone; flint chipping debris; and fire-broken rocks.

• *Zone B.* Mottled black and brown charcoal impregnated earth 5 to 12 inches deep. An occasional stemmed or triangular stone arrow point and flint chips. Moderate amounts of whole and fragmented clam, scallop, and oyster shells. Fire-broken rocks in mid-position of zone. Turtle shell (eastern box) and refuse bone material (muskrat, white tailed deer) present.

Soil is formed through an interaction of four factors: rocky soil element parent material; organic material; climate; and time of which climate is the most important. Each soil layer is referred to as a zone or a horizon.

• *Zone C.* Principle habitation zone. Color ranges from deep brown to black depending on the amount of charcoal and organic material present. Averaged between 11 and 19 inches below the surface and 8 inches wide. Some yellow streaking present, probably due to rodents tunneling down toward Zone D. Clear outlines of cooking pits, along with a few charred hickory nuts, appeared at the junction of zones B and C.

Throughout this zone were pieces of burned bone, charcoal flakes, mollusk shells, fire-broken rocks, and the majority of Woodland Period artifacts found at the site. Archaic material began to appear in the middle part of this layer and included stone tools.

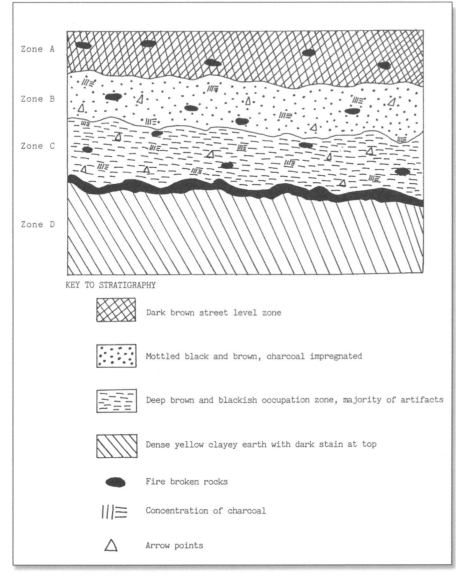

Figure 8.2
The soil profile map, or stratigraphic profile, for the Shared Site.

KEY TO STRATIGRAPHY

⬚ Dark brown street level zone

⬚ Mottled black and brown, charcoal impregnated

⬚ Deep brown and blackish occupation zone, majority of artifacts

⬚ Dense yellow clayey earth with dark stain at top

⬤ Fire broken rocks

|||≡ Concentration of charcoal

△ Arrow points

Zone A
Zone B
Zone C
Zone D

Reprinted courtesy of People's Publishing Company.

• *Zone D.* Dense yellow clay earth with an uneven, brownish black stain through the top 3 inches, most likely caused by a leaching down of organic material from the original ground cover. Archaic Period cultural material was found within this subzone.

Zone D began at an average depth of 19 inches below the surface and continued downward for some distance past the point of site excavation. No shell remains were found. A small quantity of deer bone is the only evidence of food refuse. Scattered near the top were rounded pebbles and cobbles.

Soil layers are examined not only for physical and cultural features, but also for chemical components. One technique used is measuring the ground pH (acid-alkaline balance) at various locations. Ground pH helps explain why some sites exhibit a lack of bone refuse.

Features

Hearths are the most commonly encountered feature found at prehistoric sites.

The "Features" subsection discusses a major group of cultural traits observed at an excavation site, such as the underground pits and related structures made for various purposes relating to food storage, cooking, and garbage disposal. House postmolds are sometimes included in this subsection, but not always. In the site report for the Shared Site, they were not included.

A total of sixteen features was excavated at the Shared Site. All were bowl-shaped pits, with the most (12) associated with houses. From the evidence found, five were used for food storage, seven were used for cooking, and four were used as trash bins. Note that both storage and cooking features often become refuse pits at some point in their existence.

All the pits continued into a lower zone and had pointed or round bases. The largest pit had a diameter of 4 feet, while the rest were between 1 foot and 2 feet in diameter. The deepest pit was 2½ feet deep, and the majority of pits (12) contained broken and whole mollusk shells intermixed with a compact black earth. Artifacts found in the pits consisted of potsherds and stone implements. Examples of both artifact types were found in each pit.

The hearths tended to fall into two categories—smaller ovens (5) and larger fireplaces (2). Fire-broken rocks from 2 to 5 inches long, which aided in the pit cooking process, were plentifully dispersed in the fireplaces, as were pieces of charcoal. Wall surfaces of the cooking pits were marked with a discoloring ash. Burned pieces of bone were found in all the hearths, while the charred remains of hickory nuts were found in only two.

By examining a site's features in relation to whatever else is excavated, you can get a very good idea of the inhabitants' daily camp life, including their economy, ceramic skills, trade relationships, and diet. You can also determine the types of animals that were indigenous to the area.

Artifacts

The "Artifacts" subsection is where the tools, pottery, and other material remains found at a site are listed and described. Archaeology is the study of the material remains of a culture. Typically, the archaeological purpose of a dig is to recover these artifacts. From these discoveries and the associations made through them, information is gathered about past cultures and historical items. At the Shared Site, the variety and quantity of artifacts found were similar to those of other excavated Late Woodland sites. They show that the two tribes had similar cultural traditions, differentiated only by their regional pottery and projectile point styles.

Standard archaeological procedure is for the artifacts from a site to be inventoried and described according to the material from which they are made, such as clay, stone, bone, plant fiber, teeth, or wood. At the Shared Site, clay potsherds outnumbered all the other artifacts combined, a common condition at most Late Woodland campsites.

In the stone artifacts category, broad triangular and long-stemmed points were the most numerous, implying the use of the bow and arrow as the hunting weapon of choice. Relatively few artifacts were found in Zone A, probably due to years of intensive surface collecting by enthusiastic amateurs.

In addition to the slight cultural variations between the two tribes, a small quantity of pottery from the Mississippian Culture, which flourished in the river valleys of the southeast from A.D. 750 to 1550, generated a great deal of interest. This pottery was most likely acquired by the Delaware people through a trade network with their southern neighbors. Other Late Woodland artifacts recovered were celts, axes, pipes, hammerstones, bone splinter awls, a bird bone whistle, barbed bone spearheads and fish hooks, beaver incisor tools, and stone net sinker weights.

The description of the artifacts in a site report is very important, revealing the material culture of the vanished people that once lived there.

Interestingly, the bone artifacts were better preserved at the Shared Site than at many other archaeological excavation sites because of the neutrality of the soil. Another find, a hand-worked turtle shell, may have been used as a club, rattle, or bowl.

Also found at the site, in zones C and D, were stone spear points, scrapers, and knives from the late Archaic Period (2000 B.C.) in New York. These numbered twenty-three in total and were probably used at a small, seasonal hunting camp near the edge of the marsh. Butchering marks on deer bones found in association with the tools support that conclusion.

Without artifacts, interpreting the past would be very difficult. Even with them, the correct procedures must be followed to derive the most information from them about a group's lifestyle.

Many archaeologists believe—and rightly so—that enthusiastic but uninformed amateurs have been responsible for the loss of much archaeological data. This is due to the amateur's inability to see beyond the physical artifacts. We would all benefit if urban treasure hunters would consult with professionals when they encountered significant prehistoric artifacts.

Houses

The presence of permanent or seasonally rebuilt houses at a site suggest ongoing, long-term occupation.

Houses are another important campsite component discussed in an archaeological site report and marked on a map of excavation. The Shared Site's primary evidence for the presence of at least two houses of the early longhouse variety was interpreted from postmolds. These postmolds were dark circles that formed line patterns in the lighter colored subsoil. Because of the importance of houses at a site, great care is usually taken to map each postmold. As is often the case, some of the postmolds at the Shared Site seemed to be randomly placed and may have been where drying racks stood.

The inhabitants of the Shared Site apparently used cut trees with diameters of between $2\frac{1}{2}$ and 5 inches, as measured from the postmolds, to support their houses. The depth of the ground penetration varied from 5 to 10 inches and averaged about 7 inches. Most likely, due to winter storms, parts of the houses may have needed to be rebuilt each year, as indicated by the clusters of postmolds beside the longer walls of each house.

From the sizes of the known houses (52 by 23 feet and 56 by 22 feet), the number of hearths (3) in each house and their locations along the central axis and away from the highly flammable bark walls, and from what is known about Late Woodland Period family life, we can estimate that each house was shared by three extended families composed of eight to ten people. This would place the camp's population at somewhere between forty-eight and sixty people.

Both houses had entrances on each long end, and House A also had a central opening on one side that may have been a door gap. The type of house found at the Shared Site clearly indicates a continuity of habitation because of the work that was necessary to build the structures and then to maintain them season after season.

Food Remains

Correct archaeological procedure calls for recovered food refuse, which includes animal bones, mollusk shells, and any surviving vegetable matter, to be submitted for analysis by a university or museum archaeological laboratory. After the investigation is completed, a comprehensive report is issued that scientifically classifies the flora and fauna known to have been used as food, as determined by the physical evidence.

The amount and type of food remains found at a site are clear indicators as to whether the occupants were malnourished.

In the case of the Shared Site, all the faunal remains belonged to animals inhabiting the immediate environment. A total of 7,532 bone fragments was recovered representing approximately sixty species of animals—specifically, fifteen mammals, six birds, four reptiles, and three amphibians. Some of the bones, notably those of deer, bear, and gray fox, were clearly cut by stone tools. Mollusks appeared to be the major food source, according to the presence of a very large number of their shells. In total, five types of mollusks were identified. The only vegetable material to survive was some hickory nuts.

Knowing what prehistoric people ate is important to understanding the necessities of their lifestyles and also explains some seasonal migration patterns. When archaeologists encounter food remains at a dig, they always hope that some bit of the knowledge gleaned can be used to understand the culture as a whole. Think of the animals that roamed over your city's land in its pristine state. You would most likely find them included in the faunal report of any prehistoric site in your area.

THE DISCUSSION

Any formal discussion of a site usually includes interpretive comparisons of data with other archeological sites, both near and far, to point out any possible cultural connections. The ideas expressed are only the opinions of the person who wrote the report, and you can either accept them or disagree with them, depending on your own level of knowledge.

For example, in the "Discussion" section of the report on the Shared Site, the writer noted that a survey was made of other excavated coastal site material curated at various East Coast museums, exploring for societal similarities. This research process led to the realization that some aspects of the New York group's cultural traits seemed to extend into New England. Specifically, the styles of some of the pottery and stone implements used by tribes in Massachusetts were similar to those of the artifacts found in New York.

Currently, there is no way to know whether this is due to neighborly influence, trade, or a partial dispersal of an original group in one direction or another. This last possibility is an interesting hypothesis that still remains to be tested. More conclusive evidence is required because the archaeological remains found are just a small and incomplete part of a much larger picture. There are still some interpretive hurdles to overcome here.

An important analytical point brought out in the "Discussion" section of the Shared Site report is the procedural danger in reconstructing geographically separate cultural groups by relying solely on seasonally occupied camps. People from equivalent environments and lifestyles would make use of the same types of implements to pursue parallel activities, and it is much easier to demonstrate similarities than differences.

What is definitely needed for further clarification of the matter is to locate the more permanent residential camps of the New York people. These have yet to be discovered and would certainly lead to a much broader understanding. This task may be very difficult in the long run, as those permanent camps have most likely been built over and are probably lost under New York's concrete canyons.

One train of thought that seems pretty accurate is that both the New York and Delaware tribes exhibited a closeness in house form, features, and bone and stone tools, pointing to membership in the same cultural tradition. Also important is the fact that they were able to live together in a most cooperative manner. Their only observable differences—ceramic styles and point typology—are easily explained by their prolonged geographical separation.

Lastly, a most interesting aspect of the Shared Site dig was the Mississippian pottery found at the camp. The pottery was probably brought there by the Delaware tribe, but another possibility is that migrating Mississippian people from the southeast visited Long Island for some obscure reason. Until more is learned about Mississippian migration and trade patterns, that question will have to remain unanswered.

THE CONCLUSION

The "Conclusion" is the part of a site report that ties all the separate elements together and states what has been learned from the entire excavation and interpretive process regarding the site's former inhabitants.

Basically, the Shared Site can be described as a warm weather seasonal camp occupied by two small, early Late Woodland Period bands of hunter-gatherers, one from New York and the other from Delaware, who joined together on Long Island for the main purpose of gathering shellfish and possibly also to find mates for their children. Their daily pursuits included shellfish and vegetable collecting, hunting, flint knapping, cooking, pottery making, house maintenance, and probably hide working.

Research points to a settlement pattern characterized by extended families. These families appear to have used the site for many years as a small village community. This is demonstrated by the presence of storage pits, as well as of postmolds indicating the annual reconstruction or repair of sizable longhouses.

The main sustenance of the community was shellfish, clearly indicated by the large shell midden, with a lesser portion of the food coming from hunting and fishing, as evidenced by the hunting points, fish hooks, and net sinker weights.

When early fall weather signaled approaching winter conditions, which would have made the camp's habitation difficult, the tribes returned to their sheltered inland villages, taking along provisions of dried and smoked shellfish to use as winter food supplements.

The "Conclusion" should provide the reader a complete and accurate picture of the people who occupied the site.

The discovery of both Woodland and Archaic period artifacts is significant in that it reveals that the Shared Site was an important resource for prehistoric New York tribes because it provided them with food and shelter through a long continuity of cultural evolution.

Now that you know how to read a site report, take the plunge and go to your local library or archaeological society and ask for any that may relate to your city or region. I'm sure by now you will agree that urban treasure hunters interested in archaeology and the prehistoric occupation of their city need to be familiar with this type of research document. There's quite a bit to learn!

9

Anatomy of a Park

Many urban parks are large, sprawling expanses of undeveloped land that has been used by the citizenry in many ways over the years. They will play a major role in your research and treasure hunting adventures. This is due to the numerous potentially rich subenvironments suitable for treasure hunting located within them. The general rule here is: "The older, the better."

This is not to say that you can't find treasure in newer or renovated parks. The older parks are just more consistent producers. The task of the analytical urban treasure hunter is to decipher the clues in the parkscape and then choose the section to hunt that will most likely yield the greatest number of sought-after rewards. How to do this is what we will discuss in this chapter.

GOOD HUNTING AREAS

Because of the dynamic nature of urban growth, most park grounds have probably been witness to a variety of significant human activities. Through time, the land may have been used for a prehistoric Native American village, a farm, a Revolutionary or Civil war battlefield, a temporary home for new arrivals in the growing city, a hobo jungle, a trash dump, a cache site for a family fortune, a place to hide stolen loot, and a recreational area.

Coin hunters have the most leeway here because they can use their metal detectors to survey the parkland and locate a broad selection of artifacts from different time periods. These can include coins, jewelry, weapons, pocketknives, religious medals, various types of tokens, and silverware. Some of these may be quite old and valuable.

The most obvious spots to hunt are places where people spend a great deal of time, such as athletic fields, picnic groves, hiking trails, lovers' lanes, golf courses, sitting areas, ponds, lakes, and streams. Figure 9.1 is a diagram of an urban park showing the different treasure hunting subenvironments generally offered. The park depicted is actually a typical park of considerable acreage located in New York City. Your city's parks may not have all these subenvironments, but they should have at least a few. Note that the size of a park is no indicator of its previous uses, as many urban parks were once larger, but gave up land to the developing neighborhood surrounding it.

I'm lucky enough to live near a park that does have all the subenvironments shown in Figure 9.1, which makes my treasure hunting a very varied and rewarding activity. In actuality, such parks are not uncommon in the urban setting, and you should lawfully take advantage of their treasure hunting potential.

Figure 9.1

This typical urban park offers a number of different treasure hunting subenvironments.

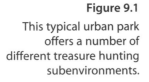

Key To Potential Finds

1. Old bottles.
2. Caches.
3. Coins and jewelry.
4. Historical relics.
5. Indian artifacts.

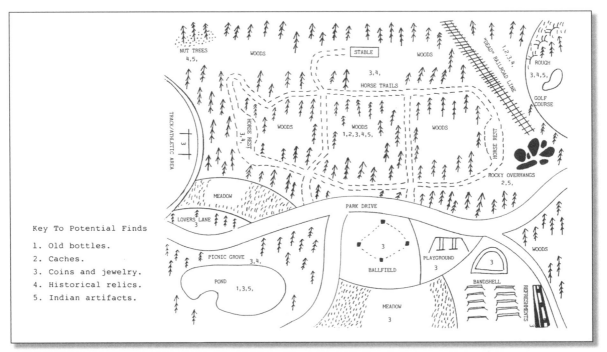

Reprinted courtesy of People's Publishing Company.

HUNTED-OUT AREAS

One bit of information of which you should be aware is that detectorists who previously hunted a park may have had similar ideas, and many of the more likely locations may have already been searched several times. Some spots may have even reached that abhorred stage commonly known in the treasure hunting trade as "hunted out."

This certainly doesn't mean in any sense that *everything* has been found. It means only that the more shallow material has been recovered, and that it might take a little more creativity, patience, and skill for you to accomplish your goal.

In truth, many excellent finds have come from areas considered hunted-out and were usually made by detectorists who were not intimidated by the going word and gave it their best shot. This is a result to be expected because people have varying problem solving abilities and the metal detectors used today have different performance characteristics.

The only thing that you know is that you never know!

OVERLOOKED HUNTING AREAS

My strategy when I detect in a park is to make a strong effort to get to the less obvious and more unlikely spots, the ones everyone else zooms past on their way to the more standard target zones. Actually, I've made a science of locating and searching overlooked places and have come to the conclusion that these sites are usually ignored because they are, to some degree, difficult to search. This includes all hills with steep or rocky inclines, muddy trails, and areas with heavy or thorny vegetation.

Most detector operators that I've observed prefer to work on a flat, clear surface because it's easier. I believe that a more vigorous approach pretty much ensures me of untouched ground and the rewards that go with it. I have made some fascinating finds while hunting on a 45-degree angle!

I also like to hunt the grass strip around the perimeter of the park, the trails leading into the park, the bridle paths, bald or dry spots, overgrown terrain, and the small, inconspicuous islands of soil that were turned over as part of a landscaping or maintenance project.

One detecting strategy in a well-hunted old park might be to search in the most improbable places. A hundred years ago things probably looked very different.

Some of the best places to use a metal detector are the entry points into a park. Over the years, the small hills of this park entrance have collected a lot of silver coins.

Bushy areas are often great spots to hunt. They may have been clear at one time, serving some long-forgotten purpose. You can make an educated guess by looking at the sizes of the trees and other vegetative growth. If most of the trees are just saplings or in any way smaller than the surrounding trees, it wasn't too long ago that the space was clear. The natural order of things in wooded areas is for the forest to reclaim previously cleared land when its upkeep is neglected—an urban given.

What now is a tangle of bushes and thorns perhaps once was where people sat on blankets under the moon while attending summer concerts at the town gazebo. Even earlier, this tangle may have been a rise where Civil War soldiers shed their clothing for a cooling dip in a now filled-in and forgotten pond. It always pays to investigate overgrown locations with an active imagination.

DO YOUR RESEARCH

I consider it very helpful to do some initial research on a park to get a good, fact-based idea of what went on there over the years. This will help you to better focus your efforts. Examples of facts about New York City parks that I've found through research and that helped direct my detecting efforts include the locations of a Revolutionary War battlefield, a nineteenth-century zoo, and the spot where a country fair was held every year. These facts resulted in my developing sensible and successful strategies for coin and relic hunting adventures.

"It is, of course, a trifle, but there is nothing so important as trifles."

—Sherlock Holmes, *"The Man With the Twisted Lip"*

When first entering a park, just look around and observe what's going on. If possible, repeat this reconnaissance several times throughout the year, as recreational activities change on a seasonal basis. If the park is old, you can be assured that people have been doing the same thing there year after year. A vintage baseball field is a fine example and can be a real bonanza for a coin hunter.

Even if you have no data on a park, you can usually determine its age by looking at the architecture of the surrounding neighborhood. Structures from the nineteenth century or earlier are a clear indication that you will most likely find old coins and bottles. However, this method can be tricky. I've encountered situations where I knew a park was old, but all the surrounding homes were relatively new looking, built within the last sixty years. What happened here was that civilization took a little more time to reach the park. My research, however, told me that the parks in question, Juniper Park and Baisley Pond Park, had been mill areas during the 1600s and had also been used for a variety of other purposes in subsequent years.

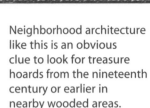

Neighborhood architecture like this is an obvious clue to look for treasure hoards from the nineteenth century or earlier in nearby wooded areas.

As you research a park, always keep a multidimensional outlook. Don't look at the park just with an eye towards increasing your silver coin hoard. Think of yourself as gathering information for a report on the park's *total* treasure hunting potential. For instance, were there old bottle parts from the eighteenth century concentrated in a specific area? How about those dropped musketballs and old British coins

In August 1857, a national contest to design a "Central Park" for Manhattan was won by Frederick Law Olmstead and Calvert Vaux. It took twenty years for the park to be carved out of bogs, glacial deposits, and pig farms. Work was halted during the Civil War.

found in the rough of the golf course? Doesn't that all tie in with the historical fact that Hessian mercenaries camped nearby during the Revolutionary War? Make associations based on facts.

In addition, try to figure out if the original ground has been covered by renovation landfill. If the trees don't have any roots showing, be suspicious. Also, if the soil is sandy and without worms, it sounds like landfill to me. Still, this can work to your benefit because the landfill may contain its own unknown treasures. It's always important to know what you're facing.

As a good example, a friend of mine was searching around in Central Park when he unearthed a fine 3-inch prehistoric stone knife while recovering a coin. Through research, he identified the artifact as being approximately 3,000 years old and belonging to the Orient Culture from the tip of Long Island, about 90 miles away from Central Park. He also learned that the original landscaping of Central Park used soil from the area the Orient people called home. The connection is obvious and shows how things may have been moved around during the formation of a city.

Every bit of information that you can find on a park is helpful and supportive of the treasure hunting process. You may be the only person to arrive at some important conclusion regarding a particular park, and the rewards for that effort will belong to you alone. This is the fieldwork part and is tremendously enhanced by the use of sound research methods.

A GOOD EXAMPLE

Former New York Senator Roscoe Conkling was found unconscious in Madison Square Park after the infamous blizzard of March 12, 1888. He suffered severe exposure and died about a month later. Alcohol consumption is suspected for his plight. A statue of Conkling now stands in the southeast corner of the park.

To demonstrate what can be found in an old city park, I would like to take you back to the now legendary relandscaping of New York City's Madison Square Park in the late 1980s. What an experience! First, though, some background information is in order.

Madison Square Park has its origins in the spirited movement for public parks that began in the 1840s and was championed by the *New York Mirror*. Editorials lamented, "The city fathers have destroyed all the green shady nooks designed as public squares." At the time, New York was growing so rapidly that the avaricious commissioners were more concerned with increasing tax revenues than planting trees.

They needed to be reminded that the "Commissioners' Plan of 1811" had specified 450 acres of public land. Another editorial demanded parks be built to serve as "the lungs of the city," to purify and regenerate the air. As a result of this steady pressure, New York opened nineteen parks for the public by 1849, and by the mid-1850s, Madison Square Park's 5 acres, with their decorative fountains and winding walks, had become a city showpiece.

Soon the rich and famous began building their homes around the park, where children and their nannies played on the manicured lawns. Comparing pictures of the park from the 1870s to ones from the present shows that basically the only changes have been to the park's surroundings, where office buildings now stand instead of fancy residences.

Permission to hunt the park was obtained by explaining to the security guard that digging would be done only after the park workers' quitting time and on weekends, avoiding interference with the project. An occasional offer of a sandwich or a beverage cemented his good feelings on the matter. However, it didn't take long for other treasure hunters to get wind of the renovation, and the obliging security guard began to put on weight.

Detecting in Madison Square Park was a very unique adventure. Rush hour stopped at the park's entranceway, where you could feel yourself slipping back into the nineteenth century. Let me set the scene. Treasure hunters readily detected long-lost old coins after bulldozers scraped away at least a foot of topsoil and revealed a New York that existed more than 150 years ago. The topsoil, piled in large mounds, was also loaded with good targets and received a thorough going-over by the rapacious treasure hunters. After a while, the mounds were respread and revealed even more treasures. Each old coin recovered brought with it a sense of New York's dynamic history.

Large cents dating back to the 1820s were regular finds. Two-cent and three-cent pieces became instant reminders of how our coinage has changed. Numerous silver Seated Liberty and Barber coins were found. But the best coin discovery, made by Digger Dave, was a 1798 over 1797 Draped Bust dime with sixteen stars and an incomplete clipped planchet mark on both sides, in very good to fine condition. (For an overview of a coin time line, see page 126, and for a discussion of coin grades, see page 178). This coin is considered a numismatic oddity because "1798" was stamped over the date on unissued 1797 coins, and only 27,550 dimes were produced in 1798. An excellent find!

Aside from coins, an interesting variety of historical relics was

A rare 1798 over 1797 Draped Bust dime found in construction debris during the legendary late-1980s renovation of Madison Square Park in New York City. Note the clipped planchet mark along the neck.

The reverse of the 1798 over 1797 Draped Bust dime found in Madison Square Park. A terrific find!

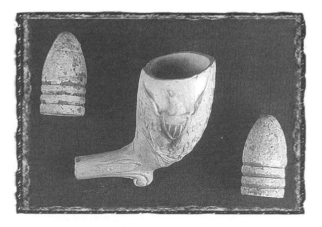

This Civil War–era double eagle pipe and Union Army three-ringer .58-caliber minie balls may have been dropped during a spirited patriotic rally held for the North in Madison Square Park. All were found in piles of dirt during the park's renovation.

These .45-caliber, 90-grain (45-90) Sharps buffalo gun bullets, part of a box, were probably dropped in the 1870s on an overgrown trail network still in use today.

also unearthed. One of these, a surface find, was most of a double eagle pipe, so called because of an eagle design on each side of the bowl. It hailed from the 1850s or 1860s. A handful of buttons was dug that spanned different worlds. Some dated from the War of 1812, while others were of Great Depression vintage and were worn by members of the Boy's Working Reserve. Also scattered around were Civil War–era minie balls, a type of ammunition used in rifles, probably dropped during spirited rallies for the North held in the park.

One exceptional find that didn't survive cleaning was a brass Abraham Lincoln presidential campaign item. Unfortunately, Abe's head popped off and went down a drain. Helping to keep the tempo of finds moving were some interesting rings of various ages, including a Melvin Purvis "Secret Agent" ring. Purvis is credited with shooting John Dillinger. Of course, plenty of antique marbles were found. A 1930s sterling silver Lone Ranger "Good Luck" token was also a notable recovery.

For six months, diehard treasure hunters dug and scraped through the mud and rubble of Madison Square Park until the rebuilding was completed. I'm sure everyone who participated in this memorable event has some interesting stories to tell. As one of my fellow urban treasure hunters commented: "This was a great opportunity to really touch the past. A Madison Square Park doesn't come along too often." Here, here!

HUNTING THE WOODS

I mentioned in Chapter 6 that my favorite hunting areas are urban woodlands, which can be part of large, old parks. Woods offer a lot of opportunity because they have persevered through hundreds of years of surrounding development and change. In most instances, their old bridle paths and other trails were the main conduits for getting around when people traveled strictly by horse or foot. It's no surprise that I've found coins and relics dating back to the 1700s along these historical, but generally unnoticed, byways.

Finds such as old coins at relatively shallow depths prove that a city's wooded areas are very stable hunting grounds. Something dropped will usually stay in the same place, since there is very little to disturb it. Aside from old coins and historical relics, modern-day equestrians lose a continuous stream of jewelry, new coins, and other items as they go galloping by or take a spill.

Clues in the Underbrush

While searching old trails, be on the lookout for signs of human activity from bygone times in the surrounding bushes. Sometimes you might encounter a leaf-covered circle of campfire rocks left by people from some past era. These will definitely be worth your while to investigate, as my finds here have included nineteenth-century coins and

Modern bridle paths were the main roads of formative urban America, where travel was strictly by horse or foot. Notice how sunken-in the grade is, an indication of many years of use. This is a proven place to find old coins and jewelry.

old sterling silverware. Back then, folks didn't have disposable utensils, so they brought "the good stuff" with them on their picnics.

Also, check around trees with light gray or white bark that have names and dates carved in them. Lost coins and pocketknives are often found next to such trees. The timeworn dates carved in them testify to years of use. Always investigate large rocks and overhangs, since they may have attracted furtive visitors looking to hide something. Put yourself in their mindset and imagine that you have something to conceal, then start searching around.

In addition, look up into the trees for old Hardy Boys–style tree houses. These may have become quite dilapidated over time, but they can be identified by structural remnants such as nailed-on walk boards, wood-slat ladders, hanging ropes, swings, and chains.

If you encounter an old, abandoned tree house site, search all the nooks and crannies surrounding the tree within a 100-foot radius. Tree houses are basically arboreal campsites, and the people who camped there needed life's necessities just like everyone else. They generally stashed those necessities close by. I happen to like climbing trees and occasionally go up to have a look around. The area below the tree house pictured in the margin produced about twenty silver coins from the 1930s and 1940s. Something definitely went on here, and maybe someone watched in disbelief as his or her small tree cache fell to the forest floor.

Remember to look up when you're in the woods. Old tree houses may indicate hidden stashes in the surrounding terrain or dropped coins underneath. Watch out for falling debris!

When hunting in the woods, you should also expect to find an interesting variety of old axe heads. At least, that's been my experience. I figure they must have gotten loose on the handle and flown off on the upswing into the brush. My oldest is a large Colonial-era tree felling model with a round poll. A basic but essential survival tool, it no doubt was used to clear the land and split trees into planks that helped to build houses on New York's Colonial frontier. I'm sure whoever lost it soon went to a blacksmith for a replacement. A man couldn't live without his axe during those rugged times.

Hidden Loot

These wooded areas have lived through good and bad times. During stressful periods of failing banks or personal misfortune, some individuals may have chosen to bury their valuables there—and then never reclaimed them. Also stashed in the woods may be the gains from illegal activities of which the perpetrator had no way to dispose at the time. Present-day criminals may also be caching their ill-gotten goods and drug money there. I know of an instance where an intrepid treasure hunter found an Uzi machine gun, complete with clips and ammo, hidden in an old stone wall, while searching for hidden drug money. The cops were sure glad to get their hands on that formidable weapon before it was used in a bloody massacre.

Actually, I've had good experiences with stone walls and consider them choice hunting spots. Once, for example, while randomly searching a stone wall for hidden treasures, I came up with buried silver tableware on one side and a Colonial-era shoe buckle in between the rocks on the other side. Quite a combination!

This large felling axe of Colonial frontier vintage helped build New York. An indispensable tool of its time and a relic hunter's prize!

Buried treasure can be anywhere, and stone walls are excellent places to search. This cache of old silver tableware was found hidden under a venerable stone wall in the Bronx.

Generally, depending on how much time they have, people caching valuables in the woods will use an immovable natural or manmade item as a landmark. This can be a large tree, a boulder, railroad tracks, a stone wall, or even a place where trails cross. Hunting the woods gives you the potential for a big strike—with a good deal of privacy. By systematically searching a likely cache area, such as where old house foundations are located, you might come up with a life changing find. Suppose you recover a miser's hoard of hidden gold coins. Just the numismatic value can help buy your retirement ranch.

In northerly climates, the woods will also provide you with year-round treasure hunting because the leafy mulch layer covering the forest floor prevents the soil from freezing, allowing the ground beneath to remain penetrable throughout the winter—a tremendous advantage when other detectorists choose to hang it up during the cold months.

Surprising Finds

This souvenir badge for a 1913 United Confederate Veterans (UCV) reunion held in Chattanooga, Tennessee, was detected along an old horse trail in Queens. A remarkable historical relic find for New York City.

The local woods might also reveal some surprising finds. I once made a very significant Civil War–related recovery along a sunken old horse trail in New York City—a United Confederate Veterans reunion badge from a May 27, 1913, Confederate Army reunion held in Chattanooga, Tennessee. This meant that someone who had fought for the South had come to New York City and lost it. Quite a surprising recovery to make, but I've learned that urban treasure hunting is filled with very unpredictable experiences.

The badge was down about 3 inches and came up in pretty good shape, with a nice coppery green patina. At first, I had no idea what it represented in terms of our country's history or of the personal bravery and sacrifice the person who lost it must have shown to earn it. All I knew was that I had something interesting to investigate, which is a great part of my treasure hunting enjoyment.

Subsequent research revealed that after the Civil War, former Confederate soldiers joined local fraternal chapters of the United Confederate Veterans (UCV), which then mustered at yearly reunions in large southern cities such as Chattanooga. Each UCV reunion had its own badge, which those in attendance proudly wore. These large reunions continued into the 1930s, but as time went by, fewer and fewer veterans showed up. Likewise, Union veterans had an organization called the Grand Army of the Republic (GAR), which convened for similar reunions in New York and other northern cities.

The last major UCV reunion was held in 1932 and was hosted by the appreciative citizenry of Richmond, Virginia, the wartime capital of the Confederacy. This forty-second annual assemblage was a grandiose affair, attracting about 2,000 grizzled old soldiers in their eighties and nineties. Majestically, they were brought to Richmond by special trains from all over the South.

The festivities were carefully planned, and Douglas Southall Freeman, editor of the *Richmond News Leader*, proclaimed: "Nothing

Confederate veterans at the last major UCV reunion, held in 1932 in Richmond, Virginia. The veteran holding a pipe is proudly wearing a badge from the 1913 Chattanooga reunion on his lapel. A perfect match to the one found in Queens!

Photo courtesy of *Confederate Veteran's* magazine and the Sons of Confederate Veterans.

TABLE 9.2 POTENTIAL COIN DEPTHS IN AN OLD CITY PARK

An old city park is an excellent place to search for vintage coins. No doubt that park has witnessed the march of time through quite a few of your city's historical eras. Coins from these eras can be found at different depths. The table below provides a general timeline showing the coin types and the depths you might expect to recover them at in an old city park.

like next week's reunion has ever been held in America. Nothing like it can ever be held again!" The reunion began on Monday, June 20, with a seventeen-gun salute signaling the arrival of the UCV commander-in-chief, General C. A. DeSaussure, and his entourage for the opening ceremony. The Stars and Bars, the first Confederate flag, was then raised over the capital.

Special entertainment, including concerts, square dancing, and old-time fiddling, was presented throughout the week. Out at the Old Soldier's Home, where many of the honored guests visited, the veterans enjoyed each other's company while guffawing at their favorite radio comedy shows.

Friday was the day of the Grand Parade, which brought tears to many eyes as the touring car procession passed in review through the streets of Richmond. These gallant old soldiers had fought in many battles, and some were sadly missing an arm or leg. They had served dutifully at Fredericksburg and Chancelorsville, fought with Beauregard at Shiloh, and charged with Stuart's lightning cavalry. They were the men who earned immortality fighting alongside Jackson in the Stonewall Brigade. All were monuments to history!

As you can see, finding that UCV badge with my metal detector connected me to some very vibrant history. Consequently, it took on a special significance for me and is now one of my favorite finds. Sometimes when looking at it, I waft away to that reunion in Chattanooga and think about what it was like to be there. When hunting in a New York City woods, you really never know what will turn up next!

Flora and Fauna

One of the things that I enjoy the most about treasure hunting in the woods is observing the flora and fauna—you know, the wild side of things! I don't mean in the most precise scientific sense, but just out of curiosity, to know what's out there staring back at me.

By now, I've reached the point where I see the world not only as a treasure hunter, but also as a naturalist. In an instant, I can become a zoologist, a botanist, or an entomologist. Even though my primary goal is treasure hunting, I consider this aspect an important part of the urban treasure hunter's world and always look forward to interesting opportunities for nature observation.

The Associated Press reported, on June 16, 2004, the death of the last-known surviving widow of a Confederate soldier. On February 2, 1934, nineteen-year-old Maudie Celia Hopkins married eighty-six-year-old William M. Cantrell in Baxter County, Arkansas. At that time, many young women married Confederate veterans for their pensions.

Successful crow calling depends on understanding crow language and what they are communicating to each other. The basic loud call of caw-caw-caw keeps the birds in touch when foraging and can indicate that food has been found, which will bring the flock in.

Honey bees were introduced into North America by European settlers. There are five different races of which the Italian variety is the least aggressive. Don't mix honey bees up with hornets!

An excellent selection of wildlife calls can be ordered from Burnham Bothers, Inc. of Menard, Texas. Contact them at (325) 396-4572 for a catalog or download their catalog at www.burn hambrothers.com/calls.html

For a big city boy, I've gotten pretty good at tracking down wild bee trees, or "following the yaller bee," as the quest used to be called in earlier days when someone got a "hankering" for honey. However, I don't carve my initials in the tree to claim it, as some early written accounts say you're supposed to do. I'm satisfied just marveling at something that not many people realize they can find in a city. I consider it another type of treasure hunting and an enjoyable pastime from nineteenth-century America. It's something that Tom Sawyer and Huckleberry Finn would have done!

I also use birdcalls with good results and have called in hawks, pheasants, and flocks of irate crows. I've also watched large butterflies sail through the forest canopy, turned over logs to observe salamanders, and picked wild asparagus. If you pay attention, there's a lot going on in an urban woods. You just have to know how to read the landscape and connect. This is where having a naturalist's perspective really enhances the treasure hunting experience.

Another kick of mine is ethnobotany, the study of how the people in different cultures use plants for food, medicine, religious practices, and so on. When I see people picking plants, I usually go over and ask how they are going to use the plants. Most of the time, these folks are recent immigrants and utilize the plants to make the medicines and cures from their home country.

Then there are the people who pick plants for food and aesthetic purposes, such as to make aromatic fragrances. I once went over to a guy picking leaves from a tall shrub and inquired what he was going to do with them. His answer of, "Have 'em for supper—this is pokeweed," said in a southern drawl, didn't ring a bell until he gave me some to try. Interestingly, the leaves tasted like pork. However, I would advise you not to start feasting on the forest unless you know what you're doing.

Urban parks are a great training ground for aspiring urban treasure hunters, as well as a constant proving ground for more-seasoned pros. Urban parks have everything you need to give your treasure hunting skills a good workout. A big, old park like the one in Figure 9.1 is a treasure hunter's dream-come-true. Try a different entrance point each time you visit for a varied perspective. Then turn your treasure awareness loose!

✿ 10 ✿

Hunting for Prehistoric Native American Artifacts

An often overlooked but very rewarding direction for treasure hunting in an urban setting is the surface collecting of prehistoric Native American artifacts. No matter where you live, you most likely will find this type of hunting potential nearby.

City dwellers tend to believe that all suitable areas for searching have been covered up by concrete and the march of progress. This perhaps is true to a certain extent, but I would say with a great deal of confidence that plenty of places to find such artifacts still exist within your city's boundaries. My hunting experiences in New York, along with the accomplishments of other urban treasure hunters, are certainly proof of that last statement.

People also tend to have stereotypic ideas about what Native American artifacts look like. Many treasure hunters expect to find only arrowheads, passing over other artifacts whose functions might not be so obvious at first. In actuality, there is quite a variety of artifacts to be found. In addition to arrowheads, these include stone axes, plummets, hammerstones, scrapers, drills, knives, pendants, pipes, celts, bolas, grindstones, spear points, hoes, bannerstones (balancing weights for spear throwers called atlatls), net sinkers, birdstones, copper items, wampum, and other decorative and utilitarian objects made of shell.

Unless people are fortunate enough to have an experienced artifact hunter from whom to learn, their first finds are usually accidental, sort of "hey-look-what-I-found!" types of experiences while doing something such as looking over soil brought in for landfill or

During early Colonial times, Anne Hutchinson and her followers settled in what is now Pelham Bay Park in the Bronx. Ignoring repeated warnings from the Siwanoy tribe to leave, they were attacked and wiped out in 1643. No trace of the small colony, which is known as "the lost Anne Hutchinson colony," has ever been found.

Some amateur flint knappers have become quite proficient at producing finely worked points. It would be an interesting project to try to replicate the point types found in your area.

probing a positive signal from a metal detector. All of a sudden, out pops an arrowhead and starts the finder thinking that their treasure hunting scope needs to be widened.

Hundreds of different tribes and subtribes lived in North America when the first colonists arrived. Finding their everyday tools, as well as the tools of their forebears, helps us to better understand the way they lived. It also affords individuals interested in early Native American culture to enjoy a more personal connection. Plus, it's a lot of fun!

In this chapter, we will discuss where to search for prehistoric artifacts and also what such a search usually entails.

RECOGNIZING A SITE

It takes a sharp eye to notice clues that you've found a good hunting site. The small telltale signs of flint chips, broken pottery, mollusk shells, bones, and fire-cracked rocks easily blend into the rest of the ground debris. The real trick is to know where to look and what you might expect to find.

Once again, visit your local museum to familiarize yourself with the typical prehistoric artifacts found in your region. Exhibits may also mention potential hunting areas that you never even imagined were there—and that are easily accessible. In addition, review professional site reports and other articles describing locally found artifacts. Research is always an important key.

For example, I used library research to locate an excellent book, *The Indians of Greater New York and the Lower Hudson*, written in 1909 by the eminent anthropologist Clark Wisler. This fine reference pinpoints all the known early sites in the New York City metropolitan area and gave me a tremendous incentive to search, since I learned exactly where to go for some very challenging expeditions. There may be a similar book about your city.

I also strongly recommend reading *Indian-Artifact Magazine*, a wonderfully informative quarterly publication, to learn from the success stories and photographs of some very dedicated artifact hunters. You may even be inspired to take up flint knapping, if you want to learn an "old skill." The necessary materials are available through the magazine, as are informative books. The magazine also offers a timely calendar of events for Native American artifact shows, atlatl throwing contests, conferences, and "knap-ins." This friendly journal has a lot of useful information for the urban treasure hunter with an interest in tracking down and understanding prehistoric North America. (For subscription information, see Appendix C.)

LOCATING A CAMPSITE

Prehistoric people tended to settle near a good water supply. Preferably, they established their camp on elevated ground above the water, both to have a good view of the surrounding terrain and to avoid being eaten alive by mosquitoes. These types of places can still be found in areas into which the city hasn't moved too heavily yet or perhaps has built around. They include shorelines, marshes, and wooded areas.

Ideally, the campsite is your main target to locate. Here's where many daily activities took place and where stone tool finds are generally most concentrated. Sometimes, the artifacts found are indicative of a site's use over time by different groups, affirming the site's desirable features. If you encounter some large stone tools such as hammerstones, axes, and celts, as well as some hearthstones, you should take it as a signal that you've probably found a campsite.

Caches of stone blades have also been found in seasonally occupied camps. These have generally consisted of unfinished preforms or completed pieces that may have been stashed for future use but were never reclaimed. Cache finds are totally unpredictable, but they have been made all over the country. Some have included fifty blades or more. I know of one cache that was found after an old tree was blown down in a storm, revealing its hidden treasure.

Over the years, my treasure hunting expeditions around New York City have led me to several productive prehistoric artifact hunting grounds. (See "More New York City Finds" on page 132.) As a surface hunter, I can only assume that these were campsites. To find such sites, I've learned to rely on the tried-and-true search strategies that have also worked well for others. These strategies include library research, topographical map interpretation, locating shellfish evidence, and browsing the ground in construction sites, farm fields, and cemeteries.

Hammerstones are the most numerous camp tools to be found unbroken. Many new collectors don't recognize them because they were used in their natural shape. Look for concentrated edge wear to be sure.

The presence of axes and other large stone tools may indicate that a prehistoric campsite is nearby. Start looking for signs of a midden.

More New York City Finds

Most of my prehistoric artifact hunting forays are very interesting adventures, and I usually wind up in some pretty obscure sections of New York City, places to which metal detecting alone would not have brought me. One spot that I enjoy searching is a woodsy park out in Queens that is geologically notable for its glacial kettle ponds. I was given that lead by a knowledgeable librarian who took an interest in my research and pointed me in the right direction.

On my first visit, I was fortunate enough to encounter a cooperative old-timer in the woods who gladly answered my questions and suggested: "You must be looking for Indian Ridge—just over the next hill. We used to go there years ago and find all sorts of things." I had never heard about this Indian Ridge before and realized I was tapping a very valuable primary source of information. He went on to describe how "back when," he and his friends would find small white quartz arrowheads along the southeastern ridge slope after a heavy rain.

All that sounded very promising, and I soon made my way to Indian Ridge, which was next to a pond and offered an excellent view of the land-

A tip from an old-timer led to Indian Ridge, where he used to find arrowheads as a boy during the 1920s. The elevated ground made this a perfect location for a village when New York City was a prehistoric wilderness.

scape. Gazing around, I pictured an active prehistoric camp up on the rise, with bark wigwams and the comings and goings of daily life. It seemed an ideal place to live, with the surrounding forest and swamp providing game, fish, and plant foods.

After hunting around for a while, I was rewarded by finding a hammerstone that fits perfectly into a female left hand. Its wear pattern shows considerable end use, probably from breaking open hickory nuts and performing a variety of other milling tasks on a stone anvil. I also found a flint scraper, but there were no white quartz arrowheads in my stars that day.

Another outing brought me to Staten Island, which has a substantial track record for artifact finds, since it was the home of prehistoric peoples going back thousands of years. It was also the home territory of the Lene Lenape (Delaware) tribe in historic times. That day, I found myself wandering through verdant green forests and tramping around on muddy shell mounds in tall rustling marsh grass underneath the Goethals Bridge—a very lonely place. That trip was a real swashbuckler, and I was rewarded by coming back with an interesting type of stone axe.

The Professional Method

Archaeologists use topographical maps to find campsites. First, they review the published literature to see if any campsites have already been found in the area. Then, they compare the topography and exposure of a potential site with the known sites for similarities. If there is a high correlation of data, including surface evidence, they undertake further exploration. You can do the same thing with equally good results.

Topo maps in a scale of 1 to 24,000 are best for the prehistoric artifact hunter and will direct you to places where there may have been, or still are, springs, ponds, lakes, or swamps. All are ideal search areas. When a prospective location turns out to be undeveloped land, you're in luck. Water resources, were generally used by many different prehistoric groups over time. If the water resource is shown on an old topo map but is not visible now, don't be discouraged. It was once there, and that's what counts. The surrounding area is still a prime location to surface hunt for artifacts. Over time, geological conditions may have been altered, and the spring may now be flowing underground.

When scales are shown on topo maps, they are usually represented as 1:24,000.

Shellfish Evidence

Shellfish were a very important prehistoric food item, and their bleached remains were sometimes piled in huge accumulations known as middens. In general, any time you see weathered, old looking clam, mussel, or oyster shells in out-of-the-way places, poke around some more. You may be rewarded by finding an eroding midden, which usually contains a lot more than shells.

These shell heaps were considered the village disposal unit and were used to discard all sorts of rubbish, including captured enemies. As a further clue, midden soil at large village sites is often recognizable because it is darker than the surrounding soil, due to the decomposition of organic matter. The presence of ash and charcoal, which are resistant to decay, also sets it apart. Many interesting museum specimens of stone tools and pottery have come from shell middens. At the very least, you will know the area contained a prehistoric campsite and can better focus your search efforts.

During the refurbishing of the Statue of Liberty, located on Lib-

An Amerindian shell mound, or midden, which extends over twelve acres near Barnagat Bay and Oyster Creek in New Jersey, is part of the Forsyth National Wildlife Refuge. This shell midden may be as old as 5,500 years and is unique because it contains large oysters up to 10 inches in length.

erty Island in New York Harbor, construction workers digging a utility trench discovered an extremely large midden composed mostly of discarded oyster shells. The Liberty Island midden covered an area of 166 feet by 69 feet and was 2 feet deep, indicating an ongoing, large-scale occupation. This occupation probably occurred during the summer months, when the oysters contained the most meat and were easily accessible.

In addition, mixed in with the shells were pieces of pottery, which enabled archaeologists to date the site as being active between A.D. 1100 and 1400, the Late Woodland Period. During this time period, many generations of prehistoric inhabitants must have canoed out to the island to harvest and feast on the rich shellfish beds. At another construction project on nearby Ellis Island, workers found a second large midden, which, not too surprisingly, contained two prehistoric skeletons.

Construction Sites

Just as in other urban treasure hunting pursuits, construction projects can be a major aid to prehistoric artifact hunting, as they occasionally cut into vanished campsites. For a good example, consider Inwood Park in upper Manhattan. This large, woodsy park is known for its rock grottos and overhangs, which served as natural shelters for some of New York's earliest Amerindian residents.

In the early 1900s, a substantial prehistoric village site was opened up by the construction of buildings across the street from the park and firmly established Inwood Park as one of the major surface collecting areas in New York City. As a result, many choice prehistoric artifacts from this part of town have been written about and are now in local museums and private collections. Current construction projects around town offer the same potential for successful surface collecting.

Shorelines

Many urban areas have grown on or near bodies of water because of the easy access to convenient boat transportation. Prehistoric people also saw this advantage and usually sought out shoreline locations for their villages, especially during seasonal fish runs. It also pays to search natural reservoir shorelines, since they have been shown to be excellent areas for hunting artifacts, particularly along any surrounding hilly terrain.

Regarding shoreline hunting, some very skilled prehistoric artifact hunters in Tampa, Florida, have found significant success after realizing that searching the Tampa Bay shoreline at low tide after inordinately high tides or storms can be very productive. Florida has a very rich prehistoric past, with many former village sites located within the Tampa Bay area. The finds include shell and stone tools, along with an interesting variety of amulets made of stone, copper, bone, or silver. Some stone spear points are more than 10,000 years old, and recovered pendants depict fish, snails, shrimp, and snakes. On occasion, early Spanish items, such as broken pottery, silver coins, and glass beads, also turn up.

Obviously, taking a walk along Tampa Bay can be quite a journey back into both early historic and prehistoric times. To their credit, the artifact hunters there have not hoarded away their finds, but have put them on view at various locations to allow the public to also appreciate Tampa's prehistoric past.

Farm Fields

While exploring out at the city limits or in nearby suburban areas, notice if there are any plowed fields around. Rural collectors have long relied on farmers to unearth many meaningful artifacts with their tilling equipment. It's best to go following a heavy rain, when the soil has been washed away and the artifacts lie exposed on top. Experienced artifact hunters prefer hunting farm fields at midday, when the sun is high, since there are less shadows to obscure potential finds.

Hunting farm fields is a tried-and-true strategy. As always, however, you need to obtain permission before entering private property. The search technique involves walking up and down the furrows while turning over rocks with what some aficionados call a "flippin' stick." This can be a broom handle with a bent nail at one end or whatever else you devise that does the same job. Over the years, numerous impressive prehistoric artifact collections have come from farmers' fields, so you're following in good footsteps here.

Take, for example, the Indianapolis treasure hunter who pursued this strategy in the suburbs and was rewarded with a large, 3-inch,

Archaeologists and collectors categorize arrowheads mainly by their notch type, such as side notched, corner notched, bottom notched, and notchless.

This 18-foot prehistoric canoe, dating back to A.D. 900, was rescued by locals from a dried-up lake in North Central Florida.

corner-notched Lost Lake spear point made from Indiana hornstone. He made this terrific find in a farm field that he had been targeting on a regular basis with good results. This variety of point dates from between 10,000 and 8000 B.C., and he was pretty surprised to make his "best find" so close to home in an area that was practically all developed. This certainly is testimony to the potential for searching the outskirts of your city for prehistoric artifacts.

The Sticks

At some point, you may cross the line into rural areas, which also have plenty of treasure hunting potential. When I was living in Gainesville, a small city in North Central Florida, I met some folks at a flea market who had rescued a dugout canoe (circa A.D. 900) from a peat bog after a lake 25 miles east of town had dried up. My polite interest created some good vibes, and they took me to a cramped warehouse where they had the canoe packed in with a bunch of old furniture.

At first sight, I was really quite impressed. In my mind, this 18-foot canoe was the second coming of the Ark. Whoever made this slender, well-balanced craft would have been very proud to learn that it had withstood being submerged for so long. It was still in good condition. Over time, the dugout had become insulated by aquatic vegetation (fibrous peat), which had protected it from biodegrading by creating an oxygen-free environment. Truly a great recovery!

The highlight of the trip back was a stop at a ramshackle trailer to see a few stone spear points that some lakeside residents had found. After the introductions, Earl and his brother, Melvin, brought

Spearpoints found by lakeside residents Earl and Melvin.

out the points, all of which were about $2\frac{1}{2}$ inches long and made of white flint. I asked where the points had come from, and the brothers said simply, "Back there," pointing in the direction of the bog.

Earl was upbeat and proudly mentioned that Melvin had found five canoes, but didn't want to go into further detail. I would have liked to learn more about the canoes's conditions and ages, and about what became of them, but Melvin was sullen and suspicious about my being there. I guess my Yankee accent didn't help, and he kept asking me what everything was worth. I certainly had no answers in that regard and contented myself with just getting a photo of the points. That was quite an interesting day in rural America for this "Big City" boy!

Peat bogs have preserved many items of archaeological importance that would have never survived otherwise. These include hides, wooden implements, textiles, baskets, fishing nets, antler artifacts, and bodies.

Cemeteries

Cemeteries are also worthwhile places to investigate, mainly because they endure a significant moving around of soil layers, sometimes bringing to the surface a remarkable variety of stone tools. For example, one cemetery out in the borough of Queens is famous for its artifact finds, which I first read about in an old 1932 newspaper article at the library. Archaeologists believe that this cemetery, which is near a good water supply, Maspeth Creek, is positioned on the site of a large prehistoric village.

The oldest known dugout canoe recovered in Florida is a 5,120-year-old specimen found at Delusia Springs near the St. Johns River.

Native Copper Areas

Some areas of the United States, the Great Lakes region in particular, have deposits of what is called "float copper" in a very pure form (99-percent pure). Float copper is native copper that was torn loose from mineral veins by glacial activity thousands of years ago and deposited over large areas of the Upper Midwest. Prehistoric people from these regions gathered and worked this metal into beads, religious ornaments, armbands, and utilitarian tools such as projectile points, crescent knives, and awls. On occasion, Old Copper Culture artifacts that date from about 5000 B.C. forward are recovered by metal detector operators and considered excellent finds.

If you live in a native copper area, make sure to bring along a metal detector to help your search. Thousands of copper artifacts have been found in Wisconsin, and Old Copper Culture tools have

For more information about the Old Copper Culture, log onto the www.copper culture.homestead.com website. A first rate educational experience!

The oldest dated copper artifact is a 2-inch socketed point. A piece of wood in the socket was carbon dated at 3940 B.C. by the University of Toronto.

A study by genetic researchers of 145 Chuckchi and Siberian Eskimos, published in the *American Journal of Genetics*, has concluded that the ancestors of those studied were in Beringia by 32,000 B.C., longer than the archaeological evidence has shown.

also been found in Oklahoma and Mississippi. This shows the presence of trade networks that brought artifacts made of exotic materials to distant regions—for example, conch shell engravings from the Gulf of Mexico to the Midwest and Knife River flint spear points from North Dakota to New York.

WHERE THEY CAME FROM

The story of the Native Americans began during a latter phase of the Ice Age glaciation in North America known as the Wisconsin. Climatic changes caused huge glaciers to form at and advance from the polar cap, while surrounding seas, rivers, and other bodies of water were reduced in volume and incorporated into the slow moving, massive ice flow.

Researchers now generally agree that in at least one instance, land that this water covered was converted into a habitable tundra environment with surrounding marshlands that allowed human migration. This occurred at the Bering Strait, which separates northeastern Asia and northwestern North America. These geological changes resulted in a walkable corridor, or land bridge, that was about 200 miles wide and that nomadic herd hunters traveled while following migrating herds of mammoth, bison, and caribou on which they depended. Called Beringia, this land bridge is believed to have been the site of several migrations.

Originating in Siberia, small groups of these nomads gradually crossed over Beringia, probably during the height of the glaciation, between 15,000 and 25,000 years ago, and spread throughout the then-uninhabited North American continent and down into South America. As a point of reference, Russian archaeologists have found habitation sites in Siberia that were occupied more than 35,000 years ago.

The existence of these nomads must have been very precarious, since stone projectile points had not yet been developed. Rather, these people possessed only spear points made of bone, ivory, antler, or fire-hardened wood. Not much is really known about them because their campsites and other items of material culture are now either covered by the Bering Sea or dispersed under so many layers of earth that locating a campsite is next to impossible. Occasional breakthroughs, however, are made during cave explorations.

Obviously, these nomads had to have been very clever and

adaptive to persevere in such a harsh environment. At present, through an assortment of widely accepted genetic, dental, and linguistic evidence, these early hunters are widely recognized as the most likely biological source of the majority of ensuing Amerindian civilization.

However, even as you read this, the prehistory of North America is being rewritten based on new theories resulting from the tracing of genetic markers that challenge the generally accepted single-source-migration and single-crossing-route interpretations. Whether they came by boat is also a point of contention, since they used skin boats, which probably would have been too fragile for such a long, non-coast-following voyage. Wooden boats certainly weren't available because there were no trees in the frozen wastes to make stronger craft.

Then there's the matter of a strange 9,300-year-old skeleton called the "Kennewick Man," found eroding in the Columbia River in Kennewick, Washington, in July 1996 and said to have Caucasian features. Such evidence strongly challenges the single-race theory of who occupied the continent thousands of years ago and has a lot of political ramifications. The political ramifications are being dealt with in the courts, as five Native American tribes want the skeleton reburied and scientists are countersuing for the right to study the very intriguing remains.

Much has yet to be learned about the peopling of North America. Many experts suspect that the story began a lot further back than has been popularly established. It seems that an almost constant flow of new physical evidence is being brought forward for evaluation. Experts in the field believe that ultimately, the most revealing discoveries will be made in Alaska and Canada, where these hardy Ice Age immigrants made first contact.

The Paleo Period

Current archaeological evidence supports the first appearance of stone projectile points in North America at about 12,000 B.C., in what is known as the Paleo Period. This period lasted to approximately 8000 B.C. and was typified by a terminal-stage Ice Age environment and the animal types just mentioned—mammoth, bison, and caribou.

In cultural terms, there is also a distinctive style of stone projec-

The first North American mammoths migrated across the Bering Strait from Asia into Alaska during a period of low sea level about two million years ago. Covered by long thick, shaggy hair, mammoths were huge and had curved tusks that reached a length of about eleven feet. They became extinct about 11,000 years ago.

tile point that is referred to as the "Paleo." The "type point" of the Paleo Period is the Clovis point, which was first found at a kill site at Blackwater Draw, in Clovis, New Mexico, in 1932. That discovery was very dramatic because the points were unearthed by amateur archaeologists in the rib bones of a long-ago-hunted mammoth.

Clovis points were chipped in a peculiar manner that left a narrow indentation called a "flute" running up from the base to about halfway across the front face. This enabled hafting the point to a piece of wood for use as a spear or lance. Such a very basic primary weapon demonstrates that Paleoindians indeed lived a haphazard and unrestricted lifestyle based on herd hunting. Based upon such discoveries as the Clovis point, archaeologists believe that they probably lived in widely dispersed bands of perhaps twenty or so extended family members who occupied seasonal camps as they followed game.

Since that initial discovery, Clovis points have been encountered all over North America and as far south as Panama. Made from different stone materials, these points testify to the meanderings of their owners. Although found in many disparate locations, they have not been found in great numbers, which has made them an artifact hunting priority and probably the most sought-after of all stone projectile points. The sites where Clovis points have been found have typically been dated at 9500 to 8500 B.C. However, with the dating systems becoming more refined, these dates may be pushed back some more.

Some Native American artifact hunters define their lifelong collecting success by their recovery of a Clovis point, which is considered the crème de la crème of finds. However, there are other similarly shaped and much desired points from the Paleo Period. These include the Holcomb, Dalton, Cumberland, Folsom, Sandia, and Quad points. The excurvate shape of Paleo stone blades is quite distinctive and thought to be particularly effective against tough hided animals such as the mammoth and bison.

Also of interest from the Paleo Period are sites that are dated earlier than Clovis. These have been found in several areas around North America, including Pennsylvania, at Meadowcroft Rock Shelter (14,000 B.C.); in Virginia, at Saltville (12,500 B.C.) and Cactus Hill (13,700 B.C.); and in Wisconsin, at the Schaefer (10,300 B.C.), Hebior (10,500 B.C.), Mud Lake (11,400 B.C.), and Fenske (11,500 B.C.) sites. None shows any evidence of being the precursor to Clovis.

There are also pre-Clovis sites in South America, such as the Monte Verde site in Chile, which has been dated at 14,500 B.P. As would be expected, a lot of controversy surrounds these pre-Clovis sites, especially those that are claimed to go back as much as 30,000 years. However, archaeology has a well-known history of rivaling interpretations and is hardly a cut-and-dried science.

The Archaic Period

The next Amerindian cultural era in North America is known as the Archaic Period. The early part of this period lasted from approximately 8000 B.C. to 4000 B.C., with the late stages extending to 2000 B.C. The late stages were marked primarily by forest adapted living.

Due to the varying climatic conditions on the continent, the more advanced Archaic Period overlapped the Paleo Period in certain areas. This is because the different Amerindian cultures did not develop at an equal pace throughout North America. In actuality, period differentiation really addresses lifestyle rather than "time zones," and both Paleo and Archaic cultures existed at the same time.

The Archaic Period is considered the horizon when a major change in prehistoric culture came about due to a restructuring of the settlement pattern and means of subsistence. More importantly, it was marked by the development of system's supporting a regular food supply.

As a result, life became more sedentary in the Archaic Period, and the population increased. In addition, early forms of villages came into being to provide greater security to clan members. Archaic peoples also tended to establish themselves in home regions, central bases to which they returned from their hunting and gathering activities.

To support their growing villages, the Archaic people turned to fishing and the collecting of shellfish, as well as to harvesting wild vegetable foods. Quite a few of the large shell mounds found along rivers and coastal areas in the South and East are attributable to Archaic people.

Archaic tools remained very functional and were augmented by barbed bone and antler tipped weapons. In addition to weapons such as spears, harpoons, and darts, the period saw such new tools as flaked and grooved axes, celts, drills, bolas, and bannerstones. (For a discussion of how stone tools were made, see page 142.) Orna-

During the Late Archaic Period, in some areas, soapstone (steatite) was commonly used for manufacturing cooking vessels and pipes.

How Stone Tools Were Made

I flaked a flint to a cutting edge
  And shaped it with a brutish craft;
I broke a shank from the woodland lank
  And fitted it, head and haft;
Then I hid me close to the reedy tarn,
  Where the mammoth came to drink;
Through the brawn and bone I drove the stone
  And slew him on the brink.

—LANGDON SMITH, "EVOLUTION" (CIRCA 1913)

In general, prehistoric toolmakers utilized two major techniques to manufacture stone implements. They frequently used these techniques in combination. The most basic is percussion. This process entails the striking of a suitable rock material, such as flint or chert, with a hammerstone to knock off large flakes.

The other technique is pressure flaking. Here, small flakes are removed from a prepared blank (large flake) through the application of pressure along the edges, usually with a bone or antler tool. Some stone points were worked on only one side, or unifacially, while others were treated on both sides, or bifacially.

Percussion alone cannot be used to produce any but the largest and most crudely shaped tools because it allows very little control over the angle of fracture. Pressure flaking and grinding were the answers to this problem, since they introduced the capability to produce more intricate and specialized tools.

Of course, the available stone material had to be workable and produce consistent conchoidal fractures. The most highly sought materials for stone tool manufacture belong to the quartz and flint families—jasper, obsidian, slate, basalt, and rhyolite. In some parts of the country, prehistoric tools made from petrified coral and wood have also been found.

It is said that prehistoric stoneworkers were the first geologists and chemists because they recognized suitable knapping materials and the changes that occur in rocks after being heat treated. Heating makes rocks easier to work. Heat treating generally also changes the color of rocks, and experts have found such evidence in Clovis points, as well as in stone points made in much later periods.

mental objects made of stone, such as pendants and gorgets, also made their first appearances in the Archaic Period.

The Transitional Period

Between the late Archaic Period and the next major phase of cultural evolution, the Woodland Period, was the Transitional Period. The Transitional Period lasted about 1,500 years and is most applicable to the Northeast and Mid-Atlantic sections of the United States.

At this time and place, prehistoric Amerindian society transformed from mainly hunting and gathering to the more permanent residential village pattern of the coming Woodland Period. Increasingly, populated zones were located along large bodies of water, such as rivers and lakes. In addition, the precursors to the ceramic industry were introduced and are considered a diagnostic criterion when evaluating possible Transitional Period sites.

The Woodland Period

The Woodland Period is considered to be the classic stage of Amerindian cultural ascendency in North America. It began about 1000 B.C. with the introduction of its most prominent feature, organized large-scale agriculture, which enabled the support of sizable village populations.

This Transitional Period Orient Culture point popped out while the author was digging a metal detector signal along a curb in Queens, New York.

Corn, beans, and squash provided stable and dependable crops and let civilization advance by freeing labor for the development of skills other than hunting. In addition, there was extensive trade and travel from region to region via the water networks that later became known as the Mississippi, Missouri, Ohio, and Tennessee rivers.

The Woodland Period is also believed to be when the bow and arrow was introduced, somewhere around A.D. 200, after slowly drifting down to the Great Plains from the Canadian Arctic. Following this development, according to some researchers, warfare increased on the continent. When encountering stone projectile points from the Woodland Period, a good rule to follow is that if the point is shorter than 2 inches, it should be considered an arrowhead; longer than 2 inches generally makes it a spearhead. Most could have also been used as knives.

The Woodland Period was also marked by a series of very significant cultural phases in the East and Southeast that brought about greater social and political development. These phases are known as the Adena Culture (1000 to 100 B.C.), the Hopewell Complex (200 B.C. to A.D. 500), and the Mississippian Culture (A.D. 750 to 1550).

These cultures used platform mound building extensively for elaborate religious and burial purposes. The most famous earthen mound, the Mississippian Monk's Mound (A.D. 1300), is located in

The Hopewell Culture (200 B.C.—500 A.D.) was named after Mordechai Hopewell. It was on his farm near Chillicoth, Ohio, that excavations in the 1890s revealed a complex moundbuilder civilization. During the Hopewell epoch, disparate Native American groups were brought together by a guiding set of beliefs and symbols, which dominated eastern North America for centuries to come.

TABLE 10.1   ARROWHEAD IDENTIFICATION

Stone projectile points were an important component of the prehistoric Native American tool kit. Whether used on spears, darts, or arrows, they were essential to survival by helping to secure wild game for food or in warfare. The arrowhead is the most widely thought of projectile point when people think about surface hunting for prehistoric stone artifacts.

Arrowheads are initially classified by their shape. Below are some of the most common arrowhead shapes that you will encounter. However, there seems to be an infinite variety of classified named types. I refer you to the *Official Overstreet Indian Arrowheads Identification and Price Guide* listed in Appendix A for a complete listing of arrowhead named types.

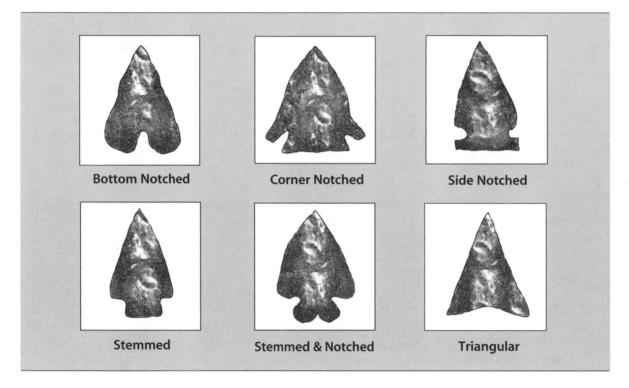

| Bottom Notched | Corner Notched | Side Notched |
| Stemmed | Stemmed & Notched | Triangular |

Cohokia, Illinois, and is considered to be the largest structure ever built by prehistoric man in North America. Meanwhile, in the Southwest, the Hohokam people (A.D. 300 to 1450) introduced irrigation farming, and their contemporaries, the Anasazi (A.D. 700 to 1400) and the Mogollon (A.D. 200 to 1400), in their later Mimbres Valley phases, became skilled potters.

As historic times approached, many villages began to form sophisticated leagues and confederacies in common defense, tribute, and trade agreements. The best known is the League of the Iroquois.

In addition, animistic beliefs provided the foundation for artistic pipes and figurines with animal designs, and wampum became a universal trade item. Potential artifact finds associated with the Woodland Period are pendants and medallions made from etched shell, along with the usual variety of stone implements, now with the addition of stone hoes used for agriculture.

THE FRATERNITY OF FLINT

Hunting and collecting prehistoric Native American artifacts is an extensive hobby area in its own right and is increasingly being recognized as a very respectable educational pursuit. Every urban area has artifacts that help to tell its prehistoric story. A great way to start out in this timeless aspect of urban treasure hunting is by attending one of the many prehistoric artifact shows held around the country and meeting up with this friendly and knowledgeable "Fraternity of Flint."

Prehistoric artifact shows are a great place to meet the Fraternity of Flint and to see what other folks are finding.

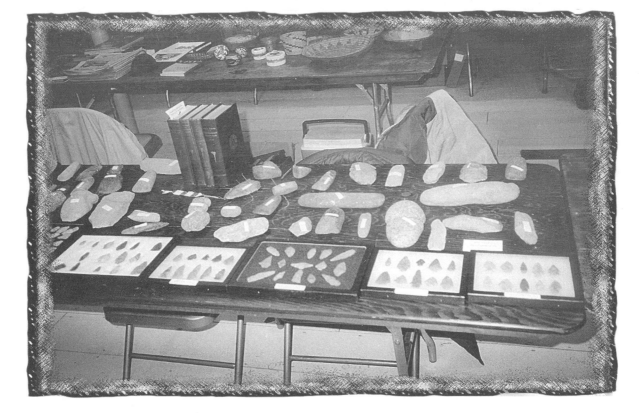

The shows that I've been to were well attended and very enjoyable learning experiences. Rows of tables were covered with an attractive array of display cases filled with prehistoric artifacts made of stone, bone, shell, quill, and clay. Also available to peruse were interesting selections of fossils and books. It's really not hard to spend the whole day just chatting, browsing, and going through a buffet of bargain bins, as well as holding some magnificent stone tools, including ancient Clovis points made by human hands thousands of years ago. You can also count on seeing folks bringing in their cherished family heirloom artifacts for identification by experts.

I think I've demonstrated that successfully hunting for prehistoric Native American artifacts around a city is not a farfetched idea and will provide you with some great adventures. Those urban treasure hunters who take up this intriguing quest usually find it to be an uncrowded and rewarding activity.

Most certainly, as you become more experienced at urban treasure hunting in general, you will develop the powers of observation and other skills necessary to succeed at hunting for prehistoric artifacts as well. All you need to start out properly is an accurate knowledge base and being pointed in the right direction, which this chapter was intended to provide.

Remember, we have little left of the original inhabitants of our country—just their stone tools, rock carvings, and other artifacts. These long-lost items of material culture offer us exciting challenges—first, to find them, and then, to use them to learn more about the early inhabitants of North America.

Your time will be well spent!

❧ 11 ❧

Bottle Digging

Antique bottle recovery is really a science unto itself, and the rewards from this endeavor can be quite good both in the monetary sense and in feelings of personal accomplishment. Due to the many levels of historical development associated with urban areas, you should have no trouble locating a sufficient number of high-potential digging sites. If you hit it right, a hoard of beautiful and valuable bottles from yesteryear can be yours!

Depending on where your research leads, you should expect to find a lot more than just bottles. Typically, the sites that contain old bottles also yield an interesting variety of other items that were discarded "way back when" and are now considered collectibles.

I gained this particular awareness early on, while excavating a Civil War–era dumpsite where I also found old silverware, coins, marbles, bisque figures, and a multitude of household items made of glass such as paperweights, inkwells, fruit jars, and dinnerware. When I related this to some of my more seasoned bottle-digging friends, they said that this was to be expected when digging an old dump.

There is a ready market for old bottles in good condition, and collectors have been known to pay top dollar for prized specimens. Many times, just such a bottle will surface after having spent one or two centuries in the ground, under a porch, or submerged in water. They are the vestiges of a formative time in America, when the increasing population and expanding need for durable containers resulted in the production of countless bottles for beverages, foods, medicines, poisons, and cosmetics.

A major stimulus to bottle manufacturing was the development of mass transportation systems and routes of travel. For example, the invention of the steamboat in 1807, the opening of the Erie Canal in 1825, and the tremendous increase in railroad lines after 1830 were important factors in the increased demand for glass products. For historians, the study of recovered bottles has revealed the development of many consequential trade networks in formative America.

In this chapter, we will discuss the history and art of bottle making in the United States, where to search for bottles and other glass items, and how to properly and safely recover them.

HISTORY OF AMERICAN BOTTLE MAKING

What makes antique bottles so appealing is that they were made by hand. The first glasshouse in the United States began operation in 1608 in Jamestown, Virginia. Between that time and the latter part of the nineteenth century, when bottle-making machines were invented, glassblowers used either long tubes called "blowpipes" to create bottles in free-blown forms or reusable molds with the desired shapes. Both methods were imprecise processes that usually left irregularities and air bubbles in the finished products, adding to their charm. Bottle collectors refer to these characteristics as "primitive features."

Antique bottles present a number of clues to their age, including their shape, the presence of a pontil scar on the bottom where the blowpipe was connected, and the height or irregularity of the seams caused by imprecise molds. Some simple rules of thumb are that free-blown bottles were used into the early 1800s, when wooden molds were developed. Wooden molds produced most of a bottle and left a seam from the base to near the top. The top was then applied separately by a glassmaker, leaving obvious traces of the attachment process. Metal molds came next and produced the entire bottle with a high-reaching seam. The typical "crown-top" look of present-day bottles did not appear until 1892.

Most bottles were produced in natural colors such as amber, olive green, and aquamarine until the mid-1800s, when the development of the food-preservation industry created a need for clear glass bottles, to allow the product to be viewed by the consumer. Still, it is

a bottle's method of manufacture and not its color that provides the key information for dating it.

Bottles of past eras manifest an appealing individuality. Finding one is a thrill, but finding only one is rare. They tend to be buried in bunches, and when one bottle turns up, you can be pretty sure others are in the vicinity.

I should point out that bottles of unusual shape, color, or artistic design are the most sought-after. You will find collectors who specialize in figurals, inks, poisons, bitters, soft drinks, and other categories of personal interest. The avocation offers many collecting possibilities.

You may also find a wide assortment of other glass, ceramic, and earthenware containers in addition to traditional bottles. Some of the earliest vessels were demijohns and carboys, which were used to transport "white lightning," cider, and vinegar.

These antique bottles recovered in New York City date from (left to right) the early-to-late 1700s, 1840, 1860, and the 1870s. All are exceptional finds. Chances are you can make similar recoveries in your own city.

EMBOSSING AND DESIGNS ON BOTTLES

Embossing makes a bottle particularly attractive. In this process, raised letters or designs were manufactured right into the glass to advertise the product and gain household acceptance. Until paper labeling began to be used with mass-produced bottles beginning in the 1890s, embossing was employed to note bottle contents. In most cases, embossed bottles are worth more than nonembossed bottles.

Flasks, which were originally intended to hold gunpowder, took on an artistic bent in the early 1800s, when they were often embossed with patriotic symbols such as the American Eagle, the flag, a bust of George Washington or Marquis de Lafayette, or the figure of Columbia encircled by stars.

Millions of embossed bottles were discarded in the late 1880s. Finding them offers a real challenge and a pleasant time-travel connection with "simpler times."

Presidential candidates of the time, such as Andrew Jackson and Henry Clay, joined the bandwagon and had their portraits put on flasks. Other flasks sported agricultural motifs such as cornstalks, cornucopias, or sheaves of wheat. A whole area of flask making was devoted to railroad designs showing locomotives with slogans such as "Success to the Railroad." Jenny Lind, the "Swedish Nightingale" promoted by P. T. Barnum, was also a very popular subject, as were scenes from the California and Pike's Peak gold rushes. Historical flasks are now considered the Cadillac of antique bottles.

It's easy to see how the trends in bottle manufacturing reflected the social imperatives of a dynamic and growing country. Antique bottles are a link with a period in American history for which many people are nostalgic because of the seeming simplicity of and satisfaction with daily life. When I recover an old bottle, I often pause to reflect on the times it lived through and the people who used it.

The figure of Columbia, which personified the United States as a woman, was a popular nineteenth-century (circa 1820 to 1850) flask design.

WHERE TO LOOK FOR ANTIQUE BOTTLES

Aside from the unexplainable pockets of bottles that occasionally surface to everyone's surprise, most bottles are found in certain places that are consistently associated with finding old glass. These include former trash dumps, old privies, construction sites, and waterfront areas.

Former Trash Dumps

An obvious place to look for old bottles in an urban area is any location that served as a trash dump over a long period of time. These sites may still be active or they may have been abandoned now that commercial landfill projects, which offer their own special bottle-hunting potential, are in vogue.

You can locate some former trash dumps by reviewing old city maps. However, many dumps never made it to a map because they were not part of any municipal organization plan. Those are the choice hidden ones you might expect to discover in a wooded area, most likely next to a neighborhood that has its origins in the nineteenth century or earlier.

This is where I found the Civil War–era dump that I mentioned at the beginning of this chapter. I located it by accident when a friend

The Dr. Henry P. Thatcher container was the first embossed milk bottle and appeared in 1884. The reassuring design of a farmer milking a cow gained it instant household acceptance.

and I were out with our metal detectors searching a network of old bridle paths near a community founded in the 1830s. An amazing find, I've named it the "Pheasant Site" after the beautiful birds that live there.

We had followed a trail into a series of gullies and had become quite intrigued by the amount of old, broken glass and bleached white oyster shells covering the ground and continuing down into the small test pits we dug. Our detectors were also locating Mason jar covers and a swath of Indian Head pennies.

This test pit dug by the author at the site of a Civil War–era trash dump led to a bonanza of silverware, old bottles, glassware, and broken dishes.

Coming back at a later date with the right tools for serious excavation, we were rewarded with a bonanza of old bottles, glassware, and crockery. Obviously, the early neighborhood residents had used the most convenient place to dispose of their trash. They probably hauled it out to the woods by horse and wagon, and then simply tossed it down the sloping sides of the gully to be covered up by nature.

I'm sure that over the years, many people have walked or ridden past this "glory hole," but nobody ever thought to dig there for old bottles, since they could not decipher the obvious clues scattered about on top of the ground. Most likely, there is a similarly overlooked wooded area near your home waiting to be explored and harvested. I know that when I'm digging and the pheasants are calling, the world seems like a better place.

Old Privies

Some of the most productive places to find a bottle bonanza in a city are long-forgotten privies in the older parts of town. Generally, most pre–Civil War houses and commercial establishments had no indoor plumbing or running water. Instead, the residents used a privy, or outhouse, in the back yard. These privies were also utilized as the household refuse disposal unit, since this was the time before regular garbage pickup.

With cities in the United States growing rapidly, the development of effective sewer systems and garbage collection became a priority. During the 1860s, as these public health efforts moved forward, the homeowners in the older neighborhoods began installing indoor plumbing, and gradually each house was connected to the main sewer system. When indoor plumbing finally became the vogue at the beginning of the twentieth century, the privy gradually drifted from the urban consciousness. Now, in the twenty-first century, privies have become known as "time capsules" because of the remarkable number of interesting and valuable historical items that can be found within them.

For example, one early-nineteenth-century privy near Wall Street was archaeologically excavated and yielded approximately 16,000 attractive glass and ceramic fragments representing the styles of dinner- and glassware in use at the time. This privy served the workers at three glass and china warehouses, and was evidently also used for dumping trash.

Privies from the late nineteenth century clearly reflect the concerns of post–Civil War living, with many types of medicine bottles found within them. After all, this was the time of the "snake oil" medicine showman. By 1880, this charlatan and hawker of cures had firmly incorporated himself into American life. He traveled widely with his assortment of bottled remedies and had shills offer fantastic testimonials that his cures would work miracles. In truth, the cures consisted mostly of ineffective herbs, opiates, and alcohol, which perhaps helped the suffering forget their illness for a while—or even started them on a new one.

It was not until 1906 that the Pure Food and Drug Act caught up with the patent medicine industry and brought about needed reform. Actually, very few of these medicines were patented, and in 1905, *Collier's* magazine ran a series of articles revealing their pernicious ingredients and exposing the quackery. At the time the law was passed, more than 100,000 patent medicines were on the market and more than 250,000 people had developed narcotic habits from their use.

Thanks to aggressive advertising techniques, these nostrums became extremely popular and even appeared in national mail-order catalogs. Quite often, the bottles were embossed with the cure's name and the sponsoring "physician," such as "Dr. Kilmer's Swamp Root, Kidney, and Bladder Remedy."

After a bottle was emptied, it was taken back to the outhouse and thrown down. Some privies were in use for quite an extended time period, explaining the large number of medicine bottles that have been dug up from this most used of all outbuildings.

An advertisement for Dr. Moore's Essence of Life appeared in the *Connecticut Courant* on March 13, 1805. This elixir was recommended for "consumption, difficult breathing, quinsy, phthic spitting of blood, flatulence, fits, and hypochondriac afflictions."

Some other exciting privy recoveries have included rare and valuable bottles and artifacts dating back to Colonial times. Even hidden caches of money and jewelry have been recovered from privy dig sites. Not many robbers of yesteryear would root around in an active outhouse, so valuables were thought to be safe there. Note that the former organic content of old privies has long since changed to a harmless and safe soil that is generally referred to as "night soil."

FINDING OLD PRIVIES

Locating old privies in rural areas and on farms is much more difficult than in the city because of the large back yards without clear property lines. It could be a long day with little to show for it.

To dig a privy, first you have to find one. This generally takes detective work, so there's something very adventurous about embarking on a dig. The only clue might be the presence of a nineteenth-century building with a back yard. Here is where your skill with a probe will come in handy as you listen for the portentous sound of crunching glass along the property line. Setting up a grid is an excellent way to start. Remember, not all people will be agreeable when you ask to excavate their yard. On the other hand, some Brooklyn privy diggers have been given lunch and refreshments by interested property owners.

In many instances, privies are located on the property line in a straight line downwind from the rear door. Keep in mind, however, that weather conditions were also a consideration when privies were built. For example, privies in cold climates were located closer to the house, while privies in warm climates were placed further away to avoid flies and odors. Privies can also be located directly outside the rear door, in the middle of the lot, or in one of the back corners. Furthermore, it's very common to find more than one privy in a yard, but once you find the first, finding the others becomes easier, since there's always a logical pattern to their placement. As a clue, follow old sidewalks or stone paths, and probe every low spot in the yard. For a typical back yard privy pattern, see Figure 11.1.

Experienced treasure hunters are always on the lookout for buildings being taken down in the older parts of town.

The most common privy shapes were square, round, rectangular, and oval. Their life span was ten to twenty years, after which they were abandoned and filled in with ashes, bricks, sand, rocks, or soil from the new privy. Some may go down very deep, to about 20 feet, with the average being about 10 feet in depth. The bottom is the sought-after trash layer. Most older privies show evidence of being dipped, or cleaned, which prolonged a privy's usefulness.

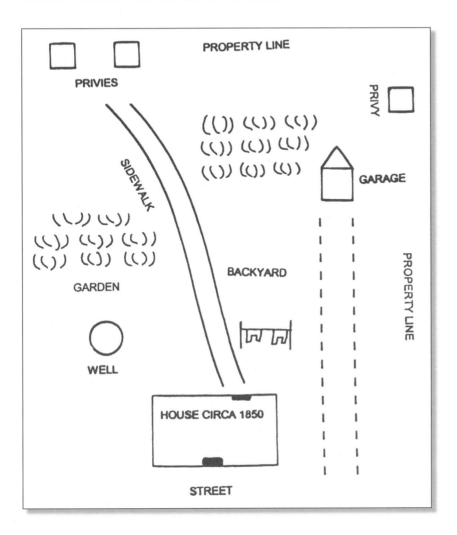

Figure 11.1
This mid-nineteenth-century house lot in downtown Brooklyn displays a typical back yard privy pattern.

While some privies were not lined with anything, others were lined with wood, brick, or stone to prevent a cave-in. In New York City, stone liners seem to have been the most common, and probing at an angle is the best way to hit the outer wall and find them. You can then define the shape and liner material by shoveling down along the perimeter.

When probing, make sure to examine the probe tip, since it may bring up a soil sample containing rust, wood, ash, coal, lime, brick, glass, or pottery—all the usual components of a ripe privy. Remember to push slowly so you don't break anything. A soft, hollow feel-

The liklihood of a cave-in made excavating this 6-foot-diameter, nineteenth-century well a risky project. Safety should always be your primary concern.

ing to the privy fill is also indicative of hitting pay dirt. If you encounter these conditions, your next step should be to dig a test hole about 2 to 3 feet in diameter to look for further concentrations of what was on the probe tip. Such a finding will strongly suggest that you've found a privy, or at least a trash pit, which may contain its own treasures. However, you can't get too excited about any dig until you're into the goods.

Note that where there are old privies, there are probably old wells and cisterns. So always be careful when breaking through subterranean walls, since a fall into a well could be fatal. One indication that you're in a cistern or well is the presence of mortar between the bricks because the lining had to be watertight. Cisterns were also usually placed close to a house so they could be filled with rainwater coming off the roof. However, digging a cistern is a lot of work, and most of the time you'll get skunked because people didn't throw refuse into their water supply.

But when a well ran dry, it may have then been used to discard trash. One such well was discovered down by Canal Street in lower Manhattan after an intrepid digger broke through a mysterious underground wall. This well was dug continually day and night, and gave up an incredible assortment of old bottles, teacups, plates, coins, ivory brush handles, silverware, clay pipes, an intact chamber pot with a floral design, plus a whale-oil lamp in excellent condition. Research revealed that the well was on the property of an 1850s hotel. No doubt, it had dried up and was put to use for dumping the hotel's trash. It also contained plenty of beautiful china marbles—not an unusual find when digging a privy. (See "The Savannah Marble King," below.)

In San Diego, an 1887 Sanborn map was used to great advantage by an urban treasure hunter to pinpoint the location of a privy that served an old 1870s Chinatown saloon, the Seven Buckets of Blood. The saloon was in the city's infamous red-light Stingaree district, where saloons and gambling parlors were concentrated along the waterfront. The area was under renovation, and the treasure hunter drove though every day, scouting around for demolition sites to

The Savannah Marble King

One veteran urban treasure hunter in Savannah, Georgia, has put together quite a large collection of marbles dating from 1840 to 1870, all recovered from his digs around town at more than 2,000 privies. This assemblage of marbles contains numerous beautiful and pricey China flowers, which are highly collectible. Privy digging has also provided this treasure hunter with a remarkable clay pipe collection. The bowl designs of some of the pipes feature notable nineteenth-century historical figures, including presidents Abraham Lincoln, Franklin Pierce, Millard Fillmore, and Zachary Taylor. Privy diggers often appear to be digging randomly, but many have a special collecting focus for their efforts.

explore. Finding a likely prospect where the old Tong building was being torn down, he brought some end-of-the-day refreshments to the workmen. After explaining his objective and asking permission, he was allowed to search around in the site after quitting time.

It didn't take long for this maestro to probe up the privy on the property line. Within a couple of days, he formed a digging team of eager treasure hunters to excavate 10 feet down into the privy, which was filled with old bottles and Chinese artifacts, including opium pipes. The bottom 3 feet of the privy was packed with ceramic beer bottles from the saloon. His best finds were a perfect Lash's Bitters bottle, a Web's Tonic bottle, a Celebrated Crown Bitters bottle, a Warner's Safe Cure bottle, Tiger Whiskey bottles, and a large, brown-glazed Chinese storage jar.

He also located the adjoining lot's privy, once shared by a livery stable and a Chinese herb store. His luck was still flying high when he came up with a variety of bitters, medicine, hometown soft drink, whiskey, and Chinese bottles. He also found a brass Civil War scabbard buckle and an ornate badge that commemorated a special 1895 train run between Los Angeles and Pasadena. Then, to top it off, his metal detector signaled a $5 gold coin dated 1905. What expertise!

Of course, downtown Brooklyn has also been a very fertile privy-digging arena, yielding many exceptional bottles. For example, a team of diggers on a streak made a great bottle strike after some initial recon with a Sanborn map. They got into an old privy on Pacific Street, where their efforts took them down 10 feet to find more than 150 bottles, including some rare soft drink bottles from New York's famous Crystal Palace, a colossal glass-and-iron tribute to the World's Fair built in the early 1850s. You can never predict what you will find in a privy-digging adventure.

The New York City Crystal Palace was built in the shape of a Greek cross topped with a 100-foot glass dome. The Crystal Palace became a symbol of the country's achievements, as well as a source of municipal civic pride.

PLAYING IT SAFE IN OLD PRIVIES

Both the San Diego and Brooklyn privy strikes demonstrate the importance of research in privy digging, as well as the type of reward awaiting the ambitious urban treasure hunter. They also show how important teamwork is. Excavating a privy must be done with great care, since you sometimes have to go down 10 feet or more. This can result in dangerous conditions, such as a cave-in. At no time should you allow yourself to become complacent about this possibility.

I've spoken with privy diggers who have had this happen to them. In each case, the person needed assistance from a digging buddy to escape. Therefore, I would advise you not to attempt an extensive privy excavation by yourself, unless probing tells you bottles are relatively close to the surface. Going in alone, with the entry hole above your head, could make it your last dig! In addition, wearing a hard hat is always a good idea for the protection it affords from falling debris and to have an attachable light source in the darkness.

DIGGING OLD PRIVIES

When excavating an old privy, for the best results dig all the way to the bottom of the pit and always check the corners. As mentioned, many privies were dipped, but sometimes the corners were ignored and are likely spots to find leftover bottles.

When you get down to the trash layer, use a pointed broomstick, which is excellent for locating bottles. The wood makes a distinctive whine when it slides over glass as you poke around, and it won't cause any scratches or other damage the way a metal hand rake can. A hand rake is more suitable for quickly scraping away soil from the walls once you define your work area.

When digging a deep hole, you will probably need to use a sturdy 5-gallon hauling bucket with a tripod and pulley setup to remove the dirt. Since privy digging is usually a team effort, one person can sift the dirt for hard-to-notice items, such as marbles, coins, and small bottles. There's nothing like a fresh bucket of bottles to keep the crew's spirits up.

Urban Renewal Sites

Urban areas always seem to be in a state of transition, which definitely means opportunity for the vigilant urban treasure hunter. When you hear that ground in an older part of town is being torn up for new development, you have to get there—fast! It's an opportunity you really should not miss because bottles and other objects from earlier times will generally appear—and then disappear just as quickly.

The Wall Street area in lower Manhattan, which is where the Dutch West India Company originally founded the settlement of Nieuw Amsterdam in 1624, is a prime example of this scenario. Construction is constantly going on down there. One intriguing consequence is that hundreds of tons of earth are always being moved around and dumped in landfill areas around the city.

The resourceful urban treasure hunter will somehow obtain permission to enter these construction sites after hours or on weekends. Sometimes, the site security guard will be cooperative if presented with a small gift of food, beverage, or cash. If this is unfeasible, you may want to follow the landfill-loaded trucks to their final destination for a good going-through.

This type of doggedness pays off especially well because much of the work is done for you. Therefore, you should always be on the lookout for piles of dirt suddenly appearing around town. I know some Colonial-era enthusiasts who become ecstatic at the thought of picking through landfill from Wall Street because of its remarkable bottle and artifact payoff record.

A persistent Philadelphia urban treasure hunter also employed this strategy with good results. It all started when he looked out his window and saw new construction activity in a vacant lot on the east side of the Schuylkill River. A large office building was going up. He didn't know it yet, but he was about to travel back in time to the Philadelphia of the 1860s.

Going over to the lot to look around, he saw workmen removing embossed bottles and other glassware from a large quantity of gray ash brought to the surface by digging machinery. Obviously, the excavation had penetrated a large mid-nineteenth-century rubbish heap that also contained broken china, animal bones, clam and oyster shells, and worn-out leather shoes. His challenge came when he couldn't get permission to search around due to insurance restrictions. Instead, he asked a helpful workman where the dirt-disposal site was. Arriving there, he was elated to see mounds of fresh gray ash and a good assortment of bottles and artifacts strewn about. This project kept him busy for the next seven months, as he kept following the dump trucks leaving the construction site and then went through the spoils.

Many of the bottles this Philadelphian recovered came from local druggists. He also found inkwells, ceramic perfume containers, the bottles from twenty-four varieties of soft drinks, barrel-shaped mus-

The sites of urban renewal projects are prime search areas for urban treasure hunters. Hundreds of antique marbles were recovered by an alert treasure hunter after a lake in New York City's Central Park was drained for repairs.

tard bottles, marbles, beautifully embossed pipe bowls, and a huge variety of food-container bottles—all rising from the ashes of West Philadelphia.

LYELL'S LAW

An integral rule of archaeology is Lyell's Law. Referring to the normal way things are buried, it states, "The oldest things are on the bottom." However, after a backhoe has scooped out an area, the soil now on top is the oldest, and the valuable relics it contains can be pretty easily picked out by eye, metal detector, or sifter. Archaeologists call this condition "inverse stratigraphy."

In New York City, bottles from every historical period dating back to the seventeenth century have been easily eyeballed on the surface after inverse stratigraphy conditions have been created at construction sites. Alert workers get first pick, but most of the time these relics are not their focus.

When an entire Dutch West India Company warehouse was excavated from a construction site on Wall Street and more than 43,000 significant artifacts were recovered, the head archaeologist said: "Never has so much material been found from this time period. It's a bit mind-boggling to find these exotic artifacts preserved so well under Wall Street." This comment should make you appreciate similar situations where you live.

ROADWORK PROJECTS

Observing routine roadwork projects can also be quite rewarding for the bottle hunter. In one instance, I was watching a bulldozer operator smoothing dirt around after removing the old, cracked sidewalk and street in an antiquated Flushing neighborhood. In one mighty scoop, he brought up, intact, a large 1870s ceramic soy sauce container covered with beautiful Chinese calligraphy glazed to the surface.

The bulldozer operator immediately jumped down to retrieve the prize, and I went over for a closer look. According to the hard hat, this was not an uncommon event because old bottles and other vintage items frequently surface when streets are torn up for urban renewal. He then related an instance where a work crew had found a cannon that appeared "out of nowhere" and sold it to a collector for $2,000.

The replacement of a vintage stone stairway revealed numerous bottles that were once tossed into the heavy vegetation lining both sides and slowly covered up.

STAIRWAY REPLACEMENT

Another time, I chanced upon an old stone stairway that was being replaced with the latest concrete model. The original stairway dated back to the 1880s and had, on both its sides, a 15-foot-wide strip of tangled overgrowth into which people had been throwing bottles and other things for years. That became readily apparent after the bulldozers cleared the area for landscaping, leaving mounds of dirt with numerous broken and whole old bottles sticking out. It was always an adventure to go over after the day's work was done and see what was lying around. These bottles were mostly 100-year-old beer bottles, whiskey bottles, and food containers. Combing through this late-nineteenth-century slice of life was an interesting experience.

The Waterfront

Another great bottle-hunting site is a waterfront under renovation. Many cities are located on a waterway such as an ocean, river, lake, or canal, and have a waterfront area that has served as a bustling harbor since early settlement times. Looking at old paintings of your city will set the scene. There's no doubt that ships' brawling crews threw many a pontil bottle overboard because modern dredging equipment brings up some choice specimens from old wharf areas. You can also try searching along the shoreline at low tide for some serendipitous finds.

I know an ardent bottle hunter who made many well-earned and wonderful finds by keeping up with a dredging project on the New Jersey side of the Hudson River that brought up tons of mud containing numerous early-1800s bottles and fine ceramics. Basically, all he really had to do was walk through and take what he wanted. His only problem came when the blazing summer sun broiled the mud into a hard pack, making the bottles somewhat difficult to extract. When pursuing dredged-up waterfront treasure, it's wise to wear wading boots and rubber gloves to protect yourself from cuts and pollution. Safety first!

Another major bottle strike took place in Queens, New York, when archaeology students from Brooklyn College found hundreds of old bottles buried in the muck along the weed-filled shoreline of Old Mill Creek, a Jamaica Bay inlet in Howard Beach. Their original intent had been to survey the area for Native American artifacts, which one of them had found nearby, at the old Brooklyn garbage dump.

Like numerous similar cases, this bottle strike was a complete surprise. Many of the bottles dated from 1900 through the 1920s, and after further investigation, the archaeology professor reached the inescapable conclusion that they had discovered the remains of a long-abandoned speakeasy. A speakeasy was a secret drinking rendezvous from the Roaring Twenties and Prohibition, which lasted from the ratification of the Eighteenth Amendment on January 16, 1919, to its repeal on December 5, 1933.

The history of Prohibition in New York City is fascinating and presents some interesting projects for urban treasure hunters. During this time period, bootleggers would use any bottle available and fill it up with "hooch" to sell. Since pilings, metal bulkheads, and chains were found, this particular speakeasy may have been a barge that picked up customers in Brooklyn and then headed for the marsh, where it tied up at a pier connected to a boardwalk. Aside from drinking, it was probably also the site of a multitude of other illegal activities, such as gambling and prostitution.

According to estimates, the number of speakeasies in New York ranged anywhere from 32,000 to 100,000 establishments. Not all were as exclusive as Manhattan's 21 Club or even the hole-in-the-wall places with the "Louie sent me!" peephole in the door. Some, such as the students' discovery, were hidden in remote areas on the outskirts of town. A bootlegger's paradise!

The point to remember here is that Prohibition was very unpop-

The remains of a Roaring Twenties speakeasy lay hidden in the marsh in Howard Beach, New York, offering a number of treasure hunting potentials.

ular nationwide, and the citizenry devised creative ways of getting around it. Tracking down these fringe-area speakeasies can be a very lucrative and fun treasure hunting direction. Chances are that you'll find yourself in some strange places having some memorable adventures. Who knows, you may even discover the remains of an old dance hall that also served "bathtub gin." Aside from old bottles, speakeasy sites also offer you a good chance to recover coins and jewelry, since people drank and caroused until they lost their concentration—among other things. A hidden cache wouldn't be out of the question here either.

A similar waterway bottle strike took place in Houston along the Buffalo Bayou, which runs right through the heart of downtown. Two urban treasure hunters paddled down the Bayou and located a hidden "monster bottle dump" that could not be seen from their boat, but rather was up and over a curve in the shoreline.

These intrepid treasure hunters had previously discovered three smaller bottle dumps in the bayou, which brought them further into the waterway to scout around. After beaching their boat and walking upstream, they saw some old broken glass eroding out of the bayou bank. When one of them found an 1880s turn-mold wine bottle, they became hopeful of finding another small dump. They could have hardly imagined that they were about to hit a bottle bonanza that would eventually yield more than 2,000 bottles from the 1880s and 1890s, all within a month of their initial breakthrough. It appears that these bottle hunters had miraculously stumbled upon an early turn-of-the-twentieth-century bottle dump that had somehow eluded the rest of Houston.

Sometimes, you have to be right on top of a site to find it. The Houston bayou hunt produced graceful wine bottles and hundreds of medicine and hometown drugstore bottles, as well as Hutchinson bottles, which inspired the term "pop bottle." Usually containing mineral or carbonated soda water, these bottles sported a new spring-operated rubber stopper patented by inventor Charles A. Hutchinson in 1879 to replace leaky corks and opened with a pop when a protruding spring was hit. An Old Hickory Celebrated Stomach Bitters bottle, worth about $150, was the prize bottle recovered. Remember, urban treasure hunting is all about being creative, and you never know how changing your perspective can increase your search potential and rewards.

INSULATORS—ANOTHER TYPE OF HISTORICAL GLASS FIND

Another type of antique glass object you will come across while treasure hunting is the insulator. Insulators were used to protect communications wires from the elements and were once a common sight along the railway and road systems in the United States. They were manufactured in many colors, including amber, green, purple, blue, and white. Some colors were used to code high-voltage wires for linemen. There are also odd types, either of unusual shape, color, or threading design. The earliest insulators had no threading and are very sought-after by collectors.

Old insulators can be recovered where there was early railroad and telegraph activity. This one has a patent date of 1870 and was found partially buried near some old and forgotten tracks.

These interesting and sometimes very valuable glass relics came into use with the introduction of the first telegraph line in the United States, between Baltimore and Washington, DC, in 1844. Flat insulators, the first style used, proved unsatisfactory and were replaced with knob-shaped insulators. More design changes followed after the first threaded designs were patented in 1865, and then again after the telephone appeared in 1876 and the electric light bulb in 1879.

The years between 1875 and 1925 were a boom time for insulator manufacturing, with many new companies springing up to meet the need. Materials such as earthenware and porcelain were also tried, but glass remained the favorite because of its ability to do the job better—even when wet—than the others. Each manufacturer had its own sales line, and thousands of varieties can now be found. As the telegraph spread across the country, so did the number of insulator types. I've dug up these "jewels of the wire" in old dumps and searched for them along now-defunct railroad tracks.

Since the telegraph is so closely associated with railroad progress, this last insulator recovery technique is quite applicable to old urban areas. In early times, the railroad snaked its way to remote outposts, many of which later became towns and cities. By reviewing old maps and train schedules, along with doing some field exploration, treasure hunters can find the location of abandoned, out-of-the-way railroad lines and stations in their areas. Of course, some may no longer be around, but others may lie forgotten in undeveloped, woodsy parts of the city.

If the tracks are very isolated and nobody with the same idea has

This railroad spur became overgrown and forgotten many years ago. A perfect place to find insulators—if nobody has beaten you to it!

beaten you to them, you may even find insulators on the remains of still-standing poles. If no poles are up, search along the tracks until you find an insulator or a piece of one. Theorizing that this is probably a spot where a pole once stood, take 40 paces (the typical spacing of poles along railroad tracks) in either direction and then search very carefully in a 10-foot radius. Your efforts may be well rewarded. Bear in mind that a rare canary yellow insulator was offered for sale at $1,500!

When hunting along old tracks for insulators, make sure you also bring your metal detector. It's been my experience that old coins are often found along parallel paths and in nearby bushes, perhaps dropped by the men who originally worked on the track. That has to be the explanation for coins I've found dating back to the 1860s, which were probably lost during midday snooze breaks. At least, that's what I like to believe!

The purpose of the early railroad systems was to move travelers and industrial goods, so also be alert for overgrown loading platforms and passenger depots, as these have their own potential for exciting discoveries. I guarantee you that searching along old railroad tracks can be rewarding in a number of ways!

PROPER BOTTLE-DIGGING TECHNIQUES

Good bottle-digging technique in woodsy areas requires that you be efficient about where you place shoveled soil. Most novices make the mistake, as I did, of shoveling onto a spot that later will need to be cleared. That's why skillful preliminary probing and test pitting are important to isolate the bottle-digging zone and should be accompanied by note taking and map drawing.

As a matter of personal pride and respect for the natural beauty of woodland sites, I always refill my holes. This can be easily accomplished in the course of digging by using a backfilling approach—that is, as you remove the soil from one area in a trench, throw it into the section you previously opened up. This will propel you in a forward direction and is a good way to excavate in a straight line. After a short time, the land will return to its previously undisturbed-looking state, with no permanent ill effects.

When digging on private property, such as someone's back yard, the standard procedure is to place the excavated soil on a tarp or pool liner and use it to refill the hole later. This also keeps things neat and showcases your digging technique. You may want to dig the property next door, and a good reference is always helpful. On occasion, curious neighbors will come by to see what's going on, and this will be a good chance to engage them. You know—future customers! After the dig, make sure the hole or privy is properly filled in and, of course, always give some of your finds to the property owner as a token of your appreciation.

Not all bottle-digging sites develop the way you would prefer. There are some sites that test pitting indicates should be excellent, but that turn out quite the opposite, containing just a bunch of sharp, broken glass. All you can say is, "That's the way it goes." To save yourself extra work, remember that a test pit should not be a major excavation—perhaps 2 feet in diameter by 3 feet deep to reveal old refuse. If nothing significant appears, try another spot. When you do make a

strike, keep digging until the vein runs out. Remember, the next buried bottle could be an inch away! Don't forget to sift for coins, marbles, small bottles, and other items that may otherwise escape your notice.

EXCELLENT READING ON THE SUBJECT

If you decide to join the "bottle brigade," *Antique Bottle and Glass Collector* magazine should become part of your regular reading. (For subscription information, see Appendix C.) This excellent monthly magazine covers all aspects of bottle digging and collecting. I really enjoy the inspiring "you are there" articles about bottle strikes from all around the country. There is also a calendar of bottle shows, and you might find one planned for your neck of the woods. These are great fun to attend to meet other bottle-digging enthusiasts to share information—and to see their beautiful bottle finds.

Bottles for sale— from inks to capers to sodas! Antique bottle shows will bring you in contact with other members of the "bottle brigade" to compare notes.

TABLE 11.2   HOW OLD IS THAT BOTTLE?

As you explore various bottle hunting sites, I have no doubt that you will come across a bottle type that you may not recognize. Hopefully, it's a bottle from the 19th century or earlier. How can you determine the age of a bottle? Well, there are several things to look for—overall shape, markings, color, imperfections, bottle opening type, and seams. These features provide an approximate timeframe to date the bottle.

If this is all new to you, then a quick bottle age identification reference will be quite useful. Below are two widely accepted methods to determine how old the mystery bottle you have just unearthed is.

Seams

As the art of glass blowing progressed, so did the way bottles were manufactured. By carefully examining the seam length of a bottle—the line that runs from the bottom of the bottle towards the top--you can quickly estimate the age of a bottle.

Lips

The opening of a bottle can tell you a lot about its age as well. As technology advanced, the shape of a bottle's lip changed to better secure its contents—from corks to caps. Pre 1840 bottles had openings that were formed when the bottle was cut free of the glassblower's pipe. With time, the process evolved from uneven rounded lips to even uniformed openings with ringed bands made by machine.

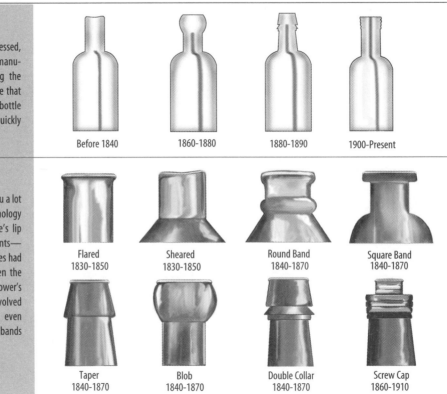

Before 1840	1860-1880	1880-1890	1900-Present

| Flared 1830-1850 | Sheared 1830-1850 | Round Band 1840-1870 | Square Band 1840-1870 |
| Taper 1840-1870 | Blob 1840-1870 | Double Collar 1840-1870 | Screw Cap 1860-1910 |

Bottle digging is always unpredictable and may take a little more energy and work than other types of urban treasure hunting. However, from my experience, after spending a glorious day probing and shoveling in the outdoors and then having a bunch of 100-year-or-older glass treasures to show for it, I guarantee that your perception and enjoyment of urban treasure hunting will take on an added dimension. Believe me, there are still plenty of good bottle-hunting spots around. Now it's your turn to be innovative and find these sites where you live. Dig one for me!

❦ 12 ❦

Caring for Finds

One of the most important things you can do as a treasure hunter is to take proper care of your finds. After all, you've gone through all the work of research and recovery, so why not make sure the financial, aesthetic, and educational values of the objects you find are maximized? The first major point to remember about this task is to start the process while the treasure object is still in the ground.

Very careful and precise recovery techniques are quite in order. Just by making the slightest scratch on a coin with a key date, you may cause the numismatic value to decline drastically. When bottle digging, be very careful not to mar the appearance of a fine specimen by being heavy handed with the shovel.

Think of yourself as a surgeon whose patient needs the most delicate touch for the operation to be a success. This is a skill that takes practice. But even before that, it requires an appreciation of why this process is so important. When a coin, metal artifact, or old bottle is removed from the ground after many years, the equilibrium that the object achieved with its surroundings is upset, exposing the object to certain physical and chemical changes. These are in addition to the changes that already occurred while the object was exposed to ground water and soluble salts. For example, an increased air temperature and exposure to oxygen may stimulate corrosion on metals. I've seen long-buried coins oxidize and change color right before my eyes.

What you want to do as soon as possible with any newly dug object is stabilize it to prevent further deterioration. Initially, you should give it a superficial cleaning by brushing off any loose soil.

You should also have appropriate field storage containers (film containers, zippered plastic bags, net bags) available to hold your recoveries. These can be carried in a small fanny pack.

In this chapter, we will discuss how to properly care for the coins, metal relics, bottles, and Native American artifacts you recover while treasure hunting. We will review how to clean them using the various methods currently available, and then how to display them with protection being a key goal.

COINS

Urban treasure hunting can turn you into an avid coin collector, even if that was not your intention originally. It's hard not to become interested in the coins that you find, and you may want to display them. I've seen some impressive "dug" collections displayed by fellow members at my treasure hunting club meetings. What these skillful diggers all have in common is a good understanding of how to make a coin recovery, clean coins, grade coins, and display them in an attractive fashion.

The gold 1881 Half Eagle
$5 coin (top) was found in
New York City's Central Park,
while the eighteenth-century
Spanish 4-reale coin (left),
1830 United States Draped
Bust dime (right), and rough
Colonial-era Spanish
"piece of eight" (bottom)
were detected in other
parks around town.

Proper Coin Recovery

When recovering coins with a metal detector, always try to pinpoint the signal precisely before opening up the ground. Of course, to do this you need a reasonable working knowledge of your machine. Next, take your digging tool and cut a small, downward slanting, three-quarter circle around the target. Then, gently lift up the ground from the perimeter of the circle in towards the center, creating a replaceable soil flap.

In the course of digging, a coin will sometimes change position in the hole. If the target does not appear right away, continue to pinpoint and dig until it does. When you locate it, carefully pick it up. If it seems to be a common coin, simply place it in your coin pouch.

If the coin appears to be old and the date is not quite legible, fight the novice tendency to rub the coin until its features are readable. Rubbing a valuable coin can cause scratches because various ground and oxidative deposits will cling to its surface when freshly dug.

Instead, wrap the coin in a tissue or place it in an empty film container, and take it home for further cleaning and evaluation. Never put a potentially valuable coin unprotected in a coin pouch with other change, since this tremendously increases the likelihood of abrasive damage.

Initial Cleaning

At home and under controlled conditions, your first step should be to do an initial cleaning of your coin finds. This should just be a simple soaking in mild dish detergent, which will loosen many of the soil particles clinging to the coins. Lightly brushing the coins with a toothbrush under running water will speed the process. Silver and gold coins usually don't need any more than this, since they have a very high resistance to the influences of air and soil, and don't form oxides. However, silver will sometimes become tarnished after com-

Resist the urge to use metal polish on valuable coins. Old coins and tokens like these may look pretty when shined up, but they lose a great deal of their value.

ing into contact with sulfur, forming silver sulfide, which presents as a gray-to-black coating.

A preliminary wash should reveal enough detail to confirm whether the coin is indeed an unusual or rare find. If it is, do not do any further cleaning because you may ruin the smooth patina that has formed on the coin after resting many years in the soil.

Patination, or the presence of a patina, can be described as a metallurgical condition resulting from the natural aging process that certain metals, most commonly copper and copper alloys (such as brass and bronze), go through. It is a chemical change that happens over time to the surface of coins and other artful metal objects, with the shiny newness becoming a more attractive, dull bluish green tone. Variables affecting the degree of patination are the type of soil and its chemical components, moisture, temperature, and length of burial.

Never use metal polish on a valuable coin. The coin may look pretty when you're done, but a rare old coin that's been shined up loses a great deal of its value. When encountering a coin with a rare date, I recommend consulting a numismatic expert to arrange for a professional cleaning. Believe me, many a valuable coin has been ruined by ignorance of the correct procedure.

Alloys

To better understand the coin-cleaning process, you should first know that most coins are alloys—a mixture of two or more elements in various percentages that require different cleaning treatments.

All American coins are struck from alloys. For example, the wartime variety (1942 to 1945) Jefferson nickel is 56-percent copper, 35-percent silver, and 9-percent manganese. It usually comes up green due to oxidation of the copper component, which may cause the finder to shout, "War nickel!" Silver coins always consist of alloys, and oxidation can occur on the nonsilver component. Therefore, you should start out using a mild copper-cleaning method that will not attack the silver.

It's always important to know what type of alloy you're facing. Suppose you find a valuable old foreign coin or even an ancient coin that a collector has lost. I know of an instance in which Roman coins were found by a detectorist in New York City. Cleaning foreign or ancient coins like more common American coins can spell disaster.

Two major categories of collectible United States tokens are Hard Times tokens and Civil War tokens. Hard Times tokens alleviated a coin shortage between 1832 and 1844. Civil War tokens were issued from 1861 to 1864 by merchants of more than three hundred towns in twenty-three states because of another coin shortage.

Mechanical and Chemical Cleaning

If your initial cleaning of a coin find does not remove all the dirt, you have two further coin-cleaning directions from which to choose—mechanical cleaning and chemical cleaning. Which route you take will depend on the metal components of the coin. Whether you choose mechanical cleaning, which can be more effective than chemical cleaning, will also depend on the metal hardness of the coin. (See "The Metal Hardness Scale," below.) An example of a mechanical method is using an ink-erasing rubber pencil on a hard-metal coin such as the war nickel I just described. The most delicate mechanical treatment is rubbing a coin with your fingers. Other mechanical cleaning materials include steel wool, wood, bone, and a glass brush. Needless to say, there is no single road to success when cleaning coins.

The chemical treatments for coins are based on the use of chemicals that dissolve the oxidative coating without attacking the coin metal itself, followed by the removal of the dissolved coating. Several methods are available, depending on the metal, but not every method gives the same result due to the differences in the coin alloys

The Metal Hardness Scale

The hardness of the metals in a coin or other metal object is what makes the object resistant to abrasion, scratching, and other types of damage when subjected to a mechanical cleaning method.

No absolute standard for metal hardness exists, but the following list provides a practical ranking from hardest (nickel) to softest (lead) of the metals that you may one day consider for a mechanical cleaning. Always proceed with caution.

- Nickel (hardest metal)
- Iron
- Platinum (precious metal with highest melting point)
- Copper
- Zinc
- Silver
- Gold
- Aluminum
- Tin
- Lead (softest metal)

Some cleaning processes will wear a coin's surface, and even though the coin will look brighter, it will lose value to a collector.

and admixtures. Always use a glass or porcelain dish for a chemical bath; never use a metal container.

If you find a bent coin that needs to be cleaned, first place the coin between hardwood blocks and gently hammer over the bend. A bent-coin repair will probably never be perfect, and a kink that follows the curvature of the coin is practically impossible to remove, but at least your find will look and feel like a coin. Afterwards, proceed with your chosen cleaning treatment.

For a comprehensive treatise on the intricacies of coin cleaning, I recommend *Cleaning and Preservation of Coins and Medals* by Gerhard Welter (Sanford J. Durst, 1987).

Keeping Things Uncomplicated

I've learned that most of my finds don't need a high level of complex attention. Here's a frequent scenario: Suppose a coin is old or interesting, but without a particularly rare date, and you want to clean it just for reference or display, or for the Find of the Month Contest at your treasure hunting club. Some common household products will achieve a satisfactory appearance. For example, if the coin is copper or brass, first soak it in olive oil for a week or so. The oil will penetrate the outer grime and loosen it without causing any pitting. You can then remove this layer by gently scraping with a toothpick. Another widely used method for oxidized copper or tarnished silver coins is to mix a paste of water and baking soda, and then, using your fingers, to gently work this compound over the coin for two minutes. This will loosen much of the outer oxidative crust. Next, rinse the coin in water, then soak it in vinegar, which is a mild acid, for three minutes. You may need to repeat these treatments if the oxidation or tarnish is heavy, but the outcome will generally be good—or, as good as possible due to the normal wear the coin received while it was still in circulation. In the case of a heavily encrusted coin, skip the water rinse and place the coin directly in the vinegar.

There are other methods for cleaning coins, including soaking them in either strong ammonia or an industrial-strength toilet cleaner containing muriatic acid, rinsing, and then rubbing on a paste of baking soda. A friend of mine has developed a technique whereby he rubs an encrusted coin with a scouring pad such as Brillo that has been coated with olive oil to loosen the oxidative deposits. His copper finds turn out beautiful, with an even green patina. However, this method takes practice to develop the right touch. A similar approach is to use a brass brush, which will remove the dirt and encrustation fairly quickly, yet is soft enough not to damage the metal of the coin.

An efficient instrument for cleaning coins is the ultrasonic cleaner, which simultaneously provides a chemical and a mechanical treatment. The coin is placed in the container with the cleaning fluid appropriate for its metal content. When turned on, the device produces high-frequency sound vibrations that force the cleaning fluid into all of the coin's surface irregularities. At the same time, the coin's surface is set into intense vibration, so that corrosion and other foreign deposits are broken loose and separated.

This device is available through metal detector dealers and jewelers. It won't always completely take off hard-crust oxidation, but it's still a worthwhile accessory because it cleans a large number of coins quickly.

A Word of Warning

Along the way, other well-meaning urban treasure hunters may tell you about their favorite coin-cleaning methods. A word of warning is in order here, since not all treasure hunters qualify for the Nobel Prize in Chemistry. Never try a new technique on a potentially valuable coin until you have first tested it on one that is expendable. Heed my words or you may destroy what you worked so very hard to find!

Clad Coins

Clad coins have a 95-percent copper and 5-percent nickel composition and, beginning in 1965, replaced the 90-percent silver coins that were in circulation. This coinage is subject to a discoloring metallurgical change after being buried in the ground for a while.

Daily city life tends to utilize enough money-taking machines that recirculation of discolored coins should not be a big problem. However, some banks and stores are not particularly keen to accept strange-looking money, and if you happen to be a heavy-duty coin hunter and find more clad coins than you can easily recirculate, the gem/rock tumbler could be your answer. This appliance costs about $50 and is commonly used by heavy-duty coin hunters to clean large numbers of discolored clad coins with excellent results. Gem/rock tumblers are sold through lapidary equipment suppliers, hobby shops, and advertisements in treasure hunting magazines.

The tumbling cycle lasts for twenty-four hours and produces a socially acceptable—and spendable—end product. The coins are tumbled in a mixture consisting of water, detergent, ammonia, and pea-size gravel. For the best results, follow the instructions that come with the tumbler, and make sure not to overload it. Too many coins per load will decrease the device's efficiency, since there won't be enough room for the proper abrasive action between the coins and the gravel.

Some treasure hunters have a creative way of using their clad coin finds. Rather than spending them disparately, having them just filter through and be gone, they apply the found money to the specific purchase of a gold coin. This is certainly a good investment and can be highlighted as an appropriate achievement when tallying your treasure hunting success.

Grading Coins

The next step after cleaning a coin is to establish its grade. The categories range from various degrees of "uncirculated" to "poor." The higher the grade of the coin, the more the coin is worth. For a listing of the commonly used coin grades and their definitions, see page 179.

When grading the luster of a coin, the standard is to grade the intensity and integrity of the coin to reflect light within the luster attributes of that coin's mintage.

Grading is a skill that you can learn by viewing enlarged, detailed photographs of expertly graded "type" coins and then comparing them to your coins. Look for similarities, such as whether "Liberty" can be read on the headband of Barber coins. You may find a 5X or 10X magnifier quite helpful here. Also helpful will be a good reference book with excellent photos to guide you in the process. I recommend *Photograde: A Photographic Grading Encyclopedia for United States Coins* by James Ruddy (Golden Books, 1996) and *Official ANA Grading Standards for United States Coins*, Fifth Edition, edited by Kenneth Bessett and Abe Kosoff (Random House Children's Books, 1997). When grading a coin, always hold it by its edges, so you don't mar its surfaces.

Standards for Coin Grading

General standards for describing a coin's condition were established by collectors in the 1940s. These have been revised over the years. The following list provides a general idea of the currently accepted standards for deciding a coin's grade. Note that I've left out the four coin grades above "uncirculated," since coins of these higher mint-state grades are considered investments that people buy and probably won't be showing up in your finds pouch—unless you land a cache fresh from the mint! Most collectors find mint-state coins very difficult to grade.

- *Uncirculated (UNC).* The coin shows no evidence of circulation and has no surface wear. All the legends (lettering), the date, and the details of the design are extremely clear.

- *About uncirculated (AU).* The coin shows small traces of surface wear on its highest design points. It may be starting to lose some of its luster from being in contact with other coins, as indicated by the presence of wispy hairline marks in the field.

- *Extremely fine (EF).* The coin shows slight wear on the highest design points and in the field. All the fine details in the design are sharp, and the coin may still have some residual mint luster.

- *Very fine (VF).* The coin shows moderate wear on its highest features, and the field also shows some surface wear. Most of the major design details are still showing. The legends may be worn, but the outline of every letter is still complete and clear.

- *Fine (F).* The coin shows considerable, even wear on all the points of the design, which is still fairly bold. This is a desirable coin, even with these weaknesses.

- *Very good (VG).* The coin shows heavy wear on all portions of the design. However, the major portions of the design are still clear, but with an absence of fine detail. All the legends are complete, although some details are absent.

- *Good (G).* The coin shows very heavy wear, with some parts of the legend faint or entirely missing. The portrait outline and the design are weak. This is the lowest grade in which a coin is still considered collectible.

- *About good (AG).* The coin shows portions of the design worn away, and the date may be partly gone. Only a very scarce coin is acceptable in this grade.

- *Fair (FR).* The coin shows features that are barely identifiable. It may have only partial dates, be dark in color, or have design parts that are completely worn away. These coins are generally used as space fillers until better coins can be obtained. Only a rare coin would be desirable in this condition.

- *Poor (PR).* This coin is sometimes unidentifiable, since it may be bent, corroded, or completely worn down.

In terms of finding coins that grade high, we should all be as lucky as the San Francisco urban treasure hunter who detected an 1850 $10 gold piece in a Bay Area vacant lot. This coin turned out to be only the seventh-known Dubosq $10 gold piece, as indicated by the word "Dubosq" on Liberty's headband, and is in the finest condition of all the known specimens.

Appropriately, this lucky treasure hunter had his wonderful find authenticated by the American Numismatic Association (ANA) and received an official ANA Certificate of Authenticity to support its estimated value of $50,000. I would like to think that one day, a coin of that stature will show up under my searchcoil.

Protecting and Displaying Coins

Now that you have cleaned and graded your coins, you need to take precautions to maintain them in the best possible condition. Your major consideration should be protecting them from physical and atmospheric damage. Of course, you can store all your coins in a moisture-proof safe, but that's no fun. Therefore, you have to take into consideration the factors relating to presentation and ease of availability. What you really want is a secure, attractive, and convenient method that allows easy access to view the coins. For security reasons, you should always keep very valuable coins in a bank vault.

Once again, you have a variety of commonly employed display methods from which to choose. Some people like to use coin folders that are made of heavy cardboard and that accommodate a particular collecting direction, such as Barber dimes, Buffalo nickels, Seated Liberty quarters, or Indian Head cents. The coins are simply pushed into prelabeled spaces in the folder according to their dates and mint marks. However, this method has one major disadvantage—it permits viewing only one side of the coin.

My preference is for a simple, inexpensive product called a "coin mount," which is a 2-inch-square cardboard frame that has a clear, Mylar-lined window the size of the coin and provides accessibility, protection, and easy viewing.

Once a mount is stapled shut, the coin inside is secure, and both its obverse and reverse (head and tail) can be viewed. You can also make notations on the mount regarding where and when the coin was found, its grade, and its current value.

After preparing a few mounts, your next step is to place them in clear vinyl loose-leaf pages that are made with rows of exact-size pockets for this purpose. These pages are readily available with coin mounts at hobby shops and coin dealers.

Your final step is to place the pages in a three-ring binder, giving you a fine, expandable medium to display your best coin finds. The process is very easy and economical, and will provide ongoing and meaningful satisfaction when you look back on the hunt that added so well to your growing coin collection.

METAL RELICS

It's always an experience to recover an old historical relic. These can be made of iron, copper, brass, lead, or pewter. Of course, you should take the necessary steps to preserve them. When cleaned and displayed properly, they are a well-earned tribute to your metal detecting skills.

Reviving Metal Relics

Iron relics are especially sensitive to oxygen, forming oxides or rust, and are seldom found in uncontaminated condition. Salts that act as an electrolyte with ground water will increase the level of corrosion, and some relics may become somewhat unrecognizable.

When it comes to removing rust and corrosion from iron relics such as guns, knives, and cannonballs, once again you have two main categories of treatment from which to select—chemical and mechanical. Chemical baths are efficient, but sometimes they take off too much of the relic and leave an uneven appearance. Therefore, you have to make sure you follow the manufacturer's directions and work the relic in a slow and deliberate manner, especially if it is heavily rusted.

The local hardware store should have a few different chemical treatments from which to choose. I would start out with the mildest. You don't want a relic that looks overcleaned, without eye appeal, but rather something that will look good on display and when photographed. For slightly rusted relics, remove most of the rust with a steel brush, holding the object under water while working. A high-speed sander/polisher with a small, soft wire wheel, such as the Dremel Multipro Rotary Tool, can be very helpful for fine detail work.

For cleaning a cannonball, I would employ a mechanical method—specifically, using a hammer to loosen most of the surface rust, followed by a good buffing with course steel wool. Remember, after restoration you have to think preservation, and applying a few coats of the spray lubricant WD-40 is the prescribed choice here. Presto, there you have it—a fine looking trophy for display!

Electrolysis

To clean heavily rusted relics, I prefer using electrolysis. Electrolysis does not utilize any hazardous chemicals, even though it is technically considered a chemical method. I learned about electrolysis from a very experienced "Son of the South" Civil War relic hunter who has used it quite extensively with good results. Electrolysis is a common method used in many industries to remove oxidation from metals by separating out its components or to add a protective metal coating.

However, be careful when using electrolysis to clean a small relic such as a buckle, skeleton key, or tool because the rust may be holding the item together. Removing the rust could cause the item to fall apart. In such a case, consider your risks ahead of time. It may be more judicious to simply clean the dirt off and have a rough-looking display piece rather than to have no piece at all.

To clean a relic by electrolysis, all you need are:

Regulated 12-volt, 2.5-amp power supply

2 wires, about 3 feet long each

Alligator clips

Stainless steel spoon or galvanized zinc strip

Pocketknife, file, and wire brush

Plastic bucket of appropriate size

Water

Salt

The steps to follow are:

1. Attach the wires to the power supply, one to the positive terminal and the other to the negative terminal.

2. Attach an alligator clip to the free end of each wire, then clip the positive line to the spoon or zinc strip, and the negative line to the rusted relic (see Figure 12.1). You may need to scrape some of the rust off the relic using the pocketknife, file, and/or wire brush to get a good electrical contact.

3. Position the spoon or zinc strip and the rusted relic about $1^{1}/_{2}$ inches apart on the bottom of the plastic bucket and add enough water to just cover the relic.

4. Add 2 tablespoons of salt.

5. Turn on the juice.

You should immediately observe a reaction taking place and a line of bubbles starting to come from the relic. If you don't see this reaction, the relic and spoon wires are probably reversed. Just turn

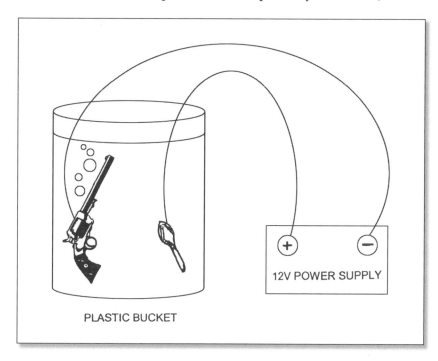

Figure 12.1

Clip the positive line to the spoon or zinc strip and the negative line to the rusted relic.

off the power and reconnect the wires. My experience has been that the cleaning process goes more rapidly when the relic is placed on an angle against the inside wall of the bucket, since this allows more surface area to be exposed.

After a while, the water will turn rusty and a brown sludge will form on the surface. Change the water and salt every two to three hours, and check the alligator clip connected to the spoon or zinc strip because it may have become corroded and need to be replaced. If the relic is large, rotate it in the bucket to attain maximum effect. Your prized relic should be pretty clean after a few treatments.

To finish, give the relic a few coats of a sealant. WD-40, Future Floor Wax, or artists' picture spray will also inhibit further oxidation. Cleaning by electrolysis is a safe and effective method and a great asset to the relic-collecting urban treasure hunter.

Copper and Brass

Copper and brass relics should be handled like copper and brass coins and treated with olive oil soaks. However, there is one added consideration. Whereas coins are usually found unbent, copper and brass relics (for example, military insignia and buckles) occasionally come out of the ground with their shapes distorted. If you try to unbend them, they usually crack because the metal at the bend has been crystallized and can't take the stress.

What should you do? *Never* attempt to straighten anything in the field. You will probably be sorry if you do! Once again, get your find home. Place it in a vise and apply heat at the bend with a butane torch until the flame turns green. This will destroy the crystallization and permit the object to be gently bent back to its original shape. However, this is a tricky procedure without a 100-percent success rate, and you may want to leave well enough alone. A bent buckle is preferable to a buckle in pieces.

Pewter

Pewter artifacts do not suffer too much from corrosion, although some soil conditions might cause long-buried pewter relics to develop an oxidative crust. If you find a pewter relic that's so affected, it's best to first gently brush it off under running water and allow it to dry. Then you can evaluate it with a magnifying glass, looking for any cracks or edge flaking.

Don't push your luck with pewter. If you find something small, such as an eighteenth-century Colonial-era army button, that does have some cracks or edge flaking, wrap it in cotton and isolate it to prevent further damage. You can still apply some gel such as Naval Jelly to enhance the button's appearance without leaving a strange shine. A light film of petroleum jelly is also an acceptable pewter protectant.

If the pewter object is larger, such as a spoon, and happens to be bent, take out your torch again. However, be particularly careful here, as pewter has a low melting temperature. If you reach that temperature— poof, it's gone! So, once again, consider stopping before this critical point and being satisfied with simply cleaning the spoon with Mr. Clean multi-purpose cleaner, which is very effective on pewter.

Lead

Lead seldom needs any cleaning treatment. However, if tarnish or corrosion does appear, you can remove it by brushing or by using a mild household cleaner that doesn't contain ammonia, such as Mr. Clean. The best-looking outcome is a smooth, white oxidative patina.

Unsticking Moveable Parts

Moveable parts, as in old toys, pocket knives, locks, and guns, should move. If they don't, soak the object in penetrating oil for twelve hours, then lightly tap it with a small hammer and try working the mechanism. If necessary, repeat these three steps. You should achieve a satisfactory outcome.

Displaying Relics

It's up to you how to creatively display your historical metal relics. Don't bury your finds *again* by sticking them in a closet or drawer. Keep them well displayed to inspire further success. Place them on a wooden stand, in a cabinet, on an étagère, or just here and there. I like using the cannonball I found in Brooklyn as a paperweight at work. It keeps me in touch.

Excavated metal artifacts and coins undergo changes as the temperature and humidity change seasonally. Therefore, when viewing them, pay attention for any signs of change on the surface, which may indicate that additional cleaning and preservation measures are

necessary. Also, try not to place your metal relics in an improper storage environment, since this can undo all your efforts.

For small, flat relics, you can use flips, an inexpensive display device made of vinyl. Flips are primarily used for protecting single coins, but they are also quite suitable for items such as buttons, religious medals, badges, good luck tokens, fobs, small militaria, keys, and dog tags. They are available through coin dealers.

BOTTLES

Bottles present different problems for the obvious reason that they are made of glass and can break easily. Wonderful specimens can and have been destroyed by careless handling. You really want to bring a bottle

I was very proud when I recovered this Revolutionary War cannonball in an area where the 42nd Regiment of Royal Highlanders saw action and not far from where the Hessians camped in New York City. This cannonball was once included in *Western & Eastern Treasures* magazine's "10 Best Finds of the Year" annual issue.

home in as mint condition as possible, or at least in as good condition as it came out of the ground. This also means no scratches, cracks, chips, or any other flaws caused by your handling.

Suppose you're digging a test pit and part of a bottle becomes exposed. That's the time to lay down the heavy equipment and reach for something like a butter knife to release the bottle from its earthy tomb. Carefully scrape away the surrounding soil and free the prize with your hand.

You can admire bottles in the field, but you should not clean them there because the right materials are necessary for the best possible outcome. Cleaning is also much more easily accomplished at home, where running water is available. Furthermore, when prospecting for old bottles, you should be prepared to wrap them in newspaper and place them in a safe carrying container.

Soaking Bottles

To properly clean a bottle, let it reach room temperature, then soak it in a thoroughly mixed solution of lukewarm water and 25-percent ammonia or bleach. If the bottle is very dirty, it may have to soak for a week. In that case, you should change the solution every two days for maximum response. When the bottle is ready, scrub it using a stiff nylon brush. Nylon brushes come in many sizes and shapes, and can be purchased at most homecare stores.

Sometimes, the outside of a bottle becomes sufficiently clean, but the inside still needs a little help. One way to clean the inside of a bottle is to mix sand or uncooked rice with water and dishwashing detergent, fill the bottle, and shake it. This usually dislodges any grime and sediment the brush couldn't reach.

The next step is to air-dry the bottle in a safe place, one where it won't be exposed to any activity that may endanger it. The kitchen sink area may seem safe enough, but to my way of thinking, it is a center for too much activity to ensure total safety for antique bottles. Find a more secure place!

Further Cleaning

On occasion, even after you have put a bottle through the entire cleaning process, it will still remain coated, inside and out, with a haze resulting from a chemical reaction between soil minerals, ground water, and the glass. This can detract from a bottle's value and display quality.

For a quick fix, you can use baby oil. A light coating will hide the haze as long as the oil stays viable. Timely touchups will maintain a less-than-perfect bottle as an attractive decoration. Just remember to handle the bottle even more carefully than normal and not let it slip out of your hands.

A permanent fix will mandate going the chemical route. Fortunately, a product called Dexter's Stain Remover will do the job very well. The treatment involves soaking the entire bottle for ten minutes and then rinsing. One treatment is usually sufficient for most mineral, rust, and calcium-deposit problems. Make sure to follow the manufacturer's instructions, and take care with this caustic fluid.

Chemical techniques are worth the trouble for a super bottle. However, for ordinary bottles, a good scrubbing followed by an application of baby oil should be sufficient. Curiously, some plain bottles take on an ancient and mysterious look when hazy. It's all in the eye of the beholder.

Displaying Bottles

When you get your bottles to an acceptable condition for display, you have a choice of ways to show them off. Some people build special cabinets with mirrored backlighting. It's a fantastic sight, and the people who do this really love their bottles. I'm more traditional and prefer to leave mine along windowsills so they can absorb sunlight.

The reason I prefer this simpler method is that the pre–World War I glass-making process included adding manganese to the mix, which caused a slight amethyst tint in clear "white" glass. However, over a period of time, when exposed to sunlight, these slightly purple bottles turn an attractive darker purple hue.

I remember the first time I noticed that a bottle had turned a darker purple and was amazed when I found out why. Some serious collectors employ a purpling box to speed up the process by shining a light bulb of a specific spectrum on their bottles. This concentrated method works in a shorter time period than day-to-day light and produces some beautiful specimens.

NATIVE AMERICAN ARTIFACTS

Native American artifacts made of hard stone usually don't need more than a washing with soap and warm water. However, porous stone artifacts are another story, since they may contain salt, which will crystallize under dry conditions and cause the artifact's surface to flake off.

Therefore, when dealing with artifacts made of porous stone, bone, antler, shell, or a similar material, first check for the presence of salt. Do this by placing the artifact in fresh water and adding a drop or two of silver nitrate, which you can purchase at a pharmacy. If salt is present, the water will become cloudy.

To remove the salt, let the artifact soak in fresh water for a couple of hours. Retest for salt, and repeat the soaking and testing process until the water remains clear.

For some good ideas on how to show off your Native American artifact finds, get a copy of *Indian-Artifact Magazine* and review the featured collections and attractive assortment of advertised display cases. You can also use these cases for displaying your metal-detecting finds.

A PHOTOGRAPHIC RECORD

A final step you can take—and should take in some cases—is making a photographic record of your finds. Some of your treasure finds may be valuable enough to be insured, so a photo record is in order. In addition, having photographs of your recoveries is an important part of recordkeeping, plus it eliminates the need to carry the finds themselves around, exposing them to the possibility of being damaged or lost.

By following my advice for the care and preservation of your finds, your enjoyment of the whole treasure hunting experience will be greatly enhanced. You will also develop useful skills that will significantly increase your overall personal versatility—the trademark of the urban treasure hunter. What could be better?

Collector display cases are a perfect way to exhibit your prehistoric Native American artifacts.

❧ 13 ❧

Cashing In

Sooner or later, you will accumulate a substantial number of valuable treasure items and may want to evaluate their monetary value. Or, you may make a particularly dazzling discovery that will start you thinking about early retirement. For whatever reason—a possible sale, insurance purposes, or plain curiosity—you should be able to ascertain the correct market value of your treasure.

Superior investigation skills brought you good fortune, so don't stop using them when the time comes to cash in. There are plenty of people who would most certainly make you an offer that would drastically undervalue your find, particularly in a big city. Unsuspecting souls are fleeced all the time. Hopefully, you're too smart for that and are willing to make the effort to receive a proper monetary return.

In this chapter, we will review how to assess the value of your treasure hunting finds and how to sell them to obtain the best returns. We will also discuss how you can market your treasure hunting skills to earn extra income.

You really don't want to earn the reputation as the blockhead who sold a $50,000 coin for $25.

GOOD REFERENCES

The first step you should take to properly assess the value of your treasure is to become familiar with the recognized identification and value guides. The following three books should cover many of the items you recover: *A Guide Book of United States Coins: The Official Red Book* by R. S. Yeoman (Whitman Coin Publishers, 2003), *Bottles: Iden-*

tification and Price Guide by Michael Polak (Avon, 2000), and *North American Indian Artifacts: A Collector's Identification and Value Guide* by Lar Hothem (Krause, 1998).

A more complete list, along with other useful treasure hunting reference books, is provided in Appendix A. These books will supply the general prices that have previously been paid or that can be expected to be paid. While some don't provide specific values, once you make an identification, you can determine a price through other means. You should be aware, though, that the true value of any treasure item is the actual price paid for it at the time of the sale. This is usually negotiable in some way, and flexibility is a virtue in that respect.

If you can't locate a reference to your particular item in any of the guides, it's probably something very uncommon and you should consult a competent professional, such as an expert at a museum or university. Also, the better auction houses in your city will have qualified people on staff who can provide an identification and a verbal estimated value at no charge.

When your treasure turns out to be something special, the auction house will even sell it for you for a small commission. This is not a bad deal considering the auction house does all the work, reaches the most interested people, and receives some good prices for quality pieces. You can also auction your treasure through an online auction service such as eBay (http://ebay.com).

AVOID THE MIDDLEMAN

You will always do better selling your collectible finds directly to a private collector than to a dealer because dealers' offers tend to be on the low side due to their legitimate need to make a profit. A collector may be accustomed to paying dealer prices, and you may be able to reach an agreement that approaches the higher range of value. First, however, you have to know that figure.

For most collectibles, aside from the supply available, condition is the most important variable in determining price. Buyers are interested in items that are as flawless as possible. The better the condition, the greater the price will be at sale.

When negotiating with collectors, you should be aware of something called the "completion factor." When a collector needs what

> Anything that you find older than fifty years is worth keeping. Somebody probably collects it and may pay you for it. If there is a date imprinted on it, all the better.

> When selling your treasure, a good rule to follow is to try to know more about the items than the buyer

you have found to fill a certain direction in his or her collection, the collector may be willing to bargain less and pay more. This should not be taken as an invitation to take advantage of the collector. However, it is something about the buyer's mentality to take into account when haggling over price.

ADVERTISE YOUR FINDS

The informed urban treasure hunter's research should include identifying local collecting organizations, such as bottle and coin clubs. These clubs generally have newsletters in which you can advertise your finds. Better yet, join the club and personally get to know the members. I'm sure you'll pick up a lot of useful information about their intriguing hobby—and maybe make some new friends.

You may also find it productive to advertise your finds to collectors through specialty magazines. For example, *Indian-Artifact Magazine* and *Prehistoric Antiquities and Archaeological News Quarterly* are excellent publications in which to place ads to sell your authentic prehistoric relics, while the mainstream metal detecting magazines always seem to have ads placed by collectors offering to purchase finds. *Antique Bottle and Glass Collector* is the premier bottle-collecting magazine and has a large "For Sale" section that reaches a very enthusiastic collector audience. Give it a try.

Aside from coins, large collector groups exist for tokens, watch fobs, antique jewelry, relics, buttons, military items, cast lead toys, barbed wire, square nails, and more.

SELLING JEWELRY

Operating a metal detector in a city should produce a good amount of gold and silver jewelry from local parks, beaches, and assorted other places. Quite commonly, the monetary value you will be offered for this booty will be based solely on the spot price of the precious metal content of the individual pieces.

Before going to sell a piece, it's always a good idea to check the latest closing spot price of its precious metal, which can be found in most newspapers and on the CNN financial page at http://money.cnn.com. This information will serve as a good baseline figure so you won't be cheated. Prices may vary slightly during the trading day, but not by much. This method of sale is perfectly acceptable, and most urban areas have many buy-and-sell shops that do business based on the daily fluctuating value of precious metals.

However, my experience has shown that you can't go into all of these places and expect to be treated fairly, especially if a gemstone is involved. You have to prepare by determining the weights of the items you would like to sell and learning how to figure the correct prices. As a good start, you may want to acquire an accurate gram/pennyweight scale to weigh the jewelry at home. You might also find it useful to purchase a metallurgical test kit to evaluate the quality of the gold in your treasures. Both the scale and the test kit are readily available from metal detector dealers and through the treasure hunting magazines.

Testing Gold

Some basic facts first. Most gold objects are alloys and contain other metals to give them hardness and strength. The simplest gold assay is based on the fact that nitric acid attacks other metals, but not gold. In a purity appraisal, some of the gold to be tested is rubbed off on a test stone, which is dabbed with concentrated nitric acid. If the gold is pure, the streak remains. If alloys are involved, a varying amount disappears. If there is no gold, the streak vanishes completely.

A more precise appraisal test, the Metal Trade Gold Assay, is based on the fact that a certain mix of acids called "aqua regia" (one part nitric acid and three parts hydrochloric acid) dissolves gold. One commercially available kit contains several vials of varying concentrations of aqua regia, along with a test stone for streaking. The concentrations are applied in order of strength to try to attack the streak, eventually revealing the gold's fineness.

The Gold Formula

The fineness of jewelry gold is indicated by its karat rating, usually noted on the underside as a number followed by a "K." The higher the karat number, the more pure gold the object contains. The highest karat rating is 24 karat, which stands for 100-percent purity. The solid gold bars in Fort Knox are 24 karat. The lowest karat rating used in jewelry, such as graduation rings, is 10 karat. The most common rating seems to be 14 karat, but 18 karat is also very common and is used mostly in gold chains.

In general, jewelers and precious metal brokers do not use the ounce system when weighing gold for cash evaluation. They use an equivalent system in which the pennyweight, abbreviated as "DWT" or "PWT," is the main measuring standard. Converting pennyweights to ounces is simple once you know the procedure.

To start, there are 20 pennyweights per 1 troy ounce of gold. Now suppose that the weight of a 14-karat wedding band on a pennyweight scale is 4 pennyweights. That, according to Table 13.1, is equal to .2 troy ounce of metal. By looking at Table 13.2, you will see that 14-karat gold has a purity of 58.5 percent. Taking the troy ounce weight of the ring (.2 troy ounce) and multiplying it by its purity (58.5 percent, or .585) will give you the total amount of pure sellable gold in the ring (.117 troy ounce).

TABLE 13.1 CONVERSION OF PENNYWEIGHTS TO TROY OUNCES OF GOLD			
Pennyweights	Troy Ounces	Pennyweights	Troy Ounces
2	.1	14	.7
4	.2	16	.8
6	.3	18	.9
8	.4	20	1.0
10	.5	30	1.5
12	.6	40	2.0

The standard weight measure of gold jewelry is by pennyweight. There are 20 pennyweights in 1 troy ounce of gold.

The next calculation is to multiply the total gold amount (.117 troy ounce) by the spot price of gold that day. For demonstration's sake, let's say that figure is $350. Multiplying .117 troy ounce by $350 will give you the honest bullion value of $40.95, which is the value of your ring. Not hard to figure at all!

TABLE 13.2 PERCENT GOLD CONTENT BY KARAT MARKING			
Marked Karat	% Pure Gold	Marked Karat	% Pure Gold
24K	100% (pure gold)	16K	66.6%
22K	91.6%	14K	58.5%
20K	83.3%	12K	50.0%
18K	75.0%	10K	41.6%

The karat marking on a piece of gold jewelry indicates its percentage content of pure gold.

The Silver Formula

Silver is the other precious metal with which you will be most involved. Jewelry and coins made of this metal also have standardized markings and silver-content weights. Most often, silver jewelry is marked "sterling." By looking at Table 13.3, you will see that all jewelry so marked is 92.5-percent pure silver.

TABLE 13.3 PERCENT SILVER CONTENT BY MARKED FINENESS	
Marked Fineness or Type of Item	% Silver Content
Marked .999	99.9%
Marked .925	92.5%
Sterling	92.5%
Marked .900	90.0%
Pre-1965 silver coins	90.0%
English silver	80.0%

German silver is a silver-colored white alloy of copper, zinc, and nickel commonly used in a variety of decorative objects. However, there is no silver content. Don't be fooled by the name.

If you have a sterling silver object and want to sell it according to its bullion value, you should use the following procedure. For our example, let's say you have a group of sterling silver objects that have a cumulative weight of 5 ounces. First, multiply the percent of pure silver (92.5 percent, or .925) by the ounce weight of the objects (5 ounces) to get the total weight of pure silver (4.625 ounces). Next, multiply the total silver amount (4.625 ounces) by the spot price of silver that day. Again, the current spot price of 1 ounce of pure silver is listed in most newspapers, but for our example, let's say it's $5.75. Multiplying 4.625 ounces by $5.75 will give you a true bullion value of $26.59 for your small hoard of sterling silver objects.

Table 13.3 also shows that United States silver coins from 1964 and earlier are 90-percent pure silver. To determine such a coin's true bullion value, use the same formula, but also try to ascertain whether the coin's numismatic value is more than its "melt value." When silver prices run high, as they did in the early 1980s, competing precious metal brokers will advertise their rates per silver coin in the local newspaper. Always shop around for the best deal.

Into the Bazaars

Never sell to a broker who asks you how much money you want or otherwise tries to back you into a corner before even weighing the item you're interested in selling. This is highly unethical. The broker is sizing you up as someone who is ignorant of the correct procedure and is hoping that you are underestimating the true value of your items or will sell them out of desperation. Head for the door because you are dealing with a shady character. Who needs that?

Out of curiosity, I decided to take a small survey of four precious metal brokers located around my neighborhood to find out who was honest. For my trouble, I received four different values for the same piece of gold jewelry, each based solely on bullion weight. Only one offer was correct. The person who gave me the lowest price even told me, with a smirk, that my 14-karat stamped butterfly pin was made of an inferior type of gold and not worth much. He said he was doing me a favor offering me his "best price"! His price was half that of the one honest broker in the experiment. The offers from the other two brokers were about 75-percent of the actual value. Cities are filled with such pitfalls, and you need to be careful.

When in a broker's shop to transact business, never let the object you would like to sell out of your sight. All metallurgical tests should be performed in front of you and not in a back room. If a precious stone is involved, be particularly careful. Diamonds can be switched with glass very quickly. For a potentially high-grade stone, first get an appraisal by a gemologist who has no interest in purchase. Once informed of its correct value, you can't be cheated, only out-negotiated. Above all, *don't throw yourself to the wolves*! They're out there waiting.

When you're in a poker game with strangers and can't figure out who the sucker is…it's probably you!

Get a Jewelry Catalog

An important aid to interpreting the value of many of the trendy jewelry items you may recover is a current jewelry catalog from a large department store or mail-order jewelry company. Such a catalog will contain pictures and retail prices of an entire jewelry line. Chances are you can locate a particular find or something similar within the catalog.

You can then offer your find to a friend or coworker at a discount, which will still be more than the bullion value alone would bring and less than what would be charged by a store. A good deal for everybody!

Antique Jewelry

Antique jewelry presents an additional problem because, once again, you may be at the mercy of someone more informed than you. In this case, I recommend a field trip to dealers in antique jewelry to look for similar items, asking about prices without mentioning that you have a piece like it for sale. That can come at a later date. This research will give you a ballpark market price to work around for whatever you decide to do. Again, auction houses can also be most helpful for evaluating antique jewelry.

THE WRITER IN YOU

At some point, you may decide to start writing articles about your adventures and finds for a treasure hunting magazine. That's how I started my writing career—as a freelancer sharing my New York City escapades in *Western & Eastern Treasures* magazine. Actually, when I'm asked what my best find is, I usually answer, "My writing career." I'm very flattered that over the years my articles have been so well accepted by the treasure hunting public. This book, *The Urban Treasure Hunter,* is a good example of how my enthusiasm for treasure hunting, combined with my gradually developing writing skills, has led to a highly respected and marketable source of useful information.

Editors are always looking for interesting how-to material from untapped sources. Perhaps you'll develop a whole new way of doing things that the treasure hunting public will be eager to hear about. Most magazines have writers' guidelines that freelancers are asked to follow. If and when you reach that point, contact the magazines to which you'd like to submit material and request a copy. This is just one more aspect of urban treasure hunting that will expand your horizons—and is also another way of "cashing in."

THOUGHTS FOR YOUR PENNIES

For you speculators out there, consider this interesting point about pennies. Since 1982, the common copper penny has no longer been composed mostly of copper. That was the year zinc took over. There were two types of pennies minted in 1982—the familiar copper (95-percent copper and 5-percent zinc) and the new "zincers" (97.5 percent zinc and 2.5-percent copper). From 1983 to the present, only the zinc variety has been minted because copper pennies are now speculatively worth more than a penny due to copper's status as a strategic metal. This has led to the hoarding of 95-percent copper cents by profiteers. I've heard of some people with over a million copper cents who are just waiting for the metal's price to rise so they can sell them off and make a killing.

There is a precedent for that logic. After clad coins were introduced in 1965, silver coins soon disappeared from circulation. When silver's spot price went up to $50 per ounce in 1980, people unloaded their hoards and took hefty profits.

Metals commodities analysts have been predicting a similar future for copper, with a significant increase in prices. That's why some treasure hunters, including myself, are saving found copper cents. I'm not getting rolls of pennies from the bank to weed them out, but rather am putting those copper pennies that I routinely pull out of the ground into a special gallon container to help pay for my retirement ranch.

Even without looking at the date, it's not hard to tell the difference between dug copper and zinc cents. While the coppers retrieved are relatively intact, the zincers may be badly corroded, as zinc is a very active metal and reduces quickly when exposed to the elements. Sometimes, after being buried for a while, zinc cents may no longer even be recognizable as coins.

FINDING LOST OR HIDDEN VALUABLES FOR A FEE

Another direction to explore to cash in on your treasure hunting talents is helping people locate lost or hidden valuables. Perhaps as a result of your public relations campaign to inform the world about the investigative services you can provide, or by an accidental field encounter, there will surely come a time when someone will need your searching skills. The most common scenarios are:

Recovered caches have contained cash, gold, stock certificates, weapons, jewelry, and ancient coins. There are probably many more hidden caches than found caches.

- Someone has passed away and the family can't locate the money or other valuables the deceased was known to have possessed.

- A person has lost an expensive or sentimental piece of jewelry while doing chores in the front or back yard of his or her home.

- A person cannot find a piece of jewelry or a set of keys after visiting a public park.

You may run into slight variations on these themes (see "Huge Silver Coin Cache Recovered in Milwaukee" on page 201), but these are the basic situations you are most likely to encounter. Most cities will have some interesting potential projects like these to explore.

Cache Hunting

In the first scenario, the relative of a deceased person who is known or believed to have stashed away money or valuables hires you to locate the hidden cache. Your first step should be to interview the deceased's relatives and friends to get a good idea of his or her lifestyle and favorite pastimes. You will need to learn how the person thought and gather information about his or her habits, likes and dislikes, and daily routines. Marcus Aurelius, the philosopher emperor of Rome from A.D. 161 to 180, said, "To understand the true quality of people, you must look into their minds and examine their pursuits and aversions." This tactic is most useful here.

Most people hide things in places within easy access so they can add to and withdraw from their cache without arousing suspicion. Such an easily accessible cache is known as a "working cache." People also like to be able to see the place in which their cache is hidden from a favorite vantage point, such as a bedroom window or a porch. Unless someone was extremely creative or devious, most working caches are findable—if they exist. Of course, some reports of hidden caches are just rumors or family lore.

If the deceased had a house with surrounding property, you may see so many potential concealment places that the job at hand may seem overwhelming. It's really not. By carefully fitting together all the pertinent facts and using analytical thinking, you should be able to develop a sensible plan of action to find the goods.

Long-time professional cache hunters say there are some favorite places that people tend to choose when hiding valuables. It makes sense to search these locations first. Therefore, when initi-

Years after Henry Ford died, his heirs continued to find cash hidden in his books and assorted other odd places. Once the habit of stashing away money begins, it can continue for years

Anyone hiding a cache lives in fear that it will be found.

Huge Silver Coin Cache Recovered in Milwaukee

A huge silver coin cache recovered in Milwaukee recently made national headlines. Treasure hunters were called in by a family to search their back yard for a large number of coin-filled milk cans that had been buried there in the early 1960s. As it happened, the person who put down this cache was the family's father, who had contracted a memory-affecting illness and could not remember where he had buried the milk cans. The treasure hunters did their job well using a variety of metal detectors and recovered a stash of silver coins weighing almost 1,000 pounds. This inspiring story demonstrates the potential out there for competent urban treasure hunters who market their talents.

ating a cache hunting project inside a house, be sure to investigate fireplaces, paneling around windows and doors, baseboards, rugs, closet floors and ceilings, sagging walls, peeling wallpaper, hidden compartments under stair steps, cabinets, the inside of pianos, bookcases, stored clothing, fishing tackle, and boxes in the attic and basement.

If your search indoors leads to a dead end, your next step should be to search outdoors. There are a number of often-used spots for stashing valuables on outer property as well. These include all outbuildings, such as garages, doghouses, and tool sheds. Other spots to carefully check are woodpiles and freshly dug areas in the garden. Also look under porches; inside clothesline poles (the caps come off); around large trees; in barbecues, disused cars, birdhouses, and birdbaths; and in any other places that look like they might conceal a cache. Try to think like the person who felt desperate enough to hide his or her belongings away from prying eyes and family members perceived to be greedy. Also, weigh that the person may not have been of sound mind—an important factor to consider.

The loss of mental faculties can be just as certain as death for keeping a cache a secret.

Protect Your Rights

Suppose you're successful and you locate the cache in the deceased's prize vegetable garden. What next? Do you stand around, humbly waiting for the family to be appreciative and give you a sandwich or a few dollars for your work?

No way! Before even turning on your metal detector or making one probe, you should negotiate the terms and conditions of the project and get a signed contract that will be valid and enforceable in a court of law. This will guarantee everyone's rights in the enterprise and is proper business procedure for any search and salvage agreement. A good example of such a contract is presented in Figure 13.1.

As the salvor, or person doing the salvaging, you are entitled to a fair, predetermined percentage of the cache or a flat fee for the services you render. I consider the salvor's proper share to be at least one-third, but not more than one-half, of the total amount recovered.

Even if you find nothing after a comprehensive search, you are still entitled to some compensation for your time and effort. Agree on a payment for this possibility beforehand and note it in the contract, unless you choose to base your fee totally on positive results. It's up to you to size up the project, make the best possible deal, and put it in writing.

KNOW WITH WHOM YOU'RE DEALING

Remember, you can't sign a binding and enforceable contract with anyone who does not have the legal standing to enter into such an agreement. For example, suppose you are approached by people who are "positive" that money is buried on property that is not theirs and offer you half to find it. You'd be very unwise to accept such a deal, since the contract would be considered invalid by a court because the people advancing the proposal did not have the legal standing to make the offer. It's not their property.

This is a very important point that can save you time, grief, and money. You may even be arrested for trespassing and get nothing for your work except a fine or worse—while making someone else rich. Always know with whom you are dealing, and ask to see proper documentation of property ownership.

When dealing with estates, do business only with the executor or court appointed guardian to ensure your rights and avoid problems. Things generally get very sticky when large sums of contested

Search and Salvage Agreement

This agreement, dated this _____ day of _____ in the year _____, is between _____, hereinafter known as the PROPERTY OWNER(S), and _____, hereinafter known as the SALVOR.

WITNESSES:

In consideration of the Salvor's undertaking to devote his/her time and equipment to search the premises described as: _____ _____ _____, the Property Owner(s) hearby agrees that the Salvor shall receive as compensation for his/her services _____ and/or _____ percent of all money, jewelry, artifacts, and _____ _____ that may have been lost or concealed in, on, or about the premises and recovered by the Salvor.

The Salvor is given full authority to work in, on, or about the above premises at any reasonable time, subject only to such notice as the Property Owner(s) may require in advance of such work. Each party waives any claim against the other for liability for any careless or negligent act or omission of the other arising out of or in consequence of the search provided for.

This agreement shall be effective for _____ days/months from the date hereof.

Executed at _____

Salvor   Property Owner(s)

_____   _____

                                           _____

Figure 13.1

A sample search and salvage agreement.

money are in question. Get your rightful share first, then let them worry about the fine details.

Piece Work

In the second and third scenarios—that is, recovering recently lost valuables on private or public land—a flat or hourly fee is the most appropriate direction to take. Other than that, follow the same advice as for the first scenario.

For quick, on-the-spot searches, I never charge. It's really my pleasure to help people out in these types of situations. Once while walking down the street with my metal detector, I passed a woman on a porch who asked me to find her wedding ring. She had lost it the day before while working in her garden. It had a lot of sentimental value, and she was distraught over its disappearance.

The woman was positive that I would find the ring somewhere in a large patch of weeds that had needed pruning. After getting this preliminary information, the first thing I asked her was if she had been wearing work gloves. She said yes, so guess where I found the ring. In the left glove! That's called starting at the beginning.

Another time, I was approached by a highly embarrassed firefighter who had lost the keys to the firehouse somewhere in a large picnic area. Of course, I found the keys in the opposite direction from where he was looking. This is common because people generally don't have an accurate idea of where they lost their valuables while enjoying themselves in the outdoors.

Lost and Found Ads

An often overlooked but steady stream of business opportunities for the enterprising urban treasure hunter can be supplied by the local newspaper's "Lost and Found" column. These columns are certainly easy enough to check on a regular basis. You'd be surprised at the variety of items listed in New York City's newspapers. The same is probably true where you live.

By contacting the advertisers and getting further details about where and when the loss took place, you can work out a plan to locate the object in question—and collect a reward. Once again, I'll mention that you might even want to place your own "Searcher

Lost and Found
Lost man's gold wedding ring. By the Coney Island pier. with the Inscription "Love Sheila 8/26/78". Reward. Email
Lost key ring w/4 Chrysler computer chip car keys. Sheep Meadow. Central Park. Reward. Email
Lost red leather wallet. Yankee Stadium. Name Cliff Soutine. Keep cash. Return wallet and papers. Reward $200. Box GH234 Times.
Lost white gold tennis bracelet with small round diamonds in square setting. Madison Square Park. Near Conkling statue. Reward. Email
Lost white and yellow gold Greek key earring. Flushing Meadow. 2" in height. Reward. Email
Lost wedding ring. Tavern On The Green area. Band with 7 diamonds. Belonged to my grandmother. $500 Reward. Email
Lost Ph.D. research in dark grey HP laptop case. Left on park bench. Greenwich Village. Reward. Email

Available" ads and leave your business card on neighborhood bulletin boards to get the word out. Customers are sure to call. I was once even contacted by a woman who saw my card and thought I was a psychic. You never know!

CONTRACT ARCHAEOLOGY

Another business opportunity for the ambitious urban treasure hunter is contract archaeology. This is a growing field and a perfect direction for urban treasure hunters to consider.

Federal law requires that land development projects financed through federal funding must conduct exploration for archaeological resources. Many states have the same requirement for use of state funds, and environmental impact statements contain archaeological resource findings as a matter of course.

The purpose of a contract archaeological dig in an urban setting is usually to assess the archaeological resources that a piece of land may have before construction projects such as highways, natural gas pipelines, and underground cable networks can begin. For example, a company may be awarded a contract with your state's transportation department to dig some test trenches in the path of a proposed overpass to determine whether the roadway will destroy any sites that may have significant historical or prehistoric archaeological value. This could be something like a seventeenth-century farm complex, an eighteenth-century smelting furnace, or a prehistoric Native American village.

Don't think that contract archaeology is leisurely work. Archaeological surveys are very demanding, and the contracts usually call for about a week's worth of heavy digging. Contract archaeology should be pursued only with serious intent and the highest ethical standards.

An archaeological resources impact study at the South Liberty Parkway, a road project in western Missouri, has revealed hundreds of arrow points, pottery shards, and other artifacts dating back to A.D. 900. The city of Liberty is funding the archaeological dig, which is required before the Army Corps of Engineers issues a construction permit.

Interpreting the Evidence

Contract digs have provided a wealth of information about the history of our nation's cities, including thousands of artifacts. Depending on which section of the country you live in, you should expect to find representative relics from every horizon of our country's historical and prehistoric past.

For example, recent contract digs in Albany, New York, revealed important sites containing pre-1625 Iroquoian pottery, seventeenth-century case gin bottles along with a Delft tile from either England or Holland, and an eighteenth-century tea set and creamer. These were all articles of everyday life from way back when.

From the evidence found, contract archaeologists recommend either preserving the site in the ground by changing the course of the road or work, or mitigating the site—that is, covering it up with asphalt so the construction project can continue. Sometimes, however, a mitigation determination will first allow the collection of data from the site through excavation.

Learning the Trade

Contract archaeology is an interesting field that is a perfect direction to follow once you have become more sophisticated in archaeological theory and techniques. The best introduction is to take a course that permits you to work at an in-progress archaeological dig under the supervision of professional archaeologists. Such a course of instruction or similar learning experience may be offered by a local college or archaeological society needing survey team members. There is definitely a place for the amateur in public archaeology!

For a more complete perspective, the Archaeological Institute of America (AIA) issues an annual *Archaeological Fieldwork Opportunities Bulletin*. If your local bookstore does not carry it, you can order it directly from the David Brown Book Company by calling 800-791-9354. You can contact the AIA by writing to 675 Commonwealth Avenue, Boston, MA 02215 or by phoning 617-653-9361.

The AIA bulletin is an excellent resource regarding the many prehistoric and historical digs in the United States and abroad that could use your help. In addition, it provides a list of state archeologists, as well as archaeological organizations to contact for additional information about nearby fieldwork opportunities not listed in the book. Also supplied are more details about archaeological field schools and programs where you can get further training.

If you think this type of work is inspiring and profitable enough to pay the bills, you won't be the only urban treasure hunter to take up this interesting pursuit as a sideline. The allure is that you never know what the next scrape of the trowel will uncover or what enigma of the past will present itself. A somewhat romantic quest!

Cashing in on your treasure hunting finds and skills is an important concept for you to incorporate into your urban treasure hunting identity—and well worth the effort. After all, treasure is treasure because it's worth something, and so are your skills. As discussed, there are many facets to cashing in, and it's up to you to creatively figure out how to best apply them to your own circumstances.

The basic points are:

- Don't do things in an uninformed or haphazard manner, or you will be fleeced.

- Never take anything for granted, and always have your own facts to back up any agreement you make.

- Deal only with reputable people when marketing your finds.

- Be trustworthy in your own actions.

The ideas and observations presented in this chapter address the basic concerns of aspiring urban treasure hunters who want to make the most financial profit from their efforts. It also points you toward the right channels and provides you with an organized framework to operate within for attaining your full potential in the field. Remember that when marketing your treasure hunting skills, your professional reputation will make you or break you. Hold yourself to high standards of ethical behavior, and your name will be thought of when a treasure hunter is needed. It's a great direction to explore.

Last Thoughts

I started out by saying that urban areas are the most diverse and rewarding treasure hunting frontier in America, and I think that I've backed up that statement quite well with the contents of this book. All the experiences of myself and other treasure hunters that I described represent what you might encounter and were chosen to help make you a well-rounded treasure hunter, confident and skillful in any situation that you may run into around town.

This book also offers you adventure, something that everyone dreams about but that is not easy to find these days without spending big bucks to be led around by a guide. Here you have adventure right down the block!

In 1925, Sir Arthur Conan Doyle, author of the Sherlock Holmes series of books and a major proponent of adventure, lamented, "The big blank spaces in the map are all being filled in—and there's no room for romance any more." I can understand his sentiments because the 1920s was a very adventure-filled era. Many daredevil expeditions were launched to the far corners of the world and brought back strange new scientific and cultural discoveries.

But, as a modern-day reply to Sir Arthur, I'd like to say that just because these spaces are "filled in" certainly doesn't mean that romantic treasure hunting potential is no longer available. My treasure hunting jaunts in New York City have shown me that adventure is always lurking around the corner—and the city is filled with corners!

Also remember that urban treasure hunting is more than just digging for and finding things. It really has multiple components. When

"There are many so-called explorers who are really travellers seeking adventure. They welcome every opportunity for a hairbreadth escape. Then they write a book about their adventures."

—Roy Chapman Andrews, Sc.D, *Leader of the American Museum of Natural History Central Asiatic Expeditions 1922-1925.*

"The three most important
qualities an explorer must
have are loyalty, unselfishness,
and dependability."

—Admiral Robert E. Peary,
Arctic explorer

artfully combined, these components transform the treasure hunter into an intrepid time traveler, sorting out the past and the present, for a very personal understanding of how his or her city came to be what it is today. A fascinating quest!

I'm sure that being an urban treasure hunter will bring out the best in you. It will also allow you to be a hero to yourself, excited by life and ideas. Few other leisure activities can provide such stimulating psychic and tangible rewards. I know that once you step into the world of the urban treasure hunter, you will never settle for the ordinary again.

It's my hope that reading *The Urban Treasure Hunter* has brought you more than the typical reader-writer connection. My intention has been to offer you the potential for ongoing dialog. If you care to occasionally check in with the expedition, you can contact me through Square One Publishers with any observations, ideas, or questions that you may have.

***Good luck
in your
treasure hunting
endeavors!***

Well, here's to *The Urban Treasure Hunter* leading you to some great treasure hunting adventures!

Appendix A

A Sample Treasure Hunting Reference Library

Although some of the following titles go back a number of years, they are classics in the field. You will find that the information they contain is as important to the urban treasure hunter today as it was when they were first published.

ARCHAEOLOGY

Cantwell, Anne-Marie, and Diana Dizerega Wall. *Unearthing Gotham: The Archaeology of New York City.* New Haven, CT: Yale University Press, 2003.

McHargue, Georgess, and Michael Roberts. *A Field Guide to Conservation Archaeology in North America.* Philadelphia: J. P. Lippincott, 1977.

Robbins, Maurice. *Amateur Archaeologist's Handbook.* New York: Ty Crowell Company, 1981.

Robbins, Roland, and Evan Jones. *Hidden America.* New York: Alfred A. Knopf, 1966.

Steward, R. M. *Archaeology: Basic Field Methods.* Dubuque, IA: Kendall/Hunt Publishing Co., 2002.

Zangger, Eberhard. *The Future of the Past: Archaeology in the 21st Century.* London: Phoenix, 2002.

BOTTLES AND GLASS

Apuzzo, Robert. *Bottles of Old New York: A Pictorial Guide to Early New York City Bottles 1680–1925.* New York: R & L Publishers, 1984.

Baumann, Paul. *Collecting Antique Marbles.* Des Moines, IA: Wallace-Homestead Book Company, 1990.

Fisher, G. W., and D. Weinhardt. *A Historical Guide to Long Island: Soda, Beer, and Mineral Water Bottles and Bottling Companies 1840–1970: Nassau, Suffolk, Brooklyn, Queens.* Bayport, NY: Long Island Antique Bottle Association, 1999.

Polak, Michael. *Bottles: Identification and Price Guide.* New York: Avon, 2000.

Webb, Dennis. *Greenberg's Guide to Marbles.* Brookfield, WI: Kalmbach Publishing Company, 1995.

CACHE HUNTING

Carson, H. Glenn. *Cache Hunting.* Dona Ana, NM: Carson Enterprises, 1984.

Carson, H. Glenn. *Cache Hunting II.* Dona Ana, NM: Carson Enterprises, 1988.

Holub, Joan. *How to Find Treasure in All Fifty States and Canada Too!* New York: Aladdin Paperbacks, 2000.

Krause, Chester, and Robert Lemke. *Standard Catalog of U.S. Paper Money.* Iola, WI: Krauss Publications, 1993.

Marx, Robert F. *Buried Treasures You Can Find.* Dallas, TX: Ram Publishing Company, 2003.

Matsen, Bradford. *The Incredible Search for the Treasure Ship Atocha.* Berkely Heights, NJ: Enslow Publishers, 2003.

Mroczkowski, George. *Professional Treasure Hunter.* Dallas, TX: Ram Publishing Company, 1979.

Patterson, Richard. *Historical Atlas of the Outlaw West.* Boulder, CO: Johnson Publishing Company, 1984.

Warnke, James R. *Search.* Boynton Beach, FL: Warnke Publishing, 1992.

Yenne, Bill. *Lost Treasure: A Guide to Buried Riches.* New York: Berkely Books, 1999.

COINS AND TOKENS

Bowers, David. *American Coin Treasures and Hoards.* Wolfeboro, NH: Bowers and Marena Galleries, 1997.

Bressett, Kenneth, and Abe Kosoff. *The Official American Numismatic Association Grading Standards for United States Coins.* New York: Random House Children's Books, 1997.

Ganz, David. *The World of Coins and Coin Collecting.* Chicago: Bonus Books, 1998.

Krause, Chester. *Standard Catalog of World Coins.* Iola, WI: Krause Publications, 2004.

Krause, Chester L., and Clifford Mishler. *2003 Standard Catalog of World Coins: 1901–Present.* Iola, WI: Krause Publications, 2002.

MacKay, James. *The Beginners Guide to Coin Collecting.* North Dighton, MA: JG Press, 1997.

Ruddy, James. *Photograde: A Photographic Grading Encyclopedia for United States Coins.* New York: Golden Books, 1996.

Rulau, Russell. *Early American Tokens.* Iola, WI: Krause Publications, 1981.

Rulau, Russell. *Hard Times Tokens 1832–1844.* Iola, WI: Krause Publications, 1996.

Rulau, Russell. *U.S. Merchant Tokens.* Iola, WI: Krause Publications, 1991.

Rulau, Russell. *U.S. Trade Tokens 1866–1889.* Iola, WI: Krause Publications, 1990.

Travers, Scott A. *The Coin Collector's Survival Manual.* Chicago: Bonus Books, 2003.

Welter, Gerhard. *Cleaning and Preservation of Coins and Medals.* Rockville Centre, NY: Sanford J. Durst, 1976.

Yeoman, R. S. *A Guide Book of United States Coins: The Official Red Book.* Racine, WI: Western Publishing, 2003.

FLORA, FAUNA, AND GEOLOGY

Bishop, A. C. *Cambridge Guide to Minerals, Rocks, and Fossils.* New York: Cambridge University Press, 1999.

Dalrymple, Byron W. *How to Call Wildlife.* New York: Funk and Wagnalls Company, 1975.

McGavin, George. *Insects, Spiders, and Other Terrestrial Arthropods.* New York: Dorling Kindersly, 2000.

Patterson, Lee Allen. *A Field Guide to Edible Wild Plants.* Boston: Houghton Mifflin, 1999.

Pellent, Chris. *The Best Book of Fossils, Rocks, and Minerals.* New York: Kingfisher, 2000.

Petrides, George. *A Field Guide to Eastern Trees.* Boston: Houghton Mifflin, 1998.

Preston-Mafham, Ken. *Identifying Bugs and Beetles: The New Compact Guide and Identifier.* Edison, NJ: Chartwell Books, 1997.

GOLD

McCulloch, James. *Nugget Shooting: Prospecting for Gold With a Metal Detector.* Dallas, TX: Ram Pubishing, 1990.

Nicola, Barbara. *The Search for Gold.* Austin, TX: Raintree Steck-Vaughn, 1998.

Petralia, Joseph. *Gold! Gold! How and Where to Prospect for Gold*. Cheyenne, WY: Sierra Trading Post, 1996.

Sierra, Jimmy. *Finding Gold Nuggets*. Sweet Home, OR: Whites Electonics, 1990.

HISTORY

Blossom, Frederic. *Told at the Explorer's Club*. New York: Albert and Charles Boni, 1931.

Calver, William L., and Reginald Bolton. *History Written With Pick and Shovel*. Charlottesville: University of Virginia Press, 1970.

Cordingly, David. *Under the Black Flag*. Fort Washington, PA: Harvest Book Company, 1997.

Edwards, Judith. *The Lindbergh Baby Kidnapping in American History*. Berkely Heights, NJ: Enslow Publishers, 2000.

Homberger, Eric. *The Historical Atlas of New York City: A Visual Celebration of Nearly 400 Years of New York City History*. New York: Henry Holt, 1998.

Key, Charles E. *The Story of Twentieth Century Exploration*. London: George G. Harrap and Company, 1937.

King, Moses. *King's Views of New York 1896–1915*. Manchester, NH: Ayer Company Publishers, 1979.

Kramer, Simon P., and Frederick L. Holborn, Editors. *The City in American Life: A Historical Anthology*. New York: Putnam, 1970.

Zeitlin, Morris. *American Cities: A Working Class View*. New York: International Publishers, 1990.

Zukin, Sharon. *The Culture of Cities*. Cambridge, MA: Blackwell, 1995.

LEGAL ISSUES

Grim, R. W. *Treasure Laws of the United States*. Rock Spring, GA: Self published, 1992.

METAL DETECTING

Baker, Lillian. *100 Years of Collectible Jewelry*. Padukah, KY: Collector Books, 1978.

Bell, Jeanenne. *Answers to Questions About Old Jewelry*. Florence, AL: Books Americana, 1991.

Carson, Glenn. *Coinshooting 3*. Dona Ana, NM: Carson Enterprises, 1994.

Fahey, Patrick. *Advanced Coinshooting*. Minneapolis, MN: Self published, 1982.

Garrett, Charles. *Treasure Hunting for Fun and Profit*. Dallas, TX: Ram Publishing, 1997.

Garrett, Charles L. *Modern Metal Detectors*. Dallas, TX: Ram Publishing Company, 2003.

Garrett, Charles L. *Treasure Recovery From Land and Sea*. Dallas, TX: Ram Publishing Company, 1988.

Merkitch, Warren. *Beachcomber's Handbook*. New York: Aperture, 1984.

Nannetti, Ettore and Diana. *New York Treasures and Metal Detecting Sites*. Brooklyn, NY: Metal Detector Distributors, 1999.

Stout, Dick. *Coin Hunting . . . In Depth*. Sweet Home, OR: Whites Electronics, 1995.

NATIVE AMERICAN ARTIFACTS

Brennan, Louis A. *Artifacts of Prehistoric America*. Mechanicsburg, PA: Stackpole Books, 1976.

Fagan, Brian M. *The Great Journey: The Peopling of Ancient America*. London: Thames and Hudson, 1987.

Fogelman, Gary L. *A Projectile Point Typology for Pennsylvania and the Northeast*. Turbotville, PA: Fogelman Publishing Company, 1988.

Hothem, Lar. *North American Indian Artifacts: A Collector's Value and Identification Guide*, Sixth Edition. Iola, WI: Krause Publications, 1998.

Overstreet, Robert M. *Official Overstreet Indian Arrowheads Identification and Price Guide*. New York: House of Collectibles, 2003.

Ritchie, William A., and Robert Funk. *Aboriginal Settlement Patterns in the Northeast*. New York: Funk and Wagnalls Company, 1974.

Swope, Robert, Jr. *Indian Artifacts of the East and South*. St. Louis: American Indian Books, 1982.

Thomas, David Hurst. *Exploring Ancient Native America*. Routledge, NY: Routledge, 1999.

Yeager, G. C. *Arrowheads and Stone Artifacts*. Boulder, CO: Pruett Publishing Company, 2000.

OUTDOOR SURVIVAL

Burns, Bob, and Mike Burns. *Wilderness Navigation: Finding Your Way Using Map, Compass, Altimeter and GPS*. Seattle, WA: Mountaineers, 1999.

Long, John. *How to Rock Climb!* Guillford, CT: Falcon, 2004.

Mattern, Joanne. *Orienteering*. Mankato, MN: Capstone Press, 2004.

Mooers, Robert. *Finding Your Way in the Outdoors*. New York: E.P. Dutton, 1972.

Schimelpfenig, Tod, and Linda Lindsey. *Nols Wilderness First Aid*. Mechanicsburg, PA: Stackpole Books, 2000.

RELIC HUNTING

Albert, Alphaeus H. *Record of American Uniform and Historical Buttons*. Alexandria, VA: O'Donnell Publishing, 1997.

Bannerman, Francis. *Bannerman Catalog of Military Goods: 1927*. River Grove, IL: Follett Publishing Company, 1988.

Dickey, Thomas, and Peter C. George. *Field Artillery Projectiles of the American Civil War*. Atlanta: Arsenal Press, 1993.

Fedory, Ed. *Relic Hunter: The Book*. Sweet Home, OR: Whites Electronics, 1994.

Friz, Richard. *Official Price Guide to Civil War Collectibles*. New York: House of Collectibles, 1999.

Hughes, B. P. *British Smooth-Bore Artillery*. London: Arms and Armour Press, 1969.

Hume, Ivor Noel. *A Guide to Artifacts of Colonial America*. Philadelphia: University of Pennsylvania, 2001.

Phillips, Stanley S. *Excavated Artifacts From Battlefields and Campsites of the Civil War*. Chelsea, MI: Bookcrafters, 1980.

Speck, Gary B. *Dust in the Wind: A Guide to American Ghost Towns*. Sweet Home, OR: Whites Electronics, 1996.

Sprouse, Deborah A. *A Guide to Excavated Colonial and Revolutionary War Artifacts*. Turbotville, PA: Heritage Trails, 1988.

Thomas, Dean S. *Ready, Aim, Fire: Small Arms Ammunition in the Battle of Gettysburg*. Gettysburg, PA: Thomas Publications, 1981.

STRANGE ENCOUNTERS

Gonzalez-Wippler, Miguel. *Santeria: The Religion*. St. Paul, MN: Llewellyn Publications, 1993.

Metraux, Alfred. *Voodoo in Haiti*. New York: Pantheon Books, 1989.

Robbins, Russell H. *Encyclopedia of Witchcraft and Demonology*. New York: Random House Value Publishers, 1988.

Turlington, Shannon. *The Complete Idiot's Guide to Voodoo*. Indianapolis, IN: Alpha Books, 2002.

Appendix B

Suppliers of Treasure Hunting Books

AUSTRALIA

Finders Books
90 Broadway
Dunolly, Victoria 3472
Phone: 03 5468 1333
Website: www.finders.com.au/books.htm
Distributes books on treasure hunting. Order online.

CANADA

Detect Enterprises
254 Bridge Street
Suite 3
Carleton Place, Ontario K7C 3H4
Phone: 888-801-6222
Website: www.detectenterprises.com
Distributes books on treasure hunting. Order online.

UNITED KINGDOM

Whites UK
35 J Harbor Road
Inverness IV 1 1UA
Scotland
Phone: 011 441 463 223 456
Website: www.whites.co.uk
Distributes books on treasure hunting. Order online.

UNITED STATES

American Indian Books
10602 Forest Lawn Court
St. Louis, MO 63128
Distributes books on Native American artifacts and archaeology. Write for catalog.

Carson Enterprises
Post Office Box 716
Dona Ana, NM 88032
Website: http://waybilltoadventure.com
Distributes books on treasure hunting. Write for catalog.

Fogelman Publishing Company
245 Fairview Road
Turbotville, PA 17772-0599
Phone: 570-437-3698
Website: www.Indian-artifact.net
Distributes books on Native American artifacts. See Indian-Artifact Magazine *or order online.*

Hothem House
Box 458
Lancaster, OH 43130
Distributes books on Native American artifacts and archaeology. Write for catalog.

K.B. Slocum Books
4401 Bouvet Court
Austin, TX 78727
Phone: 800-521-4451
Distributes books on treasure hunting.
Call for catalog.

Research Unlimited
Oscoda, MI 48750
Phone: 800-345-8588
Distributes books on treasure hunting. Call for catalog.

Western & Eastern Treasures
www.treasurenet.com/shopping
Distributes books on treasure hunting. Order online.

Appendix C

Useful Journals for Treasure Hunters

Antique Bottle and Glass Collector
Post Office Box 180
East Greenville, PA 18041
Phone: 215-679-5849

Coin Prices
Edmund Publications Corporation
2401 Colorado Boulevard
Santa Monica, CA 90404
Phone: 310-309-6400

Gold Prospectors
Gold Prospector's Association of America
43445 Business Park Drive
Suite 113
Temecula, CA 92590
Phone: 909-699-4749
Website: www.goldprospectors.org

Indian-Artifact Magazine
245 Fairview Road
Turbotville, PA 17772-9063
Phone: 570-437-3968
Website: www.indian-artifacts.net

Lost Treasure
Post Office Box 451589
Grove, OK 74345
Phone: 918-786-2182
   800-423-0029 (for subscriptions)
Website: www.losttreasure.com

*Minerva: The International Review of Ancient
   Art and Archaeology*
Aurora Publications
14 Old Bond Street
London W1S 4PP
United Kingdom
Phone: 212-355-2033 (New York)
   011-020-7495-2590 (London)
Website: www.minervamagazine.com

*Prehistoric Antiquities and Archaeological
   News Quarterly*
Box 296
7045 East State Route 245
North Lewisburg, OH 43060
Phone: 800-272-9162

Treasure Hunting
The Publishing House
119 Newland Street
Withham, Essex CM8 1WF
United Kingdom
Website: www.treasurehunting.co.uk

Western & Eastern Treasures
People's Publishing Company
401 The Alameda
San Anselmo, CA 94960
Phone: 415-454-3936
800-999-9718 (for subscriptions)
Website: www.treasurenet.com

Appendix D

Websites for Treasure Hunters

ARCHAEOLOGY

Arch Net
http://archnet.asu.edu
An online virtual library for archaeology sponsored by the Archaeological Research Institute.

Archaeology
www.archaeology.org
The online magazine of the Archaeological Institute of America.

Minerva: The International Review of Ancient Art and Archeology
www.minervamagazine.com
International online magazine of ancient art, archaeology, and numismatics.

AUCTION

eBay
www.ebay.com
An online auction site for buying and selling collectibles and other items.

NATIVE AMERICAN ARTIFACTS

www.copperculture.homestead.com
Information about the Old Copper Culture.

BOOKS

Abebooks
www.abebooks.com
For out-of-print and hard-to-find books.

Amazon.com
www.amazon.com
For current and out-of-print books.

Barnes and Noble.com
www.bn.com
For current and out-of-print books.

BookFinder.com
www.bookfinder.com
For current and out-of-print books.

BOTTLES

Bottlebooks.com
www.bottlebooks.com/basics.htm
Information about old bottles and bottle digging.

COINS

CoinFacts.com
www.coinfacts.com
A reference for United States coins.

Coingrading.com
www.coingrading.com
For information about grading mint-state uncirculated coins.

World Exonumia
www.exonumia.com
For information about collectible tokens, medals, and ribbons.

MAPS

EDR: Environmental Data Resources
www.edrnet.com/reports/historical.html
For Sanborn fire insurance maps online.

MapQuest
http://mapquest.com
For travel directions to addresses and places.

TopoZone
www.topozone.com
For maps of all kinds.

United States Geological Survey
   (USGS)
http://mapping.usgs.gov/
For USGS topographical maps.

NATIVE AMERICAN ARTIFACTS

Prehistoric American Online
www.theGIRS.com
The website of the Genuine Indian Relic Society.

SPOT PRICES

Coin World
www.coinworld.com
For the spot prices of precious metals.

Monex.com
www.monex.com
For the spot prices of precious metals.

TREASURE HUNTING

The British Museum
www.british-museum.ac.uk
An online exhibition of treasure objects found by detectorists in the United Kingdom.

Lost Treasure Online
www.losttreasure.com
The website of Lost Treasure magazine. Includes product information links.

Mel Fisher's Treasure Site
www.melfisher.com
For information for and about recovering lost shipwreck treasures.

Treasure Depot
www.thetreasuredepot.com
For information about all types of treasure hunting.

University of South Carolina Wethy Lab Home Page
http://tbone.biol.sc.edu/tide/sitesel.html
For tidal information for around the world.

Western & Eastern Treasures
www.treasurenet.com
For product information links.

Index

Urban Treasure Hunter Notes

Urban Treasure Hunter Notes

Urban Treasure Hunter Notes

Urban Treasure Hunter Notes

Urban Treasure Hunter Notes